DEAR JOAN

"The Epic Story of One of the Original Women
Commissioned in the United States Navy"

by

Marion R. Bench

COPYRIGHT 1993

by

Marion R. Bench

Bench, Marion R., 1911 -
  Dear Joan : The Epic Story Of One Of The Original Women Commissioned In The United States Navy / by Marion R. Bench.

  p. cm.
  Includes index.
  1. Bench, Marion R., 1911-. 2. World War, 1939-1945--Participation, Female. 3. World War, 1939-1945--Personal narratives, American. 4. Seamen--United States--Biography.
  5. Women sailors--United States--Biography. I. Title.

D811.B447A3   1992
940.54'5973'082--dc20
[B]   92-45116
                                              CIP
ISBN:0-942407-23-7

FATHER&SON
PUBLISHING, INC.
4909 North Monroe Street
Tallahassee, Florida 32303

FORWARD

I was only a kid of 19 when WWII broke out and when Pearl Harbor hit us. I thought I was a grown man - but found out within the next few years that I would increase considerably in wisdom.

My college buddy, Joe, and I thought that Naval Aviation would be the place to be. We both signed up and eventually we received our "wings" in the U.S. Marine Corps at the age of 21.

My sister, Marion (characterized in the book as "Joan"), had been contacted by the U.S. Navy and commissioned Lt. jg. She was one of the first three "WAVES" to be commissioned in WWII and I was so proud of her.

After completing pre-flight school in Chapel Hill, North Carolina, I had a few days of leave before reporting to flight training in Norman, Oklahoma. I stopped in Washington to spend a few days with Marion and heard all about the women's place in the Armed Forces. We had a delightful visit and I was quite impressed by what I learned, both on the serious and also on the humorous side.

One day as we walked to lunch, Marion in her "blues" with her new stripes indicating her Lt.jg rank and me in my brown cadet uniform. We found that enlisted men were quite surprised by Marion's uniform. When they spotted the insignia of an officer on a woman, they became confused and didn't know whether to salute or not. After a few incidents, I said to Marion - "I have to find out what they are saying among themselves. I will follow about ten feet behind you and thereby catch their comments." I found without fail the same question was asked - "What the hell was that?"

Marion had a lot on the ball, a college graduate, a business executive and now playing a most significant part in the war effort. She was married two years after she graduated from college and the marriage lasted about ten years. Marion was serving in Washington and her husband on the West Coast. This had a great influence on the split.

The war did strange things for all of us. I didn't have much contact with Marion from '42 to '45 and the little I had, it was evident that she was deep into the social and bureaucratic world of the military in Washington.

I began to feel sorry for her as I watched "from the wings"; her characteristics and personality change. It was a different world for her and she had to "toughen up".

Her divorce hurt her considerably and she hid these feelings from most people but I knew her too well to be deceived by this charade. She needed someone and 12 years after her divorce a fellow officer in the Navy was the one she decided would make her life complete again. They married and, I believe, lived happily until his death in December, 1986.

Marion never had children and I feel sure that there were many times in her life that she wished she had. She made up for this lack in her life by "adopting" our first child, Bonnie, and then later taking a liking first to our oldest son, Kevin, and then to our second daughter, Karen.

Her friends were closely selected which was her acquired nature, emphasized and made part of her life as, I believe, a result of her Washington training.

After the war, Marion took up a life filled with social and community activities. It always seemed to me that she was involved in a hectic lifestyle as if carried away in a tumultuous mountain stream. Would she ever let go? Could she ever let go?

God Bless you, Marion. I love you.

Deacon - M. Robert Mulligan
1st Lieutenant Fighter Pilot
U.S. Marine Corps Reserve

Dedication

To my deceased husband, Edward C. Bench, at whose urging this book was written; to my niece, Bonnie Mulligan Doherty, who patiently and uncomplainingly typed and retyped the book into her computer; and to my publisher, A. Lance Coalson, for his encouragement and faith in the manuscript.

TABLE OF CONTENTS

Chapter   Page

I   The Navy Surprises Me   1
II   The Uncertainty of Washington, D.C.   13
III   Mainbocher Uniforms and Publicity   25
IV   Tea at the White House   37
V   John's Orders and Heidi's Story   47
VI   Family Visits and Memories   59
VII   Politics and a White House Liaison   67
VIII   Friends in Washington   91
IX   Christmas and Family   101
X   Forrestal and the *USS Missouri*   109
XI   Political and Personal Turmoil   120
XII   Heart-to-Heart With John   131
XIII   A Heartbreaking "Dear Joan"   144

Epilogue

I   Friends and Family   160
II   Personal   175

CHAPTER I

THE NAVY SURPRISES ME

The perpetual sound during the High Mass was the quiet sobbing of the bride's father. The delicate smell of spring flowers permeated the church. The clear, young voice of the bride's kid brother intoned the proper responses of the Nuptial Mass. The bridal couple, consumed by love, were only aware of each other and the seriousness of their commitment. Joan, with her red-gold hair, deep blue eyes, and proportioned figure, was a beauty. With her intelligence, her analytical mind, her sense of humor, compassion and good nature, she was admired by her elders and accepted by her peers. John Evans, at 6'3" with straight brown hair and hazel eyes, had the Adonis look of the "Arrow Collar" ad popular at the time. His charm, impeccable manners, easygoing, fun-loving nature plus his unusual prowess on the dance floor made him much sought after by ladies both old and young alike, as well as admired by his peers.

It was May 1935, the middle of the Great Depression. Yet both John and Joan were gainfully employed. They had rented an acceptable apartment in the Queensboro Corporation complex in Jackson Heights which they had carefully furnished. On their wedding day, all was right for the young couple.

After their honeymoon, their days were occupied with their jobs and their ever-increasing circle of friends (including well-known, interesting, and brilliant men in journalism and radio). Nights were devoted to entertaining or being entertained, indulging in stimulating conversations, dancing at El Morroco,

Stork Club, or St. Regis, discovering odd places such as the Blue Angel, and attending Broadway theater. During these years, Joan was acquiring new skills which later would be classified as personnel manager. She advanced in the company by title and compensation. John also received increases and attended acting school one night a week at Carnegie Hall. (Joan played ostrich to her suspicion of John's possible dalliance with a member of his acting class.) Neither one compared nor gave much thought to individual successes as their monetary increases were added to their general budget.

This idyllic life style was toppled by the Japanese bombing of Pearl Harbor. Conversations turned to speculative opinions on the war; friends, acquaintances, office workers were volunteering in various military branches and applying for commissions in the Armed Services. Early in February John elected to apply for a Navy commission. About the first week in March, Joan was in the comptroller's office submitting a cost efficiency, personnel reduction procedure for the downtown cashier's department. Unexpectedly the door opened as Ruth, an intelligent, efficient secretary, entered and handed her a typed note. It read: "A Navy captain is on the phone. Insists on talking with you on an urgent matter." Ruth tossed her shoulder-length blonde hair as her blue eyes indicated impatience at this intrusion; she was fully aware of the importance of Joan's meeting with her boss.

"It's all right, Ruth," Joan responded with her ready smile. "Tell him I'm in a closed meeting and will call back."

It was more than an hour later when Joan contacted the captain, who stated he had to see her right away. "Can you give me some idea why?" she asked.

"Our procurement office is only a block away. We would be very grateful if you would come here. This matter cannot be discussed over the phone. It is a secret."

As she crossed Wall Street , the word secret had her shaking her head in wonderment. The only possible Navy connection was John's application. What in his file could be a secret?

2

When she arrived at the procurement office, the yeoman at the desk jumped up and said, "Mrs. Evans, the captain is waiting for you. I will take you to his office."

"How did you know my name?"

"We have pictures of you."

She was quite confused as he led her to the office. Entering, she was confronted by a very attractive white-haired captain and three other officers with lots of gold braid on their sleeves. They looked at her, and then they looked at each other.

"What is this all about?" she asked.

"Please sit down; we will tell you," the captain said.

When they were all seated, he continued, "We are commissioning women into the Navy. You have been selected to be one of the first women to serve. You will not be sent to an indoctrination school. You will be in Washington before the bill is passed to help with the program."

"I've seen no publicity about such a bill. Is that why you told me it was a secret?"

"It is very much a secret at this time," the captain explained. "The Navy finds itself carrying out offensive actions in all theaters of Naval operations in Europe and in the Pacific. Men are needed on the line of battle much more than at home. To release 11,000 officers and enlisted men for active duty, a law allowing a special women's contingent - Women Appointed for Volunteer Service (WAVES) - is before Congress. It specifies for 1,000 officers and 10,000 enlisted women with one Lieutenant Commander and service limited within the continental United States."

"This is crazy," she gasped. "My husband has applied for a commission in the Navy, and until he is settled I can make no commitment."

"That is no problem. At the moment, no husband and wife can serve in the same service, so we will forward his application to Marine procurement for consideration."

"There are many things to consider, such as leaving my rather responsible job."

"I'm sure this can be arranged. As a monetary consideration we will appoint you a lieutenant, junior grade."

After a few pleasantries the captain escorted her to the elevator as she experienced an eerie feeling of doors ajar and eyes peering to watch her.

She returned to her office feeling as if she were in a dream. Why had they picked her? Was it for real that they were taking women into the Navy? She had been told this was a secret. She could tell no one, not even her husband or family. Suddenly she shuddered and thought, "gosh, they seem to think that this is a fait accompli." She decided to put it out of her mind, else she just might slip and tell this secret. Her biggest problem during the next few months would be to convince John not to pester the procurement office about his application, to give them time as they must be swamped.

Then she received the letter. It was dated July 7, 1942, and signed by Captain Kenneth Castleman (the white-haired captain). It advised, in part, that Admiral Randall Jacobs, Chief of Naval Personnel in Washington, had forwarded a list of women to be interviewed by a selection board headed by Virginia Gildersleeve, chairman of the Advisory Educational Council for the Navy and dean of Barnard College. The letter was delivered by hand to her office and requested her to appear before the Board, to be prepared for a physical exam and to refrain from discussing this with anyone.

On the appointed day she entered the conference room and overheard a Navy man say to Dean Gildersleeve, "This is the woman from Manhattanville." (This was the college that Joan had graduated from in 1933.)

Turning to Joan, Dean Gildersleeve said, "Yes, I am familiar with your background. I am very impressed with the scholastic practices of Manhattanville; it is an outstanding college."

Thanking her, Joan responded that she felt lucky to have been a student there. She then asked Miss Gildersleeve, "why is the Navy interested in me?"

"Well," she answered, "the Bureau of Naval Personnel acquired a list of 68 women in the New York area qualified in personnel, management and administration. Your name was on that list. After investigating these women, you were one of the few they considered eligible for Navy duty."

Chatting about Joan's experience, she asked what she particularly enjoyed doing. Joan replied that finding the right people for the right job was very satisfying. Perhaps this conversation was one of the reasons Joan would be assigned to appoint WAVE officers.

The physical examination was cursory, taking about ten minutes: blood pressure, pulse, tapping chest and back and eye test. It did not seem to matter that she could see very little with her left eye, the result of a childhood injury. As she left the exam room, she heard the doctor say to the technician, "She's a real redhead." What an uncouth remark from a medical officer, Joan thought. Could this be a warning of how some of the older regulars might look with disdain on females entering their bailiwick?

At 2:00 P.M. on July 31st, a call came from Captain Castleman. "We want you to be at the New York Yacht Club today at 5:00 P.M. in dinner dress."

In alarm, Joan answered, "I can't possibly do that. My husband and I have a dinner date."

"You must do it and not tell anyone where you are going."

Now this is getting serious, she thought. How does one keep a secret like this from a husband or anyone else for that matter? One doesn't. She hung up bewildered. She and John were to meet at a friend's house and go on to dinner. She could not tell him. She could not even tell her own parents. Her mom and dad, Maggie and Bill Mullen, had built a house with a separate apartment for her and John. The house was further out on Long Island than their first apartment had been and she had to get there, shower, dress and be back in New York by 5:00 P.M. Her secretary accepted the fact that she had to leave, asking no questions. She subwayed home, bathed, dressed and phoned her mother.

"Can you loan me your car?"

"Certainly, but what are you doing home? What are you up to this time of day?" "I can't tell you."

"Now, Sister, what's wrong?" Sister was a name that her parents often used. "Nothing is wrong. You will have to trust me."

She phoned her friend to say she would not be with them for dinner and asked her to tell John that she would see him at home later. Although surprised, her friend did not question her.

Joan took the Chrysler which her mother had bought in 1941. Knowing her parents would not be able to get a new car for some time, probably for the duration of the war, she treated it with kid gloves.

Arriving in New York, she went to the assigned street, not sure of the location, and drove slowly to the Yacht Club entrance where two young seamen stepped out. "Park right here, madam. We will take care of your car and return it to you at the Biltmore Hotel."

"Oh, no! You don't understand," she cried. "This is my mother's car. All the signs say No Parking. The Biltmore? This is the New York Yacht Club."

"Those are our orders."

Reluctantly she gave them the keys to her mother's prized possession and walked into the Yacht Club. The place was packed with men in uniform, and there was a tremendous amount of noise, laughing and clinking of glasses. A Navy captain she did not recognize took her arm. "We are expecting you. Please come with me," he said. Not another woman was in sight. As they went up the stairs to a balcony overlooking the scene, he explained that the young men had just graduated from various Naval training schools. This party was their celebration.

Upstairs she discovered with relief that there were three other women present: Mrs. Eleanor Roosevelt, wife of the President; Mildred McAfee, who later became head of the WAVES; and Virginia Carlin, an attractive gal. They sat and talked about what one did or didn't do and how nice of the Navy to have such a great party. Joan decided this was nothing but a social event—

no one mentioned the war. After about 45 minutes, the captain came and said, "We are leaving for the Biltmore."

"Why?" Joan asked.

"There is going to be a dinner dance."

She left the Yacht Club in a trance and was put in a Navy limousine with Mrs. Roosevelt, Miss McAfee, Miss Carlin, and the captain. With police sirens blaring and motorcycles screeching, they raced down Park Avenue from the Yacht Club to the Biltmore. Escorted into the ballroom, she had one fleeting thought that the Navy was checking all their social graces. The room was filled with young men trained for war. A series of long tables, nicely decorated, each seating 12, contained place cards. The dinner seemed a bit better than the usual hotel fare. Joan danced with lieutenants, j.g.s, commanders and captains. Sometimes she wondered what John would think when she did not show for dinner. In fact, she wondered why she was at the Biltmore. While she danced with one officer, he said, "You had better ask the admiral sitting next to you to dance."

"That potbellied man? He's so old I'm sure he doesn't want to dance."

The officer smiled, "He will be your future boss, Admiral Randall Jacobs, Chief of Naval Personnel."

She was destined to clash with him. "Very well," she consented.

Back at the table, she could not ask that man to dance. She just smiled. Then, darn it, he asked her to dance or, as it turned out, to bounce around the floor. Shortly thereafter, cymbals sounded from the orchestra. A voice over the loud speaker announced, "Tonight we have the proud honor of introducing the first women who will serve as commissioned officers in the United States Navy."

They introduced Miss McAfee, Miss Carlin, and Joan. Flashlights popped. She thought, "Gosh, this is supposed to be a secret!"

All the newspaper people were there and there she was. Where had they come from? She felt helpless; it seemed so unreal.

The affair broke up shortly after the announcement. She was dutifully escorted to the entrance of the hotel. There was no "coach 'n four" waiting, but there was her mother's car. She was shocked to realize she had not been concerned about it since leaving the Yacht Club. Assuring her escorts she did not need anyone to see her home, she drove away.

On the way out to Long Island, she wondered what John and her parents would think about this night. How could she explain it to them? Reaching the house, she pulled into the garage. As she closed the doors, she noticed cars parked out front and was puzzled until the light dawned—the newspapers! She dashed for her parents' back door where they and John were waiting. They had heard her car drive in and knew what had happened—there wasn't any shock. Of course, the news had been on the radio. Her mother suggested she try to get rid of the press as quickly as possible. She went out to face them but could tell them very little until the Navy contacted her further. She tried to answer their questions. Finally, they snapped a picture of a very tired gal and left.

Her parents were extremely proud while John stood there as though in shock. He didn't seem to know what to do or say. Nervously she rattled on, trying to bring them up to date, how sometime ago they had contacted her about taking women into the Navy. She had been part of a group being considered. She told them she had said she could not make any commitment until her husband was settled. They had assured her that he would be commissioned. Relaxing a bit, she said, "At two o'clock today they called my office and practically ordered me to appear at 5:00 P.M. at the New York Yacht Club in dinner dress. From the first moment they kept telling me this was very secret as the bill authorizing the WAVES had not passed Congress. I could not tell anyone. I had no idea there was to be a dinner, and, of course, the announcement was a complete surprise. Some secret! I don't know what will happen next."

Her mother sensing how tired she was said, "It's been a long day. You two better get off to bed."

Upstairs in their apartment, preparing for bed, John said, "Why did you call Sally? Why didn't you call me?"

"Darling, I could not have kept the secret from you. I knew that, so I did the only thing I could think of under the circumstances."

Putting her arms around him she continued, "I'm sorry it exploded like it did. Let's remember soon we may both be in service doing something for our country."

"Maybe so," he agreed.

The next morning as Joan was preparing breakfast, John gave her a hug. "I must have been in some fog last night. I didn't even congratulate you."

"Well neither of us has been commissioned. Let's wait until that happy moment and congratulate each other."

The ringing of the phone interrupted further conversation. It was Sally full of congratulations and wisecracks, wanting a repeat dinner that evening with the Navy gal in attendance.

On August 4, 1942, Captain Castleman phoned her office to advise she had been commissioned a lieutenant, junior grade and was to appear in his office the following morning to be sworn in. "What about my husband's commission?" she asked.

"That's been processed to Marine procurement in Washington and should be coming through in a day or so," he assured her.

She told John and then her boss who was also awaiting word on his application to the Army. Like a splash from a rock hitting water, the news hit the office. Morgan Wheelock, son of the big boss, and other officers joined the group congratulating her. She stood in the middle of the excitement in a daze.

Morgan, guessing correctly, mentioned that after she was sworn in they would not give her much time before reporting for duty and suggested that she square away her desk. She assured him that Ruth could handle everything.

That evening Joan's household was on a high. Her mother, always conscious of clothes, exclaimed, "What will you wear?"

Joan shook her head, "That's my mom. At 10 o'clock in the morning, it won't be dinner clothes. Somewhere in my closet, I'll find something suitable."

Suddenly, she noticed her Dad looked tired. He was taking his Coast Guard volunteer work proudly and seriously. She wondered if while checking and inspecting equipment, he might be doing a lot of lifting, plus making a long subway trek each day. However, his face was one big grin. The look in his eyes pulled her up short—the pride reflected there was worth more than any Navy honor. As her eyes held his, she hoped she would never let him down.

John arrived from work, tossed her a comic military salute and hugged her. Her mother called out, "Get cleaned up you two. Dad is taking us to dinner at the Forest Hills Inn."

It was an early evening, and in spite of the excitement, Joan had no trouble sleeping. She was conscious of the fact that whenever she experienced any deep emotion, she seemed to crawl into a cocoon. There would be several other times in her life when this would happen. At breakfast, a disappointment stabbed her excitement—or her ego—when John said he had an important meeting and couldn't be at the ceremony. Pulling her cocoon a little tighter, she went forth alone, wishing that her entire family could be with her to share the thrilling moment of taking an oath to serve one's country in these days of rage against Japan's sneaky attack.

Three women, Virginia Carlin, Grace Cheney, and Joan, were entering a male-dominated Navy without any basic training or knowledge of Navy jargon. Joan was absorbed in each word as the Captain administered the oath, barely conscious of the flashlights going on around her.

At the end of the ceremony, a reporter asked, "How does it feel being a Naval officer?"

She laughed as Miss Carlin replied, "I guess I can say I entered the Navy blind. My eyes were closed with the lights."

When they pressed Joan, she said, "I've no feeling beyond thinking of the oath that I've just taken."

10

Administering the oath to new WAVES (L to R) is Captain K. Castleman, Virginia Carlin, Marion (Joan) Enright and Grace Cheney. *Official U.S. Navy photograph.*

She couldn't hear Miss Cheney's answer as one reporter was smothering her with questions. It was her first, but not last, personal experience of inaccurate reporting of the media. At home that evening, her parents, two brothers, John and she sat in the family's living room with newspapers strewn everywhere. Dad had bought several copies of every paper he could find--how lucky he wasn't near Penn Station or they might have had the out-of-town and out-of-state papers as well. The errors might have been due to the number of reporters firing questions at the three women. Chaos!

"Look," cried Joan, "they have John in a defense job. I distinctly remember saying he was a loan officer in a bank. My older brother is in a defense job."

A few minutes later Joan remarked, "Listen to this quote, 'I'm hoping they will put me to work at a very hard job.'" I recall saying I would try my best at whatever assignment I was given.

Several papers stated that she was in personnel at Macy's while both Miss Cheney and Miss Carlin were in personnel at Macy's. One paper got it straight--to a point--that she was in management at Brown, Wheelock, Harris in charge of two employees. Her department averaged twenty to thirty employees. It had to be a typographical error. One of her staff sent her the clipping with the notation: 98 percent of your staff wiped out. Her dad, having been a redhead, was proud of the red in her hair. He took exception when they called her a "blue-eyed bonde". As they picked the copy apart, the phone kept ringing until her mother took it off the hook, which must have killed her as she was too curious to ever miss a call.

CHAPTER II

THE UNCERTAINTY OF WASHINGTON, D.C.

On August 7, 1942, Joan said goodbye to her family and took the train to Washington, D.C. Her orders indicated that she was to report to the Arlington Annex as an assistant to Miss McAfee. Her small suitcase contained enough clothes for two weeks but would stretch to over a month. She had a confirmed reservation at the Hay-Adams hotel for seven nights. The Annex turned out to be across the river; buses were crowded from early dawn to late at night. It was a rude awakening to discover the transportation facilities so trying, to realize that she and John in a spurt of patriotism had agreed to sell their 1939 Pontiac to a doctor who had successfully pleaded for it. It was soon obvious that in order to maintain top physical and mental efficiency over long hours she would have to find some sort of car. Further, living out of a suitcase at an expensive hotel meant that she needed to find a more permanent place to live.

Reporting to Miss McAfee's office, not having attended an officer's training program, she had to learn quickly the various ranks, insignias, bureaus, divisions and buildings. The majority of reserve officers encountered were helpful while many of the senior Navy men were inclined to be skeptical as were the older enlisted men. It was amusing to notice a steady stream of civilian and Naval personnel going by just to peek into their office. A few officers actually stepped in with a cheery "Welcome aboard!"

The Ruler of the Navy's Waves Takes Her Oath of Office

8/4/42

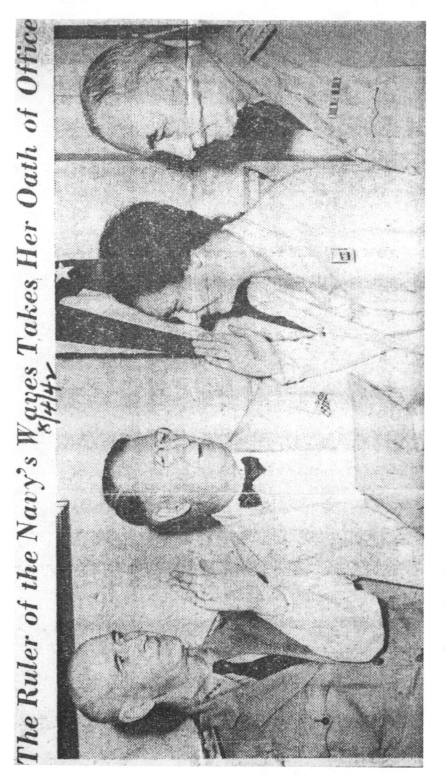

Commander Mildred McAfee, first commanding officer of the WAVES. *Official U.S. Navy photograph.*

Letters poured in from all over the country inquiring about the WAVES program, qualifications and assignments. Miss McAfee and her few assistants answered each and every one. Inquiries were sorted into categories and answering form letters were sent out. Civil Service stenographers left much to be desired. Joan was appalled by their inadequate skills in dictation, spelling and atrocious typing; perhaps she had been spoiled by her top-notch secretaries. After requesting changes three times, she was rewarded with a girl who was a help, and they worked long hours together.

Late one evening, while Joan and another gal were relaxing with a cigarette, a tall, good-looking officer came in smiling, stopped short and launched into a lecture on the dangers of smoking. He turned out to be Gene Tunney, the famous boxer who had recently quit smoking. (There is nothing more boring than a reformed smoker.)

Housing was unbelievable, almost nonexistent. From the beginning of the year, people living in Washington were cooperative in finding or offering quarters for servicemen, but Navy women had not been around. The six on duty were not yet in uniform, and their presence was unknown.

Joan and John were keeping in touch courtesy of "Ma Bell". During one of these calls, she mentioned the housing situation, and he asked the sixty-four thousand dollar question, "Doesn't the Navy have a department for housing?" Checking out the idea, Joan found out that he was right. They did have an office.

After locating the building and finding the office, she succeeded in startling the officer in charge as she was the first woman to come for assistance. They were overly anxious to please and sent her to a private home in Georgetown. The owner, a woman, was renting a large room and a small bedroom with a private entrance off a lovely garden. Joan was thrilled until she inquired about the bathroom. She would have to go up a back stairway to share a bathroom with the woman's son who was recently divorced and living with her. This fact and a feeling that she did not like the landlady, who seemed too anxious for her to take the place, made her shudder when the lady put her arm around her waist. She left a ten dollar deposit, for which she received a receipt, and made a quick exit.

She told the housing officer about her feeling and showed him the receipt. He requested a Military Intelligence report and discovered that the lady was Comtessa Loiewski Cassini. She had a history of being fond of young ladies; her son, Igor, had been tarred and feathered in Virginia for being fond of too many southern belles. The officer chuckled as he marked the card "male only."

The second place they suggested was a large manor house in Arlington that had been a beautiful private estate with formal gardens. It had been turned into a rooming house for government workers and service personnel. The lady in charge did not have any vacancies, but offered to give Joan a room whenever an occupant was on vacation and willing to sublet it. That was how Joan lived for the next six weeks, thankful and happy for the lady's kindness in spite of the many moves. Breakfast was served in a community dining room where Joan met some very attractive people. Among them was an interesting couple, Bill and Heidi Woodworth. Their friendship was to last over the next thirty years. Heidi was a remarkable woman with a fantastic background.

On August 13th, Joan was assigned to the procurement division, reporting to a Captain Andrew Lawton, a tense, acerbic Naval Academy officer temporarily in from sea duty. She had recently learned that reserve officers referred to Naval Academy graduates as "the ring club boys," and as she introduced herself this thought flashed through her mind. He was cordial and polite. He introduced her to his assistant, Commander Dick Bird. She felt that the Captain did not know what to do with this WAVE officer until his assistant said, "You will be a big help with the backlog of questionable applications from the Intelligence Bureau."

"Yes, indeed," said the Captain and led her into an office next to his. "This is Lieutenant Rockefeller who will explain what you need to do." Pointing to an empty desk, he asked, "Will it be all right for the lieutenant to use this desk?"

"Yes, of course," answered Lt. Rockefeller.

Bowing stiffly before departing, the captain said, "We hope that you will like working in our department."

Lt. Rockefeller was a serious-looking young man with a nice smile. He took her over to a table piled high with folders. "Apparently these cases represent a big headache for personnel. I go through them, analyze contents, write a condensed summary on this form, attach it to the jacket and return it to the table over there. Why don't you look through a few of them and let me know if you have any questions."

"Thank you," replied Joan, picking up several folders. Settling in at the desk, she discovered some revealing factors: the first page on each application was a letter or memo from an authoritative person, such as a congressman or an admiral; each file had been submitted to Naval Intelligence due to questionable information; each applicant had been turned down for commissioning by procurement. It was obvious that personal or political pressure had the jacket sent to Washington for review. She went over to the other table to see the type of report the lieutenant had written. She found herself staring at his signature, "John D. Rockefeller III"! One couldn't wish for more Brahmin company.

Near the end of the day, she was surprised when Lt. Rockefeller stood shyly at her desk. As she looked up, he smiled and asked if she could tell him the meaning of two words: kleptomaniac and nymphomaniac. She thought that he was joking but quickly realized that he was not. The definition of the first was easy while the second was more difficult to explain to a John D.

At lunch time the next day, he asked, "Are you eating in the cafeteria?"

"Yes. That's where I have been eating."

"Why don't we eat together?" He was ahead of her in the line, and as they reached the cashier, he turned to her and said, "I forgot to get some money. Can you loan me a dollar?" Gaining her composure, she handed him a dollar—an incident to amuse

17

THE

President of the United States of America.

To all who shall see these presents, greeting:

Know Ye, that reposing special Trust and Confidence in the Patriotism, Valor, Fidelity and Abilities of   MARION RITA ENRIGHT   I do appoint him

LIEUTENANT (JUNIOR GRADE)

in the Naval Reserve of The United States Navy to rank from the FOURTH day of AUGUST 1942. He is therefore carefully and diligently to discharge the duties of such office by doing and performing all manner of things thereunto belonging.

And I do strictly charge and require all Officers, Seamen and Marines under his Command to be obedient to his orders. And he is to observe and follow such orders and directions from time to time as he shall receive from me, or the future President of The United States of America, or his Superior Officer set over him according to the Rules and Discipline of the Navy.

This Commission to continue in force during the pleasure of the President of the United States, for the time being.

Done at the City of Washington this   FIFTH   day of   AUGUST   in the year of our Lord One Thousand Nine Hundred and   FORTY-TWO   and of the Independence of The United States of America the One Hundred and SIXTY-SEVENTH.

By the President

Frank Knox
Secretary of the Navy

99937

Commission of Marion Rita Enright (Joan) as a Lieutenant (Junior Grade)
4 August 1942

posterity. Lunch was very pleasant. On his inquiry, they swapped information about their immediate families. (That evening in her tiny bedroom recalling lunch, she chuckled thinking of the possibility of comparing backgrounds. She was a first generation Irish-American. Her grandparents and great-grandparents had raised thoroughbred horses for the gentry. Letting her imagination run wild, she wondered if maybe one of his ancestors had purchased one of their horses!)

When he inquired about how she had selected the Navy, she laughingly gave him a brief description of her introduction to the Navy. Instead of being amused, he was impressed, a reaction which embarrassed her. She quickly changed the subject, asking his thoughts on the intelligence files they were working on, which after a few comments gave him an out to return to work.

The morning of the third day, Commander Bird came in to advise Joan that she would be approving ninety-eight percent of the first one thousand WAVE officers as allotted by Congress. He took her to the enormous adjoining room in which many officers were working at desks. Turning to her escort, she said, "This could be any female's dream. The only one in the room with so many Naval men."

He laughed, "As you can see from all the stares around the room, they consider you a dream." This horseplay ceased as she spotted the tremendous pile of Naval jackets on her assigned desk.

It was a hectic month. Thousands of applications poured in from the procurement offices around the country. She worked from 8:00 A.M. until after midnight coding, setting up, classifying, preparing index cards with names and pertinent information—trying to be fair—trying to get the best-qualified people for the Navy's needs. It was a grueling job. She was astounded at the qualifications of these women. They had among them degrees in every subject of value to the Navy. There were chemists, physicists, engineers, economists, scientists, geologists, mineralogists, licensed radio operators, statisticians, doctors, lawyers, financial wizards and qualified aviators. The hardest category to get accepted were the aviators. The men in charge of aviation billets who were contacted couldn't believe these women were as qualified as their papers claimed. Finally, one officer believed and took up the cause. As a result, many women were eventually ferrying planes.

At the end of the third week, while absorbed in her work, she heard Captain Lawton addressing her. "Good morning, Lieutenant. I understand that you've been working long hours. How is it going?" She stood up and explained her procedure in handling the applications, expressing her amazement at the large number of women with outstanding education and diverse qualifications. "I'm sure, Captain, that the various procurement offices are doing a fantastic job of selecting applicants."

He smiled, even winked. "And women are not subject to the draft, but the Navy attracts good people. I appreciate the excellent job that you are doing, but try not to work such late hours." When he left, she sat back in her chair, decided that he was quite human, a nice guy.

Joan was thrilled to witness the beginning, in large numbers, of women finally being recognized for their abilities and accomplishments. Initially the Naval Academy officers were not sure women were going to work out replacing men for sea duty. However, as time went on, they became convinced and were screaming for women to be assigned to them. It wasn't too long before the law was amended to allow ten thousand more women officers as well as increasing the quota of enlisted women that could be taken into the Navy. The idea was on the way—women were placed in communications, coding, decoding, training of male pilots in Link Trainers, language translation, management, administration, medical, legal, and, of course, aviation. Approved applications of fifty or more were routed to the assignment division, orders were issued and the women were sent to Naval Indoctrination Schools established at Smith College and Mount Holyoke. Initially the women attended the program from two to six weeks, their stay dependent on personal interviews at the schools to correlate with the urgent billet requests being received. Meanwhile, enlisted women were being sent to Hunter College and its branches for indoctrination and from there to training schools around the country. In July 1944, after two years of existence of the women's reserve, it had a glowing record of expansion and achievement. Women had freed enough officers and enlisted men to crew a fleet of 10 battleships, 10 aircraft carriers, 28 cruisers and 50 destroyers.

Arriving in Washington, D.C., being thrown into the chaos of answering inquiries from all over the country, trying to find a place to live, trying to contend with inadequate transportation and inadequate secretarial help, Joan was left with little time or thought of being in a new career, new surroundings or of being separated from her family. Working weekends, eating in the cafeteria in the Annex building, all she saw of the city was while riding on the bus. Military personnel and civilians were evident in great numbers. Telephone calls to or from John and her family were her mainstay. Whatever glamour came after she was in uniform due mostly to interested stares of curiosity and admiration for the uniform.

Joan was beginning to feel more relaxed as pressure was easing off, her assignment nearing completion. She was in good spirits as she phoned John only to find him discouraged as he had not heard from the Navy or Marine Corps regarding his application. "OK, darling, let me see what I can do from this end. I know the Navy procurement system. The Marine system should be similar if not the same. However, this place is so busy everyone is working long hours. The same situation should exist for the Marines. I'll do the best I can. Give me a few days as I may have to do it on lunch hour."

"That would be great if you could find out what's going on. Art Van's orders came through this week. I guess that's why I'm uneasy." They chatted about other events at home, and she tried to pick up his low spirits. When she hung up, she told herself that he was lonesome. Being alone in their apartment was his biggest problem.

Making inquiries about Marine procurement, she located Marine Captain Ray Owens in one of the sections. Understanding how swamped he must be, she decided to barge in on him unannounced, taking her chances on the surprise tactic. It worked. Upon hearing her sad tale, he promised to locate John's file, investigate the delay and get back to her.

He kept his word and called in a day or so. "We're lucky my yeoman unearthed the jacket. It has 'expedite' clearly stamped on the cover but had been put aside for further clarification of the prior history of ulcers."

"Oh," Joan exclaimed. "He did have ulcers eight or nine years ago. There has been no trace of it for the past five years."

"Yes, the medical report has a note of that. I'll process his application and schedule him for officer's training at Quantico, Virginia, around the middle of September."

"A million thanks, Captain. I'm very grateful, and I know John will be." She'd reached the right person and acquired a future friend. In a short time she and John would be able to see each other! She could hardly contain her excitement and dashed in to tell Lt. Rockefeller the good news.

He shared her enthusiasm and said, "When he gets to Washington, let's get together for dinner. My wife would like to meet you, and this would be a good occasion."

Phoning John that evening, she said, "How would you like to have dinner with the John D's?"

"Are you serious?"

"Of course. The nice Marine captain is processing your application. You're scheduled for officer's training the middle of September at Quantico, Virginia."

"Darling, that's wonderful! You sure get things done, but how did you arrange the Rockefeller dinner?"

"Oh, John suggested that when you come to Washington, it would be a good chance to get together. It's only tentative at the moment."

"So, you're on a first-name basis?"

"Is that jealousy or envy?"

"Both, I guess."

"It needn't be either. We work in close proximity and often meet in the cafeteria for lunch. He thought it foolish to continue the lieutenant bit. I agreed. He's very comfortable company."

"Should I see about uniforms? Did he say what rank?"

"No. I'll get the information and let you know." When she discovered that he would be a second lieutenant, it never crossed her mind that she would outrank him. She was too pleased the bottleneck on his file had been unjammed to think of anything else.

CHAPTER III

MAINBOCHER UNIFORMS
AND PUBLICITY

Near the end of August, the six WAVES were advised to appear in uniform in Admiral Jacob's office; Naval public relations as well as newspaper people would be present. The other five women had received their uniforms the beginning of the week; Joan's had not been in the delivery. Miss McAfee telephoned Mainbocher's office in New York and was told that the designer had personally checked out Joan's uniform causing it to be sent out separately. It was clear that the other women wondered at this inequity; it didn't exactly endear her to them. At 3:30 P.M. the day before they were to appear, there was still no uniform for Joan. Captain Lawton notified the duty officer at the Naval Building in D.C. and the duty officer at the Annex, giving them both Joan's Manor House address and telephone number. Joan went back to work deciding to forget about it.

At 9:00 P.M. she walked into the Manor House exhausted and still with no uniform. Heidi was sitting in the lobby holding a large box. She jumped up and said, "Your uniform is here! It arrived five minutes ago. We contacted the Navy Annex to find that you had just left. Come on! We're going up to my quarters. I want to see the uniform. Bill is making tea." What a relief!

Upstairs was a lovely suite complete with living room, bedroom, kitchenette and a bathroom which had a tub and a shower. This was luxury that Joan had not seen for weeks. Heidi pushed her into a chair and took off her shoes and stockings. Bill

Rear Admiral Randall Jacobs, Chief of Naval Personnel and Commander Mildred McAfee, head of the WAVES, inspecting officers wearing their official uniforms. Joan is second from right. *Official U.S. Navy photograph.*

brought a pan of hot water in which to put her feet. "Now," Heidi said, "sit there and soak." Bill handed her a cup of steaming tea. She laughed and marveled at their kindness. Heidi couldn't wait to get the uniform out of the box. She held the jacket in front of her and paraded around the room. To Joan's horror, she discovered that the braid for the rank and the insignia were missing. Heidi found them in a separate plastic envelope. "Don't worry. I will enjoy sewing them on for you." Turning to Bill, Heidi said, "Tell Joan about the car that you located for her to check out."

"It's a ten-year-old Chevy. The body is in fair condition, and the engine is in good working order. It will need better tires. I'll scout around for them. It will serve your purpose in getting to and from work."

"Bill, that's great news! Often I am lucky to get a ride home, but in the morning I have to rely on those packed buses and hope that I get on one."

Joan had a second cup of tea while Heidi busied herself with the braid. "Bill, this tea is terrific. What is in it?"

"Just a bit of scotch. You looked like you'd been through the mill and needed to relax."

"That's amusing. On my sixteenth birthday, my parents permitted me to join them for cocktails. My father was very wise. He handed me a straight scotch with a dash of water. It was awful, tasted like medicine but it had the effect he wanted. To this day I do not like the taste of alcohol. Wait until he hears how much I liked your tea."

Joan was overtired and very sleepy. Heidi talked her into taking a hot bath, gave her a nightgown, a cup of hot soup and tucked her into the living room sofabed.

The next morning Joan awoke to find herself refreshed and relaxed. Across the room on a closet door hung the uniform, finished, pressed and ready to wear. What a thoughtful couple and how lucky she was to know them. She was dressed and waiting when Heidi appeared and said, "I'm so proud of you. Bill, hurry, come here. Look at that uniform. I'm going to file an application for the Navy. I should be doing something for my adopted country."

As the three entered the dining room for breakfast, heads turned and compliments flowed. Bill insisted on driving her to the Annex, claiming, "We don't want your uniform crushed on the bus."

At the Annex she went directly to Miss McAfee's office where the six WAVES were meeting to go as a group to the Admiral's office. Jinny Carlin told her that her remaining uniforms had arrived earlier and were in the box in the corner. Good, things were shaping up. Joan had not seen the admiral since the night of the Biltmore dinner dance. She noticed that he still retained the potbelly. He congratulated the ladies on the jobs that they were accomplishing and made a speech about duty to the Navy and the country. When the ceremony ended, the newspaper people were all over the place with lights flashing.

When this chaos concluded, two Naval officers from public relations informed Joan that she was to model the uniforms for them. They took her to an office down the hall. While she modeled the uniform, a yeoman fetched her other outfits from Miss McAfee's office. She had only seen sketches of the raincoat, dress whites and working seersucker dress and was enjoying modeling them. She was intrigued with the raincoat, and as she attached the belt, she looked up and winked as a flashlight went off. The recruiting section was to take advantage of this whimsical photo. The final photo was a close-up of Joan in the WAVE hat which was used as a recruiting poster.

Joan had not asked for this assignment and did not feel one way or the other about it. She did feel that some of the ladies were not too pleased that she had been chosen. Later, looking at the photo of the six WAVES, she burst out laughing as she thought, "This is no big deal. The young lieutenant did not have many choices."

It was rumored that Mrs. James Forrestal, wife of the then Undersecretary of the Navy, had been Fashion Editor of Vogue Magazine before her marriage. Through that connection she knew Mainbocher, the famous designer, and had selected him to design the WAVE uniforms. He had done an outstanding job, as they were perky and well tailored in very good taste. At the time the one objection—which had nothing to do with Mainbocher—was the requirement for oxfords and cotton stockings. This was shortly changed to low-heel pumps and rayon stockings (or silk if one could find them). However, on this day, oxfords and cotton stockings notwithstanding, the Navy public relations officers took the six women to lunch at one of the well-known hotels in the district. It was a happy, exciting time with all the startled stares and flattering comments on the uniform.

Back at her desk in the Annex there were so many interruptions, due to the appearance of the uniform, that Captain Lawton, who was amused, suggested that she plan to leave early. When Heidi phoned her to ask if there was any possibility of her being home about 5:30 P.M., she didn't even ask why. She just said that she'd get an early bus.

At the Manor House, Bill and Heidi were in the reception room with a man who was introduced as the owner of the Chevy. "Let's go see it," Heidi recommended. Walking across the parking area, Heidi whispered, "It's really not too bad." Looking it over, Joan thought it was fine, and after a short test drive she bought it, telling the man that she would get a check for him.

Bill volunteered to handle the transfer papers and registration and search for tires. "After all, I'm stationed on the right side of the river for this business."

The deal completed, Joan hugged Bill and cried, "There is no way I will ever be able to repay you two for your kindness and goodness."

"Shush," said Heidi. "We're just trying to help the war effort. We've decided this day has been an occasion. Further, you've had enough cafeteria dinners. It's into town for steaks tonight. We will wash up and meet you back here in half an hour."

Up in her room, Joan found a notice to call a New York operator which meant John was trying to reach her. She hurried down to the public telephone and dialed their apartment. He answered on the second ring; excited, he told her that he had seen

Composite drawing of the WAVE uniform
designed by Mainbocher.

a news reel of the first women in the Navy with their uniforms, which he thought were smashing and that his girl was the best-looking of the group.

She told him of the photos for public relations which probably wouldn't do her personal relations with the other gals any good. Then she added, "Captain Owens saw the news reel in the Navy office. He called to congratulate me. He indicated that your orders should be coming in soon. I asked him if you should see about having uniforms made. He said it would be a good idea to have them ready after you were sworn in as a second lieutenant. The exciting news—Bill found an old Chevy which I just bought."

"Do you have enough money? I can send you what you need."

"No, I don't need anything right now. Just think, I'll be able to fetch you from Quantico on weekends when you can get away." After a little sweet talk, she hung up and dashed back to her room to freshen up.

A few days after the command performance in the Admiral's office, one of the WAVE officers appeared downstairs at her desk to ask, "Have you been able to find an apartment?"

"No, I'm still at the Manor House."

"I have a large apartment and would be delighted to have you share it with me. I would only charge you a pittance."

"That's dear of you. I appreciate it but could not impose on your good nature. I feel I will locate something soon."

"The reason I would like you to move in, even on a temporary basis, is because you seem to be popular at the moment. We could invite some of these officers for cocktails."

Joan was shocked and tried to hide her reaction by quickly replying, "Thank you. My Marine husband will be stationed at Quantico and will be visiting me on weekends. I doubt that he would like the idea."

"That would be a problem," she said as she departed.

Commander Dick Cooper, a former dean at Harvard, worked at a desk fairly close to hers. He came over and said, "I'm sorry. I could not help but overhear that conversation. I can hardly believe what I heard."

Joan modeling what was referred to as "Attractive raincoat and rainproof havelock."

"Too many inconsequential things are happening. I sense their reactions. I feel like I'm slowly swinging in the wind."

"Why? What has happened?"

"First, for some unknown reason, Mainbocher personally checked out my uniform causing it to be delayed in delivery. Miss McAfee had to phone New York so they all know about that. Then public relations decided to photograph me for publicity in recruiting and assigned me to a radio show. Now this little episode."

"Don't let them get to you. They're a bunch of old spinsters. I can see your being the only married one might cause jealousy."

"I had no choice in any of these things, but I feel badly they happened."

"You've been assigned to procurement under Captain Lawton. You're out of the women's section. Don't worry."

"Maybe I'm being too sensitive."

"No, I don't think so. Anyway, we'll protect you down here." Joan had made another friend—he and his wife, Debbie, became close friends to last over the years.

Several weeks later while going through the files, Joan came across Heidi's application; nothing had been said since the night she had sewed on the braid. Her file revealed a great deal about this friend. She had been born in Germany of a German mother and a French father, a practicing surgeon who taught at Heidelberg University two nights a week. Her parents had sent her to the States to enter college. She had earned her B.A., M.A. and Ph.D. in America.

Every summer she would return to Germany to visit her family, then go on to spend a month or more in another country. She had spent two months in Russia, two months in Japan, some time in India and Africa. She spoke, read and wrote seven languages fluently. She was a photography nut and had taken innumerable pictures of coast lines, harbours, towns and cities. The officer who had taken her application had questions about the photographs which might be used in the war effort and had made a note on her file about them.

In her last year at postgraduate school, Heidi had met and married Bill Woodworth, become an American citizen and accpeted a language teaching job at Allegheny College. In 1941, Bill had volunteered for the Army and had been appointed an officer as an analyst. Heidi had resigned her job and accompanied him to Washington.

This was a remarkable woman. Joan showed the file to one of the intelligence officers and said, "I feel this woman would be invaluable as an interpreter or translator. She states she has a series of photographs which might be used." He studied the application and was obviously impressed. He copied her name and phone number, and on the basis of his feelings, Joan approved the file. She then called Heidi and invited her and Bill for dinner that evening as her guests.

She chided Heidi about being so sneaky and not telling her that she had applied for the Navy. At dinner, questions flew from Heidi, "How did you find out? Did the procurement office approve her file? Do I have a chance?"

"Whoa! The application came on my desk today. Yes, procurement approved the file. Yes, she not only had a chance, but her application was now up for orders." Heidi's excitement was joyously contagious. Bill ordered champagne and the party was on.

The following week, John was commissioned a second lieutenant in the Marines; he was given a hearty send-off by his fellow workers at the bank; he had final fittings for his uniforms; and he secured reservations for his flight to Washington. Telephone conversations during this period were lighthearted as they looked forward to seeing each other.

To further this happiness, Heidi had located a very large comfortable room with its own bath for Joan in a private home not far from the Manor House. This was an unexpected pleasure, to move in and realize that she could stay as long as she wanted with no one to return to dispossess her.

The elderly couple, Mr. and Mrs. Barnes, who owned the house were charming and gracious. They were sad not to have known about the scarcity of housing for WAVES and were delighted to have Joan and her husband share their home. The only drawback that Joan perceived was sharing the family phone. She worried that this could be a nuisance to the elderly couple. At this point she did not have too many possessions with her so that moving was simple.

At last, John was due to arrive at 7:00 P.M. at Dulles Airport on September 11th. It had been 29 days since she left home. She was at the airport an hour ahead of time. Forgetting that the WAVE uniform was still a novelty, she paced back and forth in the waiting room until she became conscious of the stares and settled into a seat. She was calmer by the time they announced the arrival of John's flight. As the passengers unloaded, she strained to watch for him; spotting him in uniform, she was filled with pride. They were in each other's arms, the crowded terminal didn't exist, it was their world alone.

On the drive to her new quarters there was so much to say they were constantly interrupting each other. They laughed and decided to take turns. While John washed and tidied up, Joan unpacked his suitcase and hung up his other uniform. "I made reservations at the Wardman Park Hotel outdoor terrace. They have a small orchestra for dancing under the stars. It seemed like a festive setting for our reunion. How does that sound to you?"

He hugged her, pecked her nose and said, "Very romantic, darling. I heartily approve."

They had finished dinner and were sitting with coffee and a cigarette when an officer from Joan's section stopped by the table. "I had to say 'Good evening' to such a happy, attractive couple."

John stood up as Joan introduced them, "Lieutenant John Hart, my husband, Lieutenant Evans."

"A pleasure! I'm glad to meet you. You have a very capable wife," he smiled and departed.

Noticing the cloud that came over John's face, she asked, "Is anything wrong? You look hurt."

"Not really," he answered. "I was just reminded of what happened when I went to be sworn in at the procurement office."

"What happened? It couldn't be that bad," she joked.

"In a way, I guess it is funny. When I gave my name to the yeoman at the front desk, he looked at me and said, 'Oh, you're the husband.'" "Don't worry about it," he laughed. "I'll get used to it."

"You're the one not to worry. After all, the 'husband' can go off to war and fight for his country while the 'wife' can only sit, worry and pray for her guy."

The awkward moment passed. She had hoped that once they were both in uniform this foolishness would end. She shuddered as she realized she outranked him. "At this moment I am with the man I love, and I want very much to have him take me in his arms to dance." The tension broken, they relished each other's closeness. Much later, they decided the double bed in the new quarters was cozy and conducive to mutual happiness.

CHAPTER IV

TEA AT THE WHITE HOUSE

Luckily, the quota for women officers had been reached. She was assigned as Assistant Director of Classification which involved various duties on special procurement problems without the deadline rush required in the job just completed. Therefore it was no longer necessary for her to work long hours, leaving evenings free to be with John. She was still expected to do publicity assignments for recruiting.

The morning following John's arrival, she was scheduled to appear on the "Mary Dorr" radio program for an interview on the various duties of the WAVES. The studio was in Washington which meant she would have to cross the river for the broadcast, due to be finished by noon. She requested and received permission to remain in the city for lunch, and made plans to meet John at the Occidental Restaurant, a popular meeting place.

Joan took the Navy bus from the Annex to the Navy main building in D.C. and then walked to the studio. Her uniform being new to the general public caused smiles, many greetings of "good morning," and officers and enlisted men saluted her. Instead of being embarrassed she appreciated the recognition of the uniform and what it signified. She smiled back their greetings and returned the salutes as she felt truly part of the war effort. She found the experience exciting; witnessing for the first time the large crowd on lunch hour, she understood she was a part of a momentous time in history. She felt grateful to Captain Castleman and the Navy committee for putting her in a position to fully appreciate and to witness the enormous display of patriotism. By the time she reached the studio she felt a keen relationship to the Statue of Liberty. She was handed a typed sheet of prearranged questions she would be asked. Her inner glow was reflected in her answers.

They were waiting at the Occidental for a table when Captain Owens, the Marine officer who had flushed out John's file, came out of the dining room. The only time Joan had seen him was that one day in his office; he had never met John. He stopped to greet them and was so friendly that he made them feel it was old home week. Before he left, they made a date to meet that night for dinner. It turned out to be a fun evening.

They ate at a small, quiet restaurant overlooking the Potomac River where Captain Owens seemed to be well-known. Conversation was devoted mainly to the war—events, theories, and speculation—until the Marines' discussed officer training school, Quantico, and possible future assignments. Captain Owens, now called Ray, was well informed, intelligent, and had an excellent sense of humor. The evening seemed to disappear. As they walked to the parking lot, Joan said, "I'm afraid we flooded you with questions. You were dear to be so patient. We do thank you."

"It's been a long time since I've had so pleasant an evening. I should thank you. It's been wild in our division. I was happy to have an excuse to leave early tonight." John shook hands with Ray and said, "I'm very grateful to you for expediting my commission."

"Don't thank me. If it hadn't been for your keen wife, that file might still be there at the end of the war."

Joan had heard hearts did flip-flops; now there was no doubt about it, for her heart performed one. Thank God he did not mention the reason John's application had been waylaid. Fortunately John was so excited about being a Marine and going to war, he did not seem to notice the remark.

When John drove her to the Annex the next morning, she took him in to see her office and meet her group. Walking down the hall, she was conscious of how proud she was of this handsome

Marine beside her. Civilian and Naval personnel arriving for work smiled and greeted them. She introduced him to Captain Lawton and Commander Bird, then took him next door to meet Lieutenant Rockefeller. After some chitchat Lieutenant Rockefeller said, "I've talked with Joan about getting together for dinner on one of your weekends here. Joan, you'll let me know?"

"Yes, as soon as John finds out about his schedule and lets me know the details."

As Joan walked him to the car, she said, "Don't forget, I've made a date with Heidi and Bill for dinner tonight. You've got to meet this fabulous couple."

Making a face, he said, "I do want to meet them, but this is the night I report to Quantico."

She kissed him, "OK, Lieutenant, pick me up at four o'clock. Our date is not until 7:00 P.M. Lots of time!"

His grin was enormous. "OK, Lieutenant," he answered as he took off for more sightseeing.

Heidi phoned to confirm the time to pick them up. Joan mentioned that she believed that John had a bellyful of WAVE conversation and hoped they could stay away from the subject, stick with the war, Bill's job, the Marines, anything else. Heidi understood and immediately promised to alert Bill.

It was only 3:40 P.M. when Joan noticed John drive into the parking lot. Suppressing a smile, she thought, "That Marine is anxious." She decided not to keep him waiting.

After an interlude of pleasure, a short nap and a shower, they were dressed and ready for the evening. Downstairs, John called goodbye to Mr. and Mrs. Barnes who wished him well and hoped that he would be back soon.

Heidi and Bill were out of the car, waiting to meet John. After introductions, Bill said, "If it's OK with you both, we'll go to Alexandria for dinner. It's on the way to Quantico. After dinner, we'll take you to the Marine base."

"Bill, are you sure you want to do this?" asked Joan.

"It will give us more time together and you won't have to drive back alone."

"That sounds great to me. I'll fetch my suitcase. It's all ready," said John.

Heidi had made reservations at a charming old inn full of atmosphere and good food. Heidi, in her usual vivacious way, was full of laughs; Bill discussed his assignment in the Army; the only mention of WAVES was when John expressed his appreciation to Heidi and Bill for being so kind to his wife. John told them that he could well understand why Joan was so taken, so enthusiastic about them; he hoped to see a lot more of them. The thirty-mile drive to Quantico, with no traffic, went all too quickly. The new lieutenant was dropped off at the gate, waved and went through to a new experience.

Three days later, John phoned her office, "Guess what, darling? I can get away every other weekend. Several staff officers drive up. There should be no problem getting a lift."

"How great! Will you be coming this weekend?"

"No. This weekend we get squared away on assignments. I understand that later on when I'm scheduled to remain on the base, it may be possible for you to join me in the mess hall for dinner. I'd love you to see this place. It's a beehive of serious activities and maneuvers. The guys are great, always helpful. We've been given a heavy study workload covering days and evenings. So far, I'm fascinated and enjoying it, even the long hours. What have you been up to?"

"A Commander John Mayer asked Captain Lawton if he could borrow me to check into some recruiting ideas. I only worked with him a day and a half. It was stimulating. He showed me a potential outline for a booklet, *The Story of You in Navy Blue*. I was pleased to give him several thoughts which he accepted. I also recommended that when recruiting offices contained any kind of display window space, it could be used to show the uniforms by using dolls dressed in the various outfits or even pictures of WAVES modeling them. Such space might also display photographs of actual WAVES at their various duties. Get local newspapers to run news items with pictures featuring local women. He seemed enthusiastic and would talk to his group about these suggestions."

"Your ideas sound good to me."

"By the way, Heidi's orders came through. She will be going to indoctrination at Smith College early in January. She is so excited."

"Congratulate her for me. She's something else. I'll phone next week when I have more information about getting to Washington."

It was only a six weeks' course. The three weekends in D.C. flew by. The first weekend, Joan was able to secure tickets for the Saturday night concert performed on a barge docked in the Potomac River off Rock Creek Park. This was one of the highlights offered servicemen and women during the war.

As they were seated, Joan sensed a quiet stirring and looked up. Sterling Hayden, in his Marine uniform, and his wife, Madeline Carroll, in a fluff of white chiffon, were entering the aisle immediately in front of them, two seats to the right. No wonder they were popular Hollywood stars. They were a gloriously beautiful couple. At intermission, standing to stretch, they noticed John in his Marine uniform and Joan in her Navy whites. They exchanged a few pleasantries. Madeline Carroll said to Joan, "You look so familiar. I can't remember where I've seen you."

This had happened on several occasions due to the poster on the REA (Railway Express Agency) trucks which carried her photograph. "The Navy has used some photographs of me for recruiting purposes. You may have seen one of those."

On Sunday afternoon, they joined the Rockefellers for a movie and went on for an early dinner. Mrs. Rockefeller was interested in the Navy women and asked many questions. John D. was interested in learning about officers training at Quantico. (Joan could not determine if he had gone to any kind of indoctrination program and assumed he had not.) While they waited in front of the Hay-Adams Hotel for John's ride, he said, "The Rockefellers are down-to-earth folk. Funny, I don't know what I expected. I've heard about the family for as long as I can

The recruiting window prepared by Lieutenant Joan. *Official U.S. Navy photograph.*

remember, mostly about their wealth. Never thought of them as individuals. That's not quite true, as I recall my father telling us the five sons were given a weekly allowance of ten cents each."

"I've heard that too. I suppose it's true. I've been around John just long enough to realize he's a good egg, a very sweet guy. I was impressed with Mrs. Rockefeller. She's delightful, charming and knowledgeable. Like John, she's very comfortable to be with."

"I'm happy he suggested the movie. I enjoyed that Rita Hayworth. She's glamorous."

Joan was about to make a wisecrack on the remark, but was cut off by the arrival of John's ride. A quick hug, a kiss and he was gone.

On his leave two weeks later, they decided to go back to the old inn in Alexandria for lunch, go to see Mount Vernon and from there go to the battlefields of Manassas. At lunch, studying the road map, John said, "Let's make a day of it. Is there any reason for us to go back to Arlington tonight?"

"None at all. We have no date."

"How about coming back here for dinner and staying overnight?"

"I'd like that if they have a room for us. Why don't you check?"

John returned, declaring, "We're lucky. They have two free rooms. After lunch, the lady suggested that you look at them and take your choice."

"OK. I better phone Mrs. Barnes. Wouldn't want her to be worried that something had happened to us. Also, if our parents call, she'll know where we are."

All arrangements made, they proceeded on their excursions. It was a bright, sunny day, beneficial to visiting these memorable sights. Mount Vernon was an impressive spectacle. It seemed particularly peaceful, overlooking the river. It was easy to imagine Martha Washington serving tea on the lawn or, not so easy, to visualize George riding hell bent up the road to an important meeting. The trip to Manassas was through scarcely populated rural country with little activity. The battlefields, left undisturbed, were deserted but soul stirring when remembering the slaughter attributed to the Civil War. They were quietly subdued as they meandered about the fields—each with his own thoughts which had to be tied into the current war situation.

They attended church the next morning at a small country chapel, ate breakfast at a convenient diner and wandered about Alexandria before heading back.

Mrs. Barnes had left a message for them to call Heidi. Returning the call, Joan heard Heidi say, "We're having a very simple cookout. We'd like you to join us." This seemed perfect before Joan drove John to D.C. to pick up his ride.

The following Wednesday, John phoned to invite her for dinner at Quantico. They toured the base and then entered the mess hall where Joan realized that she was the lone woman. Before they had finished eating, several men in John's class joined them and proceeded to ask questions about the WAVES and if the Marine Corps was going to take women into its ranks. Joan could honestly say she had no idea about Marine women.

After dinner there was no social sitting around but rather a general exodus from the mess hall as lectures were on the agenda. John walked her to the car where saying goodbye was far from private. It seemed that the entire officers' training class was in the act. The enlisted man at the gate saluted smartly. It still came as a surprise when anyone saluted her, and she thought, "Will I ever get used to it?"

Seeing the base and having dinner was a treasured experience. Those Marines were such an attractive bunch, so young, so gung-ho, so full of life—actually looking forward to going into the war zone. She shook her head, trying to erase that last thought and put her mind on the road and on driving.

On Thursday at 4:00 P.M., the initial six Navy women officers were invited to a reception and tea at the White House. This was an event anticipated with relish. Mrs. Eleanor Roosevelt greeted her guests at the entrance to the Blue Room; there was no indication that she had spent an evening with two of them a few months earlier. With her busy schedule involving traveling for speech commitments on social issues and her "My Day" column (mostly used in sponsoring liberal causes such as women's rights), she may not have recalled the event. It appeared she had little time or patience with conservative ideas. There did not seem to be any warmth in her greetings, but, in fairness, she did have a large number of people to get through the receiving line.

Wandering into the room where tea was being served, they were introduced around by the Navy procurement officers. There were several top Army women (WACS); various Secretaries of State, Commerce and Treasury; and high-ranking officers of the Navy, Army and Marines. Conversations with government officials were different, informative and exciting. Joan was enjoying herself.

Another official joined the group and said, "That is not at all necessary but extremely rude." Curiosity was aroused. He filled them in on the fact that Mrs. Roosevelt had spent the past 40 minutes off in a corner with a black enlisted WAC, ignoring the rest of her guests. Naturally, they turned to digest the subject of this information. The WAC was tall, slender and attractive. Mrs. Roosevelt was talking her head off. Fifteen minutes or so later as guests started to depart, Joan's group approached Mrs. Roosevelt to thank her for the reception. She acknowledged the gesture while continuing her conversation. It was a well-known fact that the First Lady was a sponsor of social programs. Joan had grown up in a household that held no prejudices, so that part did not bother her. But she also had grown up in an atmosphere where rudeness was taboo. She could well understand the gentleman's remark.

Outside, everyone scattered. Joan, along with other Naval personnel, returned to the Annex on the Navy bus assigned for this event.

She went to the cafeteria for supper. As she carried her tray and looked for a table, Commander Mayer called to her to join him. "Still working late, Commander?" she said.

"Yes, but it's getting better. I'm glad you're here. I've been meaning to stop by your office to tell you the booklet is being printed and your ideas were incorporated. As soon as it gets here, I'll get a copy to you." "I bet you're relieved to get that chore off your mind. Thank you. I'd love a copy."

"Your window display ideas were also accepted and are being worked on." Joan smiled, delighted. "Well, they seemed like good ideas. The uniforms are very good-looking as well as practical. They should attract women to enlist."

He grinned, "As I understand it, the gals are pouring in wanting to serve. I hear through the grapevine that the 'ring club boys' are getting the message. The gals being accepted are serious, well-qualified applicants. There has been some discussion about increasing the allotments, both for officers and enlisted personnel. Have you heard anything?"

"No, but it doesn't surprise me. Here in the Bureau of Personnel, I've had occasion to observe civil service stenos and typists and it's a sad situation. In this area alone, there would be a big demand for qualified yeomen with these skills."

"Guess I'm lucky that they assigned me a male yeoman who had everything I needed for this temporary job."

"You are lucky. I suppose once basic recruiting practices are established, they can be used for some time. At that point, where would you be assigned?"

"I hope wherever they believe I can use my alleged brain. I'm not trained for sea duty, too old to be trained." Looking at his watch he said, "Better get back to the grindstone. Come back with me. I want to show you a sketch."

The sketch was a rough outline of a proposed window display; a section showing women in various uniforms; a section picturing enlisted personnel in training programs with the ultimate inspiring assignments; and, finally, a section of hometown newspaper clippings. "We expect to get the photos together in a couple of weeks. It will take that long for those taken in the field as well as the newspaper items."

"You've truly pulled the idea together," Joan said.

CHAPTER V

JOHN'S ORDERS AND HEIDI'S STORY

John's last leave from Quantico was cut short. He was due to report back Sunday mid-morning. They agreed to spend his leave time alone, have dinner at the Wardman Park and dance away their fears. Within two days, John received his orders. He was granted four days leave before reporting to Mojave Air Base on the West Coast in preparation for being shipped overseas to action in the Pacific.

The first day, Joan left her office at noon to spend the rest of the day and evening together. The following two days John spent in New York visiting both families and friends. The last day, Captain Lawton told her not to appear in the office until John had left.

That morning they loafed around the room. Dear Mrs. Barnes, being alerted to the situation, brought up a hearty breakfast shortly after she heard them stirring. It was a serious morning.

John discussed life insurance he had taken through the Military Service Program, a plan to save money by having part of his pay withheld for him, and a trip he hoped they would take after the war. Joan wanted to slip back into her cocoon, but she realized these were things they had to talk about even if they made her unhappy. When he handed her the keys to their apartment, the tears came.

"Come on, darling. No tears on my last day. I'll phone Heidi to see if she and Bill can meet us for lunch. We'll have dinner by ourselves. I'll make a reservation for that. When I get back up here, I want to find my gal looking her pretty self." He hugged her and slapped her fanny as she headed for the bathroom and repairs.

The rest of the day turned out better than expected. Lunch with the Woodworths was a great suggestion as was the nap they snatched in the late afternoon. Joan was surprised but delighted that John had made a reservation at the Carleton and astonished when he led her to the cocktail barroom where Ray Owens was waiting for them.

Ray stood to greet them. "You were good to let me share a part of your last day."

"You've given me a new lease on life. I was anxious to tell you how much I enjoyed the program at Quantico and how much I look forward to reporting to Mojave Air Base."

Ray proceeded to give them an accurate picture of what to expect while waiting to be shipped out. It was an informative, pleasant hour. They were saying goodbye to go on to dinner by themselves when Ray said, "Don't worry about Joan. She's a super gal. I plan to take good care of her while you are overseas. In fact, I may even try to take her away from you." They all laughed.

As they studied the menu, the wine steward placed a bottle of champagne in an ice cooler at their table. Smiling, he said, "Compliments of Captain Owens."

"Thank you," John said and turned to Joan. "What a thoughtful guy."

Joan, puzzled, made no comment, but admitted the "giggly water," as she called it, helped diminish any possible gloom. The mood extended on the drive to the airport, but the actual departure nearly cracked her resolve. As he held and kissed her, the tears stood in her eyes but did not fall until the plane was off the ground.

The staff in her division was fabulous. They made the necessary polite allusions to John's departure. She was not forced to dwell on it. Heidi, bless her, phoned to ask if she could join Joan for lunch the next day in the cafeteria. Joan was grateful and said she would clear her at the gate.

The next morning disappeared quickly enough. Heidi arrived full of sunshine, excited because the Naval Intelligence Officer had called. They met to discuss her photographs. "He feels many of them may be useful. He also told me you discussed my application with him and that you had approved it. I had to see you, to thank you, and to explain why I am so anxious to be a part of the war effort."

She then told Joan the following tale.

In 1940, she discovered that her father, while lecturing at Heidelberg University, openly expressed his opposition to the Nazi party. He was taken, along with other professors, to a concentration camp. At that time, she was teaching French and German classes at Allegheny College in Pennsylvania. That summer, with Bill's blessing, she went to Germany, arranged to be introduced to a high official in the Storm Troopers and promptly seduced him.

After a few weeks of an illicit affair, she begged her trooper to help her get her father and sixteen-year-old sister across the border and out of Germany. He agreed if, once she settled them in Switzerland, she would come back to him. Of course, she promised.

Three weeks later, he told her they were ready to go. He had managed to get her father out of the camp, picked up Heidi and her sister and hid them in an Army truck. Unfortunately they were stopped as they neared the border; the stowaways were discovered; the Storm Trooper and his aide were shot on the spot. Heidi, her father and her sister were dragged to a nearby farmhouse and pushed inside. Heidi and her father were tied in straight-back chairs while seven Army men raped the sixteen-year-old girl in front of them. Heidi screamed and tried to free herself from the chair until one of the men hit her, knocking her unconscious. She awakened to find a farmer's wife attending to her bleeding wrists caused by her efforts to free herself from the ropes that had bound her.

Two other women were down on the floor taking care of her sister who was mumbling incoherently and bleeding profusely. They tried to calm Heidi's hysterics and assured her they would help get them across the border. When she asked about her father, she was told he had been taken away in the truck with the two dead Army officers.

The women were very kind and patient in spite of their fear of being caught. The underground who came to their aid was the epitome of courage and caring. They succeeded in taking Heidi and her sister across the border to a hospital in Davos, Switzerland.

After consultation with several doctors, Heidi was informed that her sister was in a state of temporary insanity caused by shock, but with proper care and treatment, she would probably be all right.

Physically, the wounds she suffered would, with proper care, heal eventually, but it would take a while to straighten out the mental disorder. Heidi perceived the kindness, sensitivity and compassion of one of the doctors and sought him out. She explained her situation: having to return to America, to her husband and to her teaching job. She asked his recommendation about what she should do. He advised against moving her sister and offered to take care of her for whatever time necessary until she was well again. Heidi gave him her home address and telephone number, and she assured him that she would send him money every month for expenses.

To her amazement, he turned down her offer. He claimed this case would give him personal satisfaction to get even with the Germans for such atrocities. Heidi flew back to the States; the doctor kept in touch about the condition of her sister.

It was almost a year before Heidi's sister began to recover her memory, but progress after that was fairly rapid. The doctor took her on excursions outside the hospital—at first for sightseeing trips, then for concerts and dinners. By the end of the second year, they had fallen in love and were married.

A wonderful ending to a horrible story.

Now Heidi felt certain her father, if not dead, would be in a concentration camp. She wanted to do her part to bring this war to an end. Her eyes filled with tears as she said, "It is impossible for anyone living in America to understand the fear that exists in a police state, the knock on the door at any hour of the day or night. One is suspicious of one's neighbor or the person behind you on the street."

"Dear Heidi," Joan began, "try not to think about it. I will pray very hard for your father's safety." They sat silently for several minutes until Joan realized that she had work waiting for her.

She walked Heidi to the exit door and watched her go down the sidewalk, shoulders straight and head high. How she admired that woman!

That night she wrote a very long letter to John relating Heidi's story and telling him how proud she was of his being in the Marines. After all, they were always first into any real action. She told him of her love and how she missed him.

In addition to her regular duties on procurement programs and meeting with public relations, Captain Lawton advised Joan that she had been cleared to deliver top-secret papers to the underground military office at the White House. She recognized the responsibility of this assignment and was awed by the solemnity of the procedure.

She arrived at the gate in her battered Chevy. A Marine parked her car and escorted her down the ramp into the Situation Room occupied by a Navy Admiral, a Marine General and an Army General plus several lower-ranking officers. The routine was a pleasant formal greeting, signing a receipt for the documents, and a "thank you and goodbye." The Marine escorted her back to her car and let her through the gate.

Returning from her first experience on this duty, Lt. Rockefeller asked her, "What was it like?"

"It's hard to describe, John. There's all this brass, admirals and generals. It's in the bowels of the White House in a room where you just know important decisions are being made daily. It's awesome."

"I can understand what you mean. Incidentally, Commander Bird mentioned that some USN officer complained to him about your picture being in the Naval Officer's Guide.

"I didn't know that. Why would they put it there?"

"As I gathered, it is in the section describing officers' uniforms. This officer claimed the WAVES are a temporary unit for the duration of the war and as such should not be included."

"It is an emergency service. He could be right. I'm surprised. I wish they had picked someone else."

"Why do you wish that, Joan?"

"I have a gut feeling the gals upstairs are tired of seeing my face here and there. Anyway, what did the commander tell him?"

"He said that he didn't know anything about it. Did you see the message from the housing section?"

She went to her desk and read the message. "Great. Hope they've found something for me," she exclaimed as she dialed the number.

When the officer she requested came on the line, he said, "An apartment in a private home has just come to my attention. I wasn't sure of your present situation."

"An apartment with more than one room? I now have a bedroom and bath in a private home."

"It's a basement apartment. The house is built on the side of a hill, so the living room, bedroom, and bath are above ground. The furnace and laundry room are at the back into the hill with side windows for ventilation. It's located in Arlington, Virginia, not too far from the Annex. The living room is pine paneled with a brick fireplace and sliding glass door leading to a small patio."

"It sounds fantastic. I've always loved fireplaces. Does it have any cooking facilities?"

"Yes, a kitchenette arrangement, nothing elaborate. If you can get away at lunch time, I'll get an appointment for you to see it. You can make your own deal with the landlord."

"How very nice of you. I can be free between 12:30 and 1:30 P.M."

He called back to say it was arranged and gave her the address and directions for finding the house.

The landlord was a bit stuffy; he wouldn't rate as God's gift to women—maybe he didn't expect a female officer—perhaps he was sensitive about renting out a part of his home. Joan loved the apartment. The appointments were practical, comfortable and attractive. It did have a working fireplace complete with kindling and wood boxes filled for immediate use. The kitchenette was merely adequate. A private telephone line had been installed. He would not give her a lease and wanted two months' rent in advance, payable monthly thereafter. Needless to say, she grabbed it.

The housing officer was delighted with her enthusiasm.

Having missed some time at her desk, she stayed late to catch up; then she grabbed a quick salad supper in the cafeteria. She planned to phone John about 8:30 P.M. which would be 5:30 P.M. his time at the base in California. She was excited to tell him about the apartment. Arriving home, she discovered no one there and was hesitant to use the phone without permission. She stood wondering whether to wait a bit longer or to go to Heidi's to call when the phone rang. It was John.

"Darling, this must be mental telepathy. I was about to call you. I found an apartment today. I want to give you the address and phone number."

"That's terrific, Dear. I have an address I want to give you. This one is overseas but the story Heidi told you makes it easier to get out and do something."

This was it. He was being shipped out to the Pacific War Theater; there was no need to discuss it further. They swapped addresses. She tried to be cheerful, then he asked, "Have you seen Captain Owens? I hear he is much favored in aviation circles. He might be in a good position to advise you on what is going on."

"No, I haven't seen him, but he has called. In fact, he invited me to go horseback riding one of these Sundays."

"That sounds like a good idea. You love to ride. I believe you can learn a lot from him about the war area."

"OK. Now that I have this apartment, I'll ask mother to come down for awhile and bring my jodhpurs and boots. You're right. It will be helpful to get whatever information I can about you."

53

"I'll be here for a spell, but it may be difficult to contact each other. Things are hopping."

"Maybe I can get a military pass to fly out to see you for a few days. Is there anything against my doing that?"

"Would you really try? Lots of guys have wives here."

The next day, Captain Lawton not only arranged the pass but was able to get her on a Navy plane going to San Diego that afternoon. It was a rush to return home, pack and drive to Anacosta. She was breathless as she boarded the plane to face eight young Naval officers. They were being sent as replacements to the West Coast for active sea duty in the Pacific. They were intrigued with having a female officer aboard. As soon as they were airborne, they besieged her with questions about the WAVES.

One officer asked, "Are you going to the West Coast on an assignment?"

"No, I'm on a special leave to visit my husband, a Marine Aviation Officer, scheduled to leave for duty in the Pacific."

They were concerned and sympathetic and changed the subject. After being in the air for several hours, the pilot announced an overnight stop in Dallas, Texas; reservations had been made for them at one of the city hotels. She did hear correctly when someone said, "The Navy does things up right." Having boarded at the last minute, she had no idea of this stop; she discovered the men were looking forward to it, an extra junket for them.

A Navy bus took them into the city. These officers facing the unknown became what they were—young, exuberant, boyish men. When they learned not one had ever been to Texas, it established instant mutual interest in the scenery, the buildings, and the city in general. Stepping out of the bus at the hotel, Joan let out a shriek. There was a crunching sound under her feet. It felt like the sidewalk was moving. Indeed it was with a solid covering of live locusts.

Amidst much laughter, "up, up and away", two of the officers each grabbed an arm and lifted her across the walk into the

54

lobby. The doorman shrugged, accepting the phenomenon that occurred at this time every year.

One ensign pointed to a large sign advertising their famous restaurant with dancing through dinner and said, "That sounds like what we need. Let's check in and meet in the restaurant in half an hour. Is that OK?"

He made a point of including Joan. Agreement being unanimous, he went off to make the reservation. It was a happy evening. The food was good, the music great, and with the eight escorts she spent most of dinner on the dance floor. Being a female was an obvious distinction, yet they accepted her as a Naval officer, just one of them.

As they were leaving the restaurant, her attention was drawn like a magnet to a table of six women of varying ages. The looks she received left no doubt that they disapproved. She was an envied female. It wasn't the first time nor would it be the last. She felt embarrassed and sad, strangely enough not for herself but for these women who seemed to lack acceptance of any alleged progress or success accomplished by a member of their own sex.

The next day during the remainder of the flight, the atmosphere seemed a lot more quiet, more serious. Joan could only speculate whether they had stayed up later than she or if they were beginning to face the reality of their mission. The pilot had notified the Marine Base at Mojave of their arrival time at San Diego, so John was waiting for her.

She introduced John to her traveling companions, and then the pilot said, "I have orders to transport her back to Washington. The plane should be returning in two or three days. Where can I reach you?" John had a reservation receipt from the hotel in his wallet and gave him the name and number.

This time their reunion was not lighthearted. They couldn't shake the uneasiness even while indulging in idle chatter. Touring the Mojave Base compounded the apprehension, as a state of preparation and readiness saturated the area. She smiled as smiling faces welcomed her. The servicemen appeared to be excited about going off to war, or else they put on a good show.

At the bar in the Officer's Club, she noticed a few drinks produced gaiety and laughter. To her it sounded forced, mechanical and hollow like the talking doll that she had bought a cousin's child that said "Ma Ma." Perhaps her nerves were playing tricks. Perhaps she was over reacting. After all, reports from the Pacific War Zones were frightening, particularly as they applied to our fighting Marines, and her husband was going into that theater.

They joined another Marine and his wife for dinner at the La Jolla Hotel where they were all staying. Her heart went out to the pretty young wife who would soon return alone to her New Jersey apartment to await her husband's return while taking care of three small boys ages 3, 5, and 8.

When they broke up after dinner, Joan's mind was still sorting out the dilemma whether under these conditions being childless, as she and John were, was a blessing or whether having children would be comforting. That first night physical contact, making love, was intense, erasing tensions. They were able to enjoy the next two days before the Naval Air Station called to advise the plane would take off for Washington at 8:30 A.M. the next morning. Before boarding, tossing aside the fear it may be the last time they would be together and determined to avoid a morbid departure, they succeeded in containing their tears. She struggled, wrapping herself in that convenient cocoon.

After a half hour in the sky, an attractive older officer offered her a welcome cup of coffee plus some comforting words. There was no stopover on this trip. Settling in for the long flight, she thought about how lucky they were to have had these few days together. She remembered the pretty young wife going back to her small children. This reminded her that she would be going back to a real apartment.

She thought about the afternoon that she had rushed back to her room to pack for this trip. She had told her landlady about the apartment, about John going overseas and how her captain had arranged a pass and got her a ride on a Navy plane. As she collected her things, she was bubbling with excitement. Mrs. Barnes had put her arms around her and told her not to worry. She and Mr. Barnes would take her few belongings to the apartment on Sunday and explain about the trip to her new landlord.

How kind and good people were when you needed them. Feeling a bit more relaxed she fell asleep wondering about the three civilians who stayed up front glued to reams of paper and engrossed in serious discussions.

At Anacosta, she found her car and went straight to the apartment. Bless Mrs. Barnes. Not only were her belongings in place, but her mail was on the counter. Bills were cast aside. Letters from her mother and brother, Bob, brought the news that they wanted to visit her. She contacted them immediately to let them know they could stay with her in the new apartment.

CHAPTER VI

FAMILY VISITS AND MEMORIES

It was therapeutic to be in new surroundings at this time, better still to have her mother and brother coming for a visit. She was extremely proud of Bob. He had been accepted in the Navy V-5 program in June and sent to R.P.I. (Rensselaer Polytechnic Institute), then to Chapel Hill, North Carolina, where he had just completed the program. He was given leave before having to report to the Naval Reserve Aviation Base in Norman, Oklahoma. Mother and Trudy, a girlfriend of Bob's, would come down from New York. Bob would come up from North Carolina.

The new setup would come in handy. The bedroom had twin beds where Joan would put Mother and Trudy. She and Bob would use the two couches in the living room, or so she planned. She had some fixing up to do before they arrived.

The next morning at work, she and Lt. Rockefeller were discussing a classification problem when the phone rang. It was Captain Owens. John, sensing it was a personal call, left her desk indicating he'd be back.

"Hi, Lieutenant. How about having dinner with me? I want to hear about your trip."

"Gosh, Ray, I can't. My brother just finished his course at Chapel Hill and he's coming to visit. My mother is coming down from Long Island at the same time. I have a million things to do."

"Like what?"

"Did you know I found an apartment in Arlington?"

"No. You didn't tell me."

"Well, it only just happened. The living room floor is Mexican tile. I want to wax it. In fact, I want to get the place sparkling before they arrive. I've also got to figure out about meals as the kitchenette only has a two-burner electric plate plus an electric frying pan."

"When are they coming?" he asked.

"This Saturday, which gives me two evenings to get ready."

"I've got an idea. I'll grab a Marine coverall, hop the Navy bus and be at the Annex about 5:00 P.M. to go home with you. I'd like to see the apartment. I'll wax the tile floor while you shine up whatever you have to shine up. That shouldn't take two hours; then you can wash your silly face and I'll take you to dinner."

She couldn't change his mind. John had come back into the room so she gave in and agreed.

Ray not only waxed the tile floor, but scrubbed it first, waxed it, let it dry and polished it with a dry cloth. Meanwhile, she attacked the bedroom and the bathroom. He was right. In less than two hours things were shining.

He took the laundry room which had a zinc sink, and she used the bathroom. They washed, dressed and went out to dinner. The whole procedure took her by surprise. If this was the way Marines took over, no wonder they had the top reputation as fighting men. At dinner, he insisted that he would take care of the evening meal that Saturday night. He wanted to meet her mother and brother. What better way to become friends than to feed them?

"I really should know what you plan in the way of food, so I can be prepared with dishes and cutlery," Joan said.

"Let's see, how about barbecued chicken, potato salad and tossed green salad? I can prepare it at my place. Does that sound OK to you?"

"Yes, but where will you get it? Do you have enough coupons? I insist on paying for it."

He let out a belly laugh and said, "How can I make time with your family and have you pay for dinner? I know exactly where to get it, and, yes, I do have enough coupons." As far as he was concerned, the matter was settled.

Realizing that there would be five for dinner, she bought extra plates and cutlery as the apartment supplied only four settings. Now it would boast a service for six. She hadn't counted on glasses. He brought Scotch and soda. Luckily, he and her mother were the only takers, which didn't discourage him at all. It was quite an evening.

Ray was most entertaining. Bob was fascinated with his knowledge of the Marines. Her mother fell for his flattery but, tired from the trip and a long day, announced that she was going to get ready for bed. Leave it to Mother! She could not get to the bathroom without coming out into the hall. She appeared in a very feminine pink peignoir. Leave it to Ray. He christened her "Pinkie," a real doll. To Joan's astonishment, Ray proclaimed that he and Bob would stay up longer. If no one objected, he'd sleep on one of the couches. It looked like the ax for Trudy or Joan— they were dismissed—no thought of where they would sleep. Mother howled and pushed the twin beds together. She decided that it would be fine for three skinny people. Ray certainly took the place by storm.

The next morning he was up before anyone awakened, cooked bacon, made toast and set up cups for instant coffee. Joan had arranged to go to late Mass. Heidi and Bill had invited them for a picnic lunch. She wondered how Ray would react to the plans. She should have guessed. He took it in stride, asking if they would drop him off on the other side of the river on their way to church.

Mother, Trudy and Bob stayed on for a few days. Ray called twice to chat with "Pinkie." At some point, he told her that he was going to take Joan riding on Sunday. The only time he mentioned riding to her was "some Sunday," and now she learned it was this Sunday.

61

It was pretty lonesome when the family departed. Joan looked forward to Sunday and wondered if he would let her in on his plans. He finally called and said, "That's a nice family you have. I can see why you're OK."

"Thank you. You were a hit with them."

"That was the point. We're all set for Sunday. I have reservations at the stables for 10:30 A.M. Sound good to you?"

Checking the impulse to be facetious about the "some Sunday" date, she said, "That's fine with me. I'll go to 9:00 o'clock church and meet you after that."

"When you get across the bridge, turn left on Rock Creek Park Road. It will be on your right. You can't miss it."

Church was over sooner than anticipated, and she arrived ahead of Ray. She walked through the stables looking at and talking to the horses when a nice groom came over to her. She introduced herself, saying that she was joining Captain Owens. He obviously knew Ray and asked, with a twinkle, "Tell me, Lass, do you like to ride as well as you enjoy nuzzling these animals?"

"Oh, yes!" she said as she noticed him eyeing her boots and jodhpurs.

"Aye, the Captain must be taking special care of you as he wanted you to have a nice, quiet horse. I'm a mind that you'll enjoy the Park better on a more spirited mount. Aye. He won't take no notice."

"Thank you, sir. You are very observant. You are right. I left the school-horse days some while back."

"Aye, Lass. I know."

Ray arrived, looking sharp as a tack. His high boots were polished to the nth degree, his tweed jacket tailored to perfection. He greeted her, commenting on how lucky they were to have such a perfect day. Turning to the groom, he said, "I see that you've met the young lady. Do you have a nice horse for her?"

"Aye. The stable boy will be bringing both horses presently."

The horse he had picked for her was a lovely, well-mannered bay gelding. Ray watched like a mother hen as she mounted. Satisfied everything seemed fine, he led the way to the riding path. At the path he reigned in and told her to go ahead. The weather was crisp, not cold, just right. Joan felt happy trotting along, enjoying every minute. She spotted a narrow creek crossing on the trail up ahead and decided to jump it. The bay was smooth as silk in that easy carry. However, Ray, close behind, had not been alerted soon enough. His horse refused and stopped dead, sending him into the stream. She held her breath, not being at all sure of his reaction. He was superb. He recovered the reins, brushed off his damp pants and proceeded to laugh his head off, his only comment being, "And I was worried about you."

It was an enjoyable ride, discovering they each knew a little bit about horses. At lunch, he complimented her on her riding. "Thank you. You're not so bad yourself. I'm afraid any ability I may have is, in part, in the genes, plus my mother's patient coaching."

"Why do you say 'the genes'?"

"My maternal grandparents were born in Ireland not too far west of Dublin in a rural area called Ballinahowna. Their farm covered acres of lush green, lawn-like fields—where before dawn large, yummy mushrooms popped up for the taking while delicate bluets pushed through the buttercups. It was ideal land for grazing horses, sheep and cattle; horses were the primary stock. My Grandmother Kelly died before I was born. Aunt Gigi, mother's oldest sister, keyed me in on the lady. She was a blonde, blue-eyed, fun-loving beauty who probably willed her strain to extend into future generations. Aunt Gigi felt very tender towards her. She married a handsome, black-haired, brown-eyed member of the Gavin clan. He was a wiry string bean with a keen sense of humor, tender sensitivity and abundant generosity. They were a religious, hard-working couple and respected in the community. They had eleven children—nine female and two male; nine were dominated by black hair and brown eyes, one had auburn hair and brown eyes, and one, my mother, came along with platinum hair and violet eyes—grandmother's child. Numerically she was number eight. They named her Margaret and called her Bob. As a little tyke she could be found in the fields eating wild mush-rooms, singing to the wildflowers, or in the barns petting or trying to comb the horses. By the time she was four, she was riding bareback through the fields, first on the work horses and then on the thoroughbreds which grandfather raised for the gentry. No one admitted hoisting her aboard. At age twelve, grandfather was training her to show the horses. Now do you believe it's in the genes?"

"I have no doubt whatsoever. How did your mother show the horses?"

"Haven't you had enough of my family for today?"

"No. I knew Pinkie was special. I want to hear more."

"At certain times there were fairs in Ireland to sell horses, cattle, sheep, pigs or whatever. I can still hear Aunt Gigi's description. I'll try to mimic her: 'Dada and one of the lads would take the child and a string of horses and ride to whatever town was holding the event that year. They managed to keep the little one hidden until she appeared in the ring on a seventeen-hands stallion or an outstanding brood mare. It was a sight to see, this blonde, child-angel putting the horses through their paces. There would be ohs, ahs and glory-bes, then a quiet hush before the loud voices broke into the bidding. So help me the gentry bid high on any horse she rode.' That's how it worked."

"She must be a truly experienced horsewoman."

"Yes. She rides in hunts, teaches and has been in horse shows."

"When she comes again, I have a lot of questions to ask her."

"Ray, it's late. I have laundry and ironing to do. I must go."

The next day she telephoned his office to thank him for the ride and was delighted to learn that he had survived without catching pneumonia.

Heidi invited Joan for Christmas Eve and to stay over for Christmas Day. She was very grateful but couldn't resist saying, "Tell Bill on this visit I will not need to soak my feet or drink tea with scotch." As she hung up the phone, nostalgia hit with a bang.

This would be her first Christmas away from family, husband and home.

She was temporarily lost in a flashback of bittersweet memories: decorating the house; the stable Dad had built of old wood for the creche figures; the balsam tree protecting the collection of handmade ornaments, the little village nestled at its base, the music box church that played "Silent Night", the oval mirror for a lake, small cardboard houses, fake trees; china figures—the carolers, milkmaid with her cows, shepherd with his sheep, even a pigman with his pigs. Then the Christmas wrapping paper and ribbons, carefully saved, added to the joy of rummaging through the box for the right size paper, sometimes ironing the ribbon, finally finding the proper cache for the gift. The smells of baking mingled with the aroma of balsam. The devotion, the innocence, the joy of Midnight Mass was indescribable. These were the delights of growing up with caring parents in a home full of warmth and love. Leaving the nest at any age, even under the exhilaration of being in love, marriage, a new adventure, is new lifestyle. Yet certain customs remain the same. Or, as the French express it, "Plus ca change plus c'est la meme chose" (the more things change, the more they remain the same).

After her marriage, Joan insisted on a small live tree, a small creche from Woolworth's, plus jingle bells on the door of the apartment. She came out of her reverie to recall that, although she had written regularly, she had not heard from John. When she had called Ray to thank him for the horseback ride, he had told her that John was assigned to an SBD (Scout Bombing Division) heading for particular islands in the Pacific. He assured her that it was too early to receive mail from the War Zone. She assumed the situation was the same.

Bob was still on leave at home with her parents for the holidays. Ma Bell was kept busy between Long Island and Arlington, Virginia. Heidi and Bill were a Godsend for her at Christmas. Their place was decorated with holly, bells and mistletoe, and, of course, their very own vivaciousness brought everything to life. Midnight Mass at the Cathedral in Washington was jampacked, standing room only; yet, the priest's voice and the magnificent choir were the only audible sounds in that immense basilica. Here she found the God that she trusted with all their lives. During Christmas week Heidi received her orders to report to Smith College for indoctrination classes on January 3rd. Joan invited some of the Manor House people to her apartment to celebrate the occasion.

CHAPTER VII

POLITICS AND A WHITE HOUSE LIAISON

Christmas festivities were quickly forgotten as the New Year approached. January 1, 1943, would have been like any other wartime working day with one exception. Captain Lawton sent for Joan. He formally advised her that a new billet had been established for his office, and he requested her for the assignment. "Lieutenant," he began, "you are now assigned to the Personnel Procurement Division as Liaison Officer with the White House, Senate, House of Representatives, Secretary of the Navy, Secretary of War, and various Chiefs of the Bureaus. You will replace a Lt. Commander USN being sent to sea duty."

Standing in front of his desk, bewildered as to what would be expected of her in this assignment, Joan was speechless. The captain smiled and walked around to stand beside her. "This office has been deluged with calls from across the river concerning inquiries on commissioning of favorite sons. You will be given a WAVE secretary and male yeoman to assist you in handling this annoyance. I have every confidence that you will make this new endeavor a success."

"Captain, I'm truly grateful for your confidence and will do my utmost to retain your trust. Where will I be working?"

"You'll be right here in my office," he said pointing to a desk to the left of his. "This will be your desk. I've requisitioned a secretary desk and a small table which they promised to move in next to your desk as soon as possible."

67

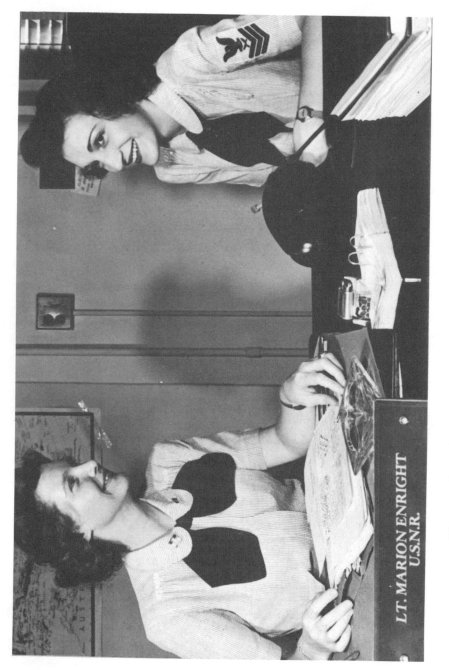

Lieutenant Joan with Yeoman Stephanie Budd. *Official U.S. Navy photograph.*

Within the week, Yeoman Stephanie Budd reported. She was a complete joy—attractive, efficient, and energetic. Yeoman Frank Walsh, already attached to the Division, was introduced to Joan as the able person who would retrieve and return whatever jackets she needed. Walsh was an all-around super guy who, because of his age, was not subject to the draft, but, like many other patriots, had enlisted anyway. Stephanie's desk, with typewriter, was barely in place when Joan realized how hectic and political her job would be. How grateful she was to have Stephanie and Walsh, who would be invaluable to her.

She quickly discovered that if a Congressman called requesting Mr. X be commissioned in the Naval Service and she reported that it was not possible for such and such a reason, within twenty-four hours or less, another call would come from a different Congressman or a Senator. When the political connections were great enough, calls came from the White House or Secretaries' offices. She hurriedly devised a system of 3x5 index cards which carried the man's name, address, pertinent information on education, job qualifications, and the reasons for his not being commissioned. The back of the card listed the date and the name of the individual or individuals interested in the man. Therefore, as soon as a second call came in, she could pull the card and inform the person, "Oh, yes, Mr. Robert Jones of Pittsburgh, Pennsylvania. He has been carefully considered for a commission. Congressman So and So is also interested in him. Unfortunately, we regret because of...we are unable to commission this man."

After the first call, the second caller, as well as further callers, were taken by surprise when she seemed to know all about the favorite son. They were more or less convinced and let the matter drop.

As always there were exceptions. On the whole, most were reasonable gentlemen and understood the reasons given. As a matter of fact, Joan received several letters expressing appreciation for her help even though their particular applicant had not been commissioned. There were unpleasant moments with a senator from Massachusetts who was demanding, argumentative, and unreasonable, yet she adhered to Navy principles and did not commission his henchman.

The assignment was challenging and kept her stimulated and busy. The days flew by, each one leaving her tired but satisfied as the original theory of the WAVE program had been to free men for sea duty. She felt part of that plan.

It was almost the end of January before she received mail from John. Then three letters written at different times arrived on the same day. He was gung-ho about the Marines, described some of the men in his unit, and told how he admired them. He was delighted to find one of their friends, Art Van, in the Ordnance Section of his outfit. They had real gabfests when they could get together. He did not know where they were headed and couldn't tell her if he did. He cautioned her not to be alarmed if he was too busy to write. He, too, was receiving her letters in packets of two or three at a time. He mentioned he had a letter from Bob from Norman, Oklahoma, in which Bob told him it was a kind of weeding-out stage with difficult night flying, night maneuvers, and risky landings and takeoffs. He was concerned about making it. She had not heard from Bob; learning this she set out on a campaign, "You can do it" as the theme song.

The pitch worked. On February 15th she had a letter from him that read: "When I get through this program (not if), I'm afraid I will have to blame you for a large part of my success. Your letters are wonderful and really inspire me to do better. You wrote that we are so much alike. Thanks for the compliment."

So far, February 1943 was a good period. Her brother was out of his gloom, and a week ago she had a call from Northampton. "Is this Lt. Evans?"

"Yes," Joan confirmed.

"This is First Lieutenant Woodworth, United States Marine Corps."

"Why you turncoat. How come?"

"I figured most of the top Navy jobs in the Washington area would be filled. The Marines are just starting. Our class is the first to have a choice. The opportunities seem better."

"I'd heard some rumors about the Marines taking women. This is a surprise."

"You're not unhappy I chose the Marines?"

"Oh, no!"

"Our uniforms have been approved but are not available for a few weeks. When you see me in two days, I'll still be in the Navy Midshipman outfit. I had to call. I couldn't wait to tell you."

Joan's mother flew down in April for a week or so. It was fun having her around. Joan's friends adored her. She did so much for Joan around the apartment in addition to being there when she returned from work. Once Ray learned "Pinkie" was visiting, he showered her with attention. He took them out to dinner and even cooked a meal in his apartment. He seemed pleased to show off his flat and was satisfied with his culinary accomplishments.

It was a lovely time of the year. The cherry blossoms were out in Washington; the days were longer and the weather warmer. Joan was happy to arrive home one afternoon to find her mother sitting in the little patio reading. "So good to see you sitting out here. Did you have a fair day?"

"It is much warmer here in the sun. I've been lazy today. Didn't do much of anything. A Mrs. Bagley phoned to invite us to dinner tomorrow night. She said you and her daughter, Kathleen, were friends. I don't remember hearing about them."

"It's only since I've been in Washington that I have known them. Kathleen went to Manhattanville, many years before me. She read in the alumnae news that I was attached to Personnel in the Navy. She wrote me a nice letter saying that she had applied for the Navy and was anxious to be commissioned. Could I help expedite her file as her husband was commissioned in the Army as a colonel and was being sent out West? It came at an opportune time. I was in the middle of all those applications. In checking the index cards, I found her name in the A group. I thought she would be excellent material for Recruiting and Personnel jobs. However, like Heidi, she fooled me and joined the Marines. She's stationed in Washington. She looked me up. We've been friends

71

ever since. Kathleen's mother rented a house in Georgetown to be with her. They are both very attractive and good fun. You'll like them."

"I said you'd call when you came home. If it's all right with you, I'd enjoy meeting them."

"OK, I'll call."

Mrs. Bagley and mother were "best friends" from the start with the common denominator being their daughters and their pride in them. After dinner, coffee was being served in the sun room when Mrs. Bagley said, "We've been hoping that Joan would move in with us. We have lots of room in this big house, and we both love her. We'd make sure she was well taken care of and see she had the proper food."

Joan was surprised to hear her mother say, "That would be a great relief to me. Her apartment is very damp. With summer coming, it will probably be full of mildew. It's a cute apartment, but it is not healthy."

"Joan, we really would love to have you here with us," Kathleen said.

"I didn't realize Mother was unhappy about the apartment. I appreciate how good you both are to me. My rent is paid to the end of the month. Perhaps, I should move in then while I try to find a decent apartment. Would that inconvenience you too much?"

"Of course not. Forget about looking for another apartment. You can stay here as long as we do," Mrs. Bagley assured her. They were so happy with her decision Joan felt maybe they were right, and so another move was in the making.

The disruption of moving was nil compared to the upheaval in the office the next morning. Congressman Lyndon Johnson came down from the Hill and stormed into the office. Four-letter words punctuated his highly abusive accusations. Joan stared angrily at him and turned to Stephanie and asked if she would like to take a break. "No, thank you. This may be a tale to tell my grandchildren."

This picture of Lieutenant Joan, wearing the propeller anchor WAVE insignia, appeared in an article telling how "WAVES Free Men For Duty At Sea". *Official U.S. Navy photograph.*

The Congressman must have overheard these remarks, yet they had no effect whatsoever. He continued to rant, rave, and be obnoxious. Captain Lawton, a quiet, dignified, and reserved gentleman, stood and glared at him. Joan handed the captain the index card which he glanced at. He said, "We have no authority to commission this man. You will probably want to see Admiral Jacobs, Chief of the Bureau. I will call and tell him you are here."

Captain Lawton made the call only to discover that the admiral was out of the building at a conference. This was not what the Congressman wanted to hear. He stomped out, slamming the door behind him. Captain Lawton and Joan were at a loss to understand why any member of the House would be interested in an individual who had a record of disobeying orders, shirking duties, being defiant to superiors, and was an outspoken homosexual. This enlisted man had been reprimanded on numerous occasions. There didn't seem to be any reason for Johnson's interest except, Joan thought, but did not say aloud, "Could it be the nonacceptance of homosexuals might make such a person a safe risk as a confidant due to the fear of blackmail?"

The next afternoon, the admiral sent for this file. Thanks to Yeoman Walsh, the jacket was temporarily missing. Johnson never let up on his harassment of the admiral. It became impossible to keep the file hidden.

Joan prepared a memo giving the details and attached it to the jacket. She sent it to the Secretary's office. Captain Gingrich, Aide to the Undersecretary of the Navy, studied it and phoned Admiral Jacobs, advising him that the case had come before their office and the man could not be commissioned. The matter was dropped. Joan called Captain Gingrich to thank him for his backing and was told, "Any time the pressure gets out of hand, let me know." At a convenient moment, Joan reported the incident to Captain Lawton who smiled broadly and said, "Good. Better keep that friend in the Secretary's office. We may all need him."

Bob completed the Norman, Oklahoma, training program and was sent to Corpus Christi, Texas, where he finished his flight training as a V-5 cadet. He phoned Joan to announce that he'd made the top ten percent in his class and had been given his choice of service. "What did you choose?" Joan asked.

"The Marine Fighter Pilot Division."

"My God, Bob, a fighter pilot."

He laughed, "Well, that's my preference. Now you have two Marines to look after. That ought to keep you busy."

"Do you remember Heidi?"

"Who could forget that live wire. What's she up to?"

"Just before she was to graduate from the Navy program at Smith, the Marines appeared on the campus and announced they were taking women. She elected to go with them. Her reasons were sound. She wants to stay in the Washington area because of Bill."

"That's what this Marine does not want. I received my wings and have been ordered to San Diego for operational training for combat duty."

Later, she mentioned this to one of the Marine officers in the Annex, and he expressed concern. It appeared that for every six or seven pilots, there was one SNJ (an open cockpit plane) for training purposes. However, he said the new F-4U Corsair Fighter should be delivered in a few weeks so they could get extensive combat flying maneuvers.

At work one morning things seemed fairly normal when Admiral Jacobs called down over the intercom requesting an enlisted man be commissioned. When Joan started checking into the file that Walsh had brought her, she could hardly believe what she was reading. The enlisted man was from Canada and had joined the U.S. Navy, thereby gaining temporary asylum from justice as he was wanted by police forces around Europe and Canada. It was only when and if he was discharged that the police could nail him. He listed several occupations on his record sheet: art dealer, painter, sculptor. The intelligence report showed that he had stolen art, had stolen paintings, had sold paintings he never delivered, and had taken money for sculpture he never finished. This was a beaut; even if the file was lost, she was certain it wouldn't wash.

After careful thought, she composed a memo listing the many reasons he should not be commissioned and attached it to the cover of the jacket. Walsh took it to the admiral. Before he was back in the office, the intercom buzzed. The admiral instructed Joan to report to him immediately. When she entered his office, she was shocked to find this enlisted man—whom she recognized from the photo in his jacket—busy working on a bust of the admiral. The admiral was mad as hell and shoved the file at her saying, "I order you to commission this man!"

"Yes, Sir," was all she could manage in a weak voice while she had a mental vision of this potbellied guy bouncing her around the dance floor at the Biltmore. She returned to her office and stood in front of the captain's desk. When he looked up, she said, "You won't believe this." Then she gave him the details.

The captain was obviously disturbed and agreed the man must not be commissioned. "Any ideas?" he asked.

"How about our friend in the Secretary's office?"

He grinned, "You're in charge."

Again she enlisted the help of Captain Gingrich. Walsh took the jacket with the attached memo over to Gingrich. He asked Walsh to wait. Walsh was back in the office in short order having taken the bus over to the District and back. With an enormous grin, he handed Joan the file. Written across her memo was "NO JVF" (meaning, No James V. Forrestal) and stamped underneath, "Undersecretary of the Navy."

"That was quick," Joan said.

"It took about ten minutes before I got the jacket back. Did you see this guy in Jacob's office?"

"You bet I did. With that amount of egotism, something had to be done fast," answered Joan.

"I think the secretary called the admiral with the bad news, not Captain Gingrich. How did he ever get to Jacobs in the first place?" Walsh wanted to know.

"Who knows? But from his file, he's not the shy type. He also does pretty well rounding up suckers. He might have conned

This photograph was widely printed to show uniforms for women serving in the Army Air Corps, Marine Corps, Navy and Army. Lieutenant Joan is second from right. *Official U.S. Navy photograph.*

one of the admiral's friends. Captain Lawton will be relieved on this one."

A few months later, Admiral Jacobs was transferred out of the Bureau, and Admiral Louis Denfeld took over. This jolly man's attitude seeped down through the ranks producing a light-heartedness—a perceivable new and surprising change in the Bureau. There were a few wisecracks in the office as to whether or not Jacobs ever got a finished bust.

Mrs. Bagley and Kathleen were, by nature, gracious, kind, and affectionate, making her stay at their Georgetown house comfortable and memorable. Kathleen was stationed at Marine Headquarters in the Navy Annex in the Plans and Policies Section, which she referred to in Marine lingo as "Pots and Pans." This was located on the far side of the building from Joan's office.

Usually at dinner at home with them, Joan could keep them amused with some happening at her job. On July 1, 1943, this routine was changed dramatically as Joan was quiet and subdued. Her well-mannered friends did not pry. On that day, Captain Lawton had her deliver top-secret material to the White House. The documents were delivered and signed for. As she turned to leave, the door opened to President Roosevelt in his wheelchair. There was no way she could describe or forget those piercing, cold, blue eyes or the toothy grin. "Why, Lieutenant," he said, "what a pleasant surprise. A little sunshine in this dreary place."

"Good morning, Mr. President."

He blocked her way out. "You must stay. I may have a nice surprise to show you."

The officers in the room looked shocked. She suddenly felt chilled and uncomfortable. She was trapped. He ordered her to bring a chair and sit next to him. The admirals and generals were stumbling around, confused. The contrasts she witnessed were astounding: the man in the wheelchair faced the straight-backed, physically fit military men; the man in the wheelchair held absolute power; the military men were questioning but deferential; the man in the wheelchair displayed bizarre egotism, probably exacerbated by his disability; the military men showed normal concern.

"Well, gentlemen," the President's voice was a little sharper. "Let's see the plans we discussed. After all, the lieutenant is cleared for top-secret material."

Instantly confusion was replaced by serious respect. Buttons were pushed and out of one wall slid a large panel on which was a map of Europe stuck with various colored pins. The top officers explained in detail the strategy of the invasion of Sicily to take place in nine days. Joan was horrified. She did not want to know about this. She had no right to know. How could the President insist on her hearing it? It was incredulous! She looked at him as he smiled at her. He was very pleased to show off to a mere woman officer. She caught a fleeting expression on one admiral's face which indicated that he understood and was sympathetic.

The experience and the days and nights that followed were a nightmare. She felt guilty having been allowed to absorb information so crucial to the war effort and to national security. Through sheer determination and will power, she carried on a normal routine but could not forgive the President's arrogance and stupidity. She was terrified that she might let slip what she knew. She agonized over the many leaks detrimental to security and what percentage occurred through egotism. The incident was appalling and increased her anxiety for John and Bob as no recent letters had been received. She was thankful when July 10th slid by to free her from the reticence that imprisoned her; fifteen years would disappear before she told anyone, and then it was someone very special.

A few days later, Kathleen appeared in her office bursting with happiness and expectation. Her husband, an Army Air Corps officer, was coming home on leave. He would be arriving in time to join them for dinner. Her excitement was infectious, and Joan looked forward to meeting Ed Hogan.

She was surprised to find him such a big man. He was quite tall, broad, and handsome with a deep voice. Perhaps her reaction was due to the fact that Kathleen, although of average height, seemed petite, very feminine, always looking as though she stepped out of a bandbox whether in uniform or out of it.

Having him around sure pepped up the household. Colonel Hogan was still there near the end of July when an invitation was delivered to Joan's office by a Navy yeoman which caused another flutter of excitement in the Georgetown household. They were enjoying a cocktail before dinner when Joan could no longer contain her news. "I received an invitation today. Do you mind if I share it?"

"Please," Kathleen cried.

"OK, here goes, 'The Secretary of the Navy and Mrs. Forrestal request the pleasure of the company of Lt. Evans on August 1st at 1642 29th Street at 8 o'clock. Buffet dinner in honor of ranking WAVE officers of the Navy.'"

"How great!" Kathleen exclaimed. "Will you wear dress white uniform?"

"I guess so. It's a formal RSVP. I'll check upstairs. I still have a few friends in the Women's Reserve," Joan joked.

It was indeed a formal party. As Joan dressed, she recalled the last time she wore "whites" was at the Wardman Park Hotel with John before he left for the West Coast. She decided that if she didn't receive mail soon, she'd have to call Ray.

The grounds of the Forrestal home were more natural than manicured. "Lovely," thought Joan. The interior was warm, friendly, comfortable, family oriented, and charming but not fussy. It turned out there were more ranking male officers and male civilians than women. Mrs. Forrestal was an attractive, intelligent lady. Joan knew she was interested in the WAVES from its conception, having obtained Mainbocher to design the uniform, which she approved. She knew that she traveled, giving speeches at various clubs and gatherings to promote the WAVE program. Joan was instantly attracted to her.

She watched Mrs. Forrestal circulating among her guests, greeting each one as though he or she was special. Joan, always eager to assimilate multifarious opinions, was an ardent listener as she ambled about during the cocktail hour. At dinner she was

delighted to be a part of serious political and bureaucratic rumi-
nations. She was surprised to hear one high civilian official relate
a few of the blunders that occurred in his offices. On the other
hand, it was refreshing to know that, in order to make a point,
someone was honest with no intent of covering up. Joan felt elated
to be part of this erudite evening.

The night after the Forrestal's dinner, Kathleen was determined to hear about the affair and invited Heidi for dinner to hear
the details and to meet Col. Hogan. Heidi was in charge of setting
up and managing a Marine barracks in the Washington area for
enlisted girls. She had been so busy that neither Kathleen nor Joan
had seen her. They were delighted that she was able to get away
for dinner. Joan's account of the buffet was not too long in the
telling. Most of the evening, Heidi entertained them with hilarious
incidents she encountered in her assignment, such as urinals being
delivered for the bathrooms and shaving mugs arriving when
ordered for Quantico male barracks. "Not to worry, Heidi," Joan
volunteered, "such goofs creep up in more serious matters. I heard
of one last night. In mentioning the difficulties encountered in
getting supplies to the War Zones, one Army Air Force officer sent
in three separate requisitions for supplies of a certain screw when
the same screw could be used in the three different types of
airplanes."

Hearing this tale, Col. Hogan wasn't a bit upset as he
guessed that happened often. He hoped the mechanics could be
convinced to check out this sort of duplication. Heidi finished the
evening with her rendition of her speech to the gals on the dangers
of dating. It was uproarious.

The next morning, Joan received a hand-delivered note
from Mrs. Forrestal asking her to stop by her house after work. On
occasion the Public Relations Department still photographed Joan
for publicity purposes. She wondered if this was what Mrs.
Forrestal had in mind, particularly since the upsurge in requests
for the services of officers and enlisted WAVES had spurred
Congress to raise the quotas from 1,000 officers to 10,000 and
from 10,000 enlistees to 100,000. She was unprepared for the

reason. Mrs. Forrestal wanted her as an aide on an inspection tour of Naval bases where WAVES were on duty.

Joan, delighted with the idea, said, "Mrs. Forrestal, I'm flattered and happy for the opportunity to see the women at work."

"Good. I'll have the secretary's office advise Captain Lawton to make the necessary arrangements."

The captain seemed pleased the secretary's office had chosen an officer from his section and told Joan the schedule was to visit the Navy Yards and Procurement offices in Philadelphia and Boston. The bottom line was that they would leave on August 5th—two days away!

Looking at the captain, she smiled, "I guess men at sea and pilots don't get much advance notice."

"No," he confirmed. "Take what time you need to get ready for the trip."

Stephanie volunteered to write John and send him the itinerary. "I do thank you. Yes, that would be the best thing you could do, as I suspect I will not get time during this trip."

On the morning of August 5th, a Navy chauffeured car was sent to pick up Joan. Thoughtful Mrs. Bagley was sad and disappointed that the driver did not have time for coffee and muffins. He picked up Mrs. Forrestal, and they were on their way.

The trip to Philadelphia wasn't that long, but Mrs. Forrestal was so easy to travel with, it seemed like no time at all. Capt. T. T. Patterson was gracious and helpful while touring the Yard and the Procurement office. It was the first time Joan had seen enlisted girls working heavy equipment or even in the Communications office. It was a revealing visit.

Leaving Philadelphia, they were driven to New York City to the Bradford Normans' apartment at the River House. They were accepted with open arms. Joan was enchanted with their two children, a boy and a girl. She was puzzled when Mrs. Norman cautioned that sometimes the existence of children could cool a romantic relationship with a mate.

During cocktails at the apartment, attention was focused on the interesting discussions between Mr. Norman and Mr.

Firestone about defense needs and procurement thereof. Joan was pleased to meet and chat with Lt. John Falter, a Reserve officer and an artist who was working on publicity. They went to dinner at the Stork Club and were ushered into the back room by the owner, Mr. Billingsly, who summoned a waiter to take drink orders.

Recognizing Joan, he said, "Mrs. Evans, I haven't seen you in a while. Your usual ginger ale?"

Laughing, she replied, "Being in the Navy has brought some changes. I've learned to appreciate very dry martinis."

"We can arrange that."

Embarrassed, she explained the milk, ginger ale, and double scotch period of her life. "Years before the war, my husband had ulcers and was on a milk diet. I had not acquired a taste for liquor. Our constant pal, Bill Carey, was a double scotch drinker. That was the way we worked our way through several night clubs."

It seemed to amuse everyone that the lady lieutenant had succumbed to the wickedness of hard liquor. To ease the moment of truth, Lt. Falter said, "Never mind, Joan. Here's a present for you."

Reaching across the table, he handed her a sketch he had drawn of her on the back of the menu. Joan's big smile and thank you pleased Lt. Falter. Mrs. Forrestal was quick to take advantage. "I thank you, too, and will thank you further if you get my ideas for publicity accepted in the New York area." She rattled off several suggestions for magazines and newspapers to carry stories about women working there. It was a foregone conclusion that her thoughts would have priority the next day.

General conversation prevailed at dinner with breaks for dancing. Joan, observing Mrs. Forrestal, was amazed at how little effort and time she expended in roping in the publicity men as though she was engaged in ordinary chitchat.

Before leaving New York and heading north to Northampton, Mrs. Forrestal mentioned they would go by way of Southampton, New York, to see some friends. They would be the guests of Mr. & Mrs. Shields on Ox Pasture Road. "What a coincidence," exclaimed Joan. "My family's house was just down the road. As a teen-ager, I had a crush on Mrs. Shields' beautiful daughter, Rocky, who later married Gary Cooper."

"I think Rocky's daughter, Maria, is staying with her grandparents. You will have a chance to see her."

It was a nostalgic thrill for Joan to see the old area and meet this happy, beautiful little girl, to sit at dinner and recall how she had stared at Maria's mother, and to surmise that Maria would have her share of ogling. The next evening, a Saturday, Mrs. Shields arranged a theater night at Guild Hall in East Hampton. It was a preview of Philip Barry's new play, "Without Love." The play was entertaining, and everyone seemed to enjoy it. Afterwards they went back to Philip Barry's house on Dunemere Lane which was packed with well-wishing friends and family. Joan was excited, meeting and talking with Mr. Barry, and was aware that theatrical conversation was the mode of the evening. The scene was farfetched from the realities of a war. Appraising the happy faces and considering the occasion, perhaps this was not a bad idea.

Sunday lunch was at the Bathing Corporation (Southampton's Beach Club) where Joan ran into one of her peers. Joan got a quick impression that although her friend expressed admiration for serving in the Navy, she was happier spending her summer at the beach. This was what our men were fighting for—freedom and choices.

Monday, August 9th, they left for Northampton. Arriving in the enchanted New England town, Joan was anxious to see the old colonial home of President Calvin Coolidge where they would be guests of his widow, Grace Coolidge. Her name fitted her, as she was a most gracious, charming lady who made one feel she had been waiting all her life to welcome her guests to the quiet allure of the old house. The home was a treasure. Mrs. Coolidge harmonized with its patina. Dinner—from the delicate china, crystal glasses, heavy silver flatware, and handmade doilies—was an experience in gracious living. They walked across to the Smith campus where Mrs. Forrestal was introduced to the Officer

Candidates. She talked of her recent trip to England where she conferred with leaders of several women's services. "One big difference in their services and ours is English women are conscripted at eighteen years of age, leaving little chance to complete formal education. This is a pity as many will not return to studies after the war."

One midshipman asked, "Are the British, as a group, attractive?"

"Yes, I found them attractive. However, you must realize I'm prejudiced. To me, the WAVES are tops."

The next day Captain Herbert W. Underwood, commanding officer of the school, escorted them on a tour. They attended classes in personnel and physical education and witnessed a field drill—a moving sight to watch the women go through the precision movements.

They went to Filene's store to observe a fitting of midshipmen's uniforms. After lunch they attended a lecture on the difficulties of fighting a war in the Pacific Islands. This was given by former Senator Hiram Bingham in the John M. Greene Hall. He looked and acted like what most would envision a senator to look like: he was tall, erect, had graying hair and positive opinions. It was an informative hour. He had the highest praise for the Naval action in the Battle of Midway.[1]

Later Mrs. Forrestal gave a dinner preceding the benefit performance by Argentintia and her troop of Spanish dancers. Proceeds from the concert were used for the Smith College club Scholarship Fund and Ginling College in China. Her guests were Mr. and Mrs. Robert Kentor, Major and Mrs. Charles MacArthur (Helen Hayes), Lt. Frances Rich, Lt. Joan Evans, Lt. Col. Martin Sommers, Lt. George Abell, Lt. Drew Dudley, and Captain and Mrs. Vincent Astor. That last night in Northampton, climbing

---

[1]Joan did not know at the time that in October 1945, working for Norman Bel Geddes, the famous industrial designer, her first job would be to organize, supervise, and direct the photographing of scale models depicting the Battle of Midway.

into bed, Joan thought of the interesting people she had met. She amused herself trying to imagine the important folk who might have slept between the heavy linen sheets.

The final stop was Boston, where Captain L. H. J. Kepplar squired them through the Boston Navy Yard. To Joan this appeared to be the busiest place they had encountered so far— certainly the largest complement of WAVES at work with a diversity of jobs that was enlightening.

Again she found the group attractive, serious, and capable. The captain arranged a 1:00 o'clock luncheon with Mr. Arthur C. Sullivan, National Vice President of the Navy League. Again, Joan was fascinated watching Mrs. Forrestal charm the men, then convince them into cooperating in the recruiting of WAVES. After lunch they proceeded to the Procurement Office where Mrs. Forrestal chatted with the officers, captivating the men and encouraging the WAVES. Joan noted her pitch generally offered good common sense towards recruiting in all categories.

They were driven to the hotel where the Undersecretary would join them. He had been attending conferences at the submarine base in New London, Connecticut. Joan was intrigued about meeting him face to face after seeing him at a distance in and around the Navy building. She knew very little about this impressive man: a graduate of Princeton University, President of Dillon, Reed (a Wall Street Investment Banking House), and Undersecretary of the Navy beginning in 1940. She also had heard he had been instrumental in having his friend, Robert Lovell, appointed as Assistant Secretary of War for Air.

They arrived before he did and were taken to a suite of two bedrooms separated by a spacious sitting room. While waiting for their luggage, Mrs. Forrestal said, "I'm almost sorry to have our trip end tomorrow. We did a good job getting lots of publicity for the WAVE program. Don't you think so?"

"Indeed I do. It was a great privilege and pleasure traveling with you and watching you captivate your audience. I admire you for devoting so much of your time to the WAVES and for persuading Mainbocher to design the uniforms which are terrific."

The Undersecretary and the luggage arrived simultaneously. After greeting his wife, he turned to Joan, "Nice to see you, Lieutenant. The word is you two gals have been doing a good job on publicity. Let's wash up and meet here in the sitting room. You can bring me up to date over a cocktail. We will have dinner downstairs in the hotel."

A quick bath and change of clothes left her marveling at her luck at having cocktails and dinner alone with the Undersecretary and his wife. Getting back to the sitting room as fast as possible, she found him already mixing drinks. The forty-five minutes with him while Mrs. Forrestal dressed for dinner was one of the highlights of her Navy career. He asked her specific questions about the trip, asked for her opinions, and seemed to listen to her conclusions. She mentioned Mrs. Forrestal had worked very hard for the recruiting program and was an inspiration. It was a wonderful opportunity to see the Navy women at work in their varied assignments. No matter where they went, the WAVES were all business, intent and serious about their jobs and the war effort. She said, "Having commissioned about ninety-eight percent of the women officers, I am well aware of the extraordinary and varied qualifications and experiences. However, with the exception of yeoman's skills, I did not completely understand the outstanding experience and Navy training of the enlisted women until this trip. And I realize I've seen only a fraction."

He talked about his trip to the submarine base, of his feelings about the country and the war and his concerns about them. He was truly worried about the communist infiltration in the United States; he was distressed that other high officers and officials did not share his opinion. He made the point he did not trust third-party communication on the subject.

Mrs. Forrestal joined them looking refreshed and elegant, an exceedingly handsome woman. As he handed her a drink, she asked him about his visit to the submarine base. She listened attentively then commented on how well he understood the problems which she knew he would straighten out. "I called home.

The boys are fine. I gather they enjoy the freedom of no parental interference. Everything seems to be in order...."

At dinner he wanted to know about the success of her luncheons, dinners, and speeches. He was particularly pleased on hearing Senator Bingham's praise in connection with the Naval action at the Battle of Midway. He did not mention details of the battle, only commented on the unfortunate but necessary loss of life, indicating he was thankful it had not been a lot more. Joan wanted the night to go on forever. Of course it never does. There has to be an end.

Preparing for bed, Joan had no doubt he was one of the great patriots of the century. She admired his keen, concise mind. She remembered hearing he took his job very seriously, that lights burned in his office late into the night. She recalled at some point during the trip, after Mrs. Forrestal had talked with him on the phone, she had mentioned how worried she was about him, that he had not taken a vacation or even a day off since 1940. His entire time as a civilian administrator was devoted to building and sustaining a Navy unprecedented in size and power, one which in World War II would destroy the Japanese fleet and the German submarine threat, as well as provide amphibious support for every landing operation in the Atlantic and the Pacific.

Captain H. W. Underwood, Mrs. Jo Forrestal and Lieutenant Joan.
Official U.S. Navy photograph.

Mrs. Forrestal, seated, with (standing L to R) Rear Admiral R. Theobold, Lieutenant Parker and Lieutenant Joan. *Official U.S. Navy photograph.*

CHAPTER VIII

FRIENDS IN WASHINGTON

Returning to Washington after the inspection trip, Joan was disappointed to find no mail from John or Bob. She was pleased to receive several letters from her mother and friends enclosing newspaper clippings with photographs about the trip.

Returning to her office, she found that Captain Lawton had been replaced by Captain Carl Fink. She had come to understand Lawton's seriousness and appreciate his dry humor and she felt sad to find him gone. Captain Fink was an entirely different personality. He was a large man with a ready smile and happy, outgoing nature. She discovered from Walsh that Fink had lost his ship at Pearl Harbor and had just come in from sea duty having commanded another ship in the Battle of Kiska. He obviously deserved shore duty. It didn't take long for everyone to fall in love with this teddy bear.

Commander Bird introduced Joan to the captain. She was nonplussed by his warm, friendly welcome. "I'm delighted, Lieutenant. It seems I've inherited a very popular young officer. Capt. Lawton gave you a 4-0 rating and claimed our office had a political plus with you as a favorite in the secretary's office. Stephanie and Walsh gave me a clear picture of how they feel about you and kept me up-to-date with newspaper clippings. I'm sure Commander Bird is relieved to have you back. He won't have to work so hard. I'm lucky you're my assistant. Welcome back."

"Thank you, Captain. Captain Lawton may have mentioned this trip was part of an extracurricular assignment in public relations connected with publicity for recruiting purposes. I understand the quotas are being reached more quickly than expected. This need should ease off proportionately. Of course, Captain," Joan added with a big smile, "you must know it's the Navy itself that attracts the ladies."

"I'm just catching up with the need for women in the Navy and how well it is working out. I was given a copy of your itinerary. Did it go well?"

She told him how impressed she'd been to observe the seriousness of the women, how enlightened she'd been to witness the exacting duties such as welding, heavy equipment mechanics and communications. "Mrs. Forrestal saw to it the press followed us to luncheons, schools and wherever to record her speeches. She's a remarkable woman, intelligent, charming and forceful. I'm glad she's on our side."

"Did you make any speeches?"

Joan laughed, "No, Sir. Officially, I was her aide. She never needed aid of any kind. I did join in on conversations, answered questions and tried to be inspiring as a happy, contented WAVE."

Further chitchat was ended by a telephone call from the Housing Section. She was overjoyed to find out that Metropolitan Life Insurance Company was building a complex in Arlington not far from the Annex. It was to be completed in September. They put her on a list for a one-bedroom apartment. She was to see them and fill out an application. The Metropolitan office was on the grounds of the development, which was a five-minute drive from her office.

She went over on lunch hour and introduced herself to the lady representative who said, "Yes, Lt. Evans, you're on our list. The Navy is most anxious for you to obtain an apartment. I understand that you've been moved about many times from hotels and furnished rooms since you arrived in Washington."

"I've been living with a friend and her mother since June. It's uncomfortable to overstay one's welcome in another's home even though they are wonderful to me."

"I understand. Fill out the application. I'll get it processed right away. While you are here, there are two types of apartments still available. We'll show them to you."

The development was very attractive, two-story brick buildings, nicely landscaped even in its unfinished state. She chose a one-bedroom, ground-floor apartment with a small patio. Within the week, the lady called to say her application had been approved.

She got in touch with Kathleen to meet in the cafeteria for lunch. Seated at a table Joan said, "I've been accepted at Parkfairfax. I know you understand, but do you think your mother will? You've both been so good to me. I don't want to hurt her. Will she recall I moved in until I could find a decent apartment? And this is so close to the Annex."

"She's very attached to you, but I'll break the ice. When will you be able to move in?"

"It should be ready in three weeks, around the middle of September. I wanted to check with you as to how soon I should tell her."

"Your birthday is coming up. We've planned a small party at the house. Maybe we should tell her after that."

"How dear and thoughtful. I didn't realize you knew the date. I knew yours from your file." The matter being settled, they talked of other things until time to return to work.

The afternoon produced a new experience in procurement problems. An officer from the Secretary's office called Joan to ask her help. The son of Larry McPhail, manager of the Brooklyn Dodgers, was unable to pass the Navy physical due to high blood pressure although several private physicians attested his pressure was normal. She agreed to talk with him and alerted Walsh to advise the doctor in the dispensary at the end of the building of the situation in the event she might need him.

She had no idea that an hour of fun was ahead for her. The attractive young man, tall and sandy-haired, unsure with a contagious smile, appeared at her desk. Sensing the fact he was uncomfortable standing in a Naval office containing five uniformed persons, she suggested they go outdoors. Walking around the parking lot, she avoided any mention of his current problem. They talked about the crowded conditions in the area, but small talk did not ease his tension. Acting on impulse she burst out laughing and said, "You need to be dumped into a large tub of liquor like Dumbo and Timothy Mouse."

He stared at her as she described the scene in the movie "Dumbo," and then he was laughing. Still alluding to the movie she led him to the side door into the dispensary. Before he had a chance to think about the man in the white coat, Joan laughed and said, "OK, Timothy Mouse, stop giggling and roll up your sleeve." It was over, his blood pressure was normal and he was commissioned.

Next morning presented a different episode. Public relations informed her she was to go to the White House at 10:00 A.M. At that time some fifth grade school girls visiting Washington were due to stop. She was to greet them, talk with them and answer their questions. They were a sweet bunch of children definitely aware of the fact they were in the President's house. They were wide-eyed and curious as they walked around with Joan. Once they decided they had seen everything, they turned their attention to Joan and the WAVES. She gave them a quick idea of what these women were doing around the country for the war effort. She encouraged them to try on her jacket and her hat. Immediately they wanted to know if they could be junior WAVES. Joan was sorry to have to disappoint them. Eighteen years old seemed unreachable at that moment. Two pretty little nymphs, Emily and her sister Connie, pleaded for Joan's address to write to her. Joan wrote it out fully believing the thought would be forgotten before they were back home in Marlborough, Massachusetts. To her surprise, Emily did write thanking her for speaking with them. She enclosed a photograph of them in pseudo uniforms, saluting smartly. Correspondence faded as homework became heavier. Christmas was coming soon.

Driving back, Joan did a bit of daydreaming, hoping one day to have a little girl of her own. Her mind wandered, remembering some unhappy moments that slid by. While still in New York, before coming to Washington, she had vibes of outside forces entering her life. Since being in the Navy, several incidents alerted her to the difficult position John was in from the beginning: hearing about the WAVES program on his car radio, "you're the husband" bit, outranking him and the deluge of publicity photographs. A sixth sense warned her that uncontrollable factors could eventually upset her existence. For instance, her family, John's family and well-meaning friends, all anxious to keep John supplied with mail, had swamped him with newspaper clippings and publicity photos.

The inspection trip with Mrs. Forrestal was blown up in the papers for obvious reasons, publicity for recruitment. Stephanie sent John the itinerary for information but gave her own viewpoint, "The delight and pride of the Captain to have his assistant chosen.... It sounds very exciting, she will make a big hit as she does with anything she undertakes.... She's so wonderful, we all love her."

She recognized all this must sound like child's play to anyone in a War Zone. He'd had a bellyful of it. A later letter from him confirmed her fears as he indicated how glad he was she was having such a good time while he was being shot at and watching his buddies die. It was short and cool. She tried to convince herself that it was the strain he was under and wars were tough. She didn't attempt to justify the fact she was following orders. It seemed too incongruous. She slipped into her cocoon while merely increasing her affections in her letters.

She had trouble shaking off the heaviness of her thoughts even with the interesting and unexpected facets of her work. Then an invitation came from Mrs. Forrestal for dinner at her home. Once she admitted such events could not be avoided, she had to accept them and be amiable. Mrs. Forrestal was a clever hostess who knew how to gather interesting guests at her dinner parties. Joan noticed that the Undersecretary was conspicuously absent,

95

that Mrs. Forrestal missed having her husband around, that she shouldered the responsibility of their two teen-age sons, that she was gay, witty, and charming—a brave, courageous wife who accepted the fact her husband was a dedicated man. She hid her true feelings.

At cocktails, Joan discovered two old friends from New York, now Naval officers stationed in Washington. They caught up on family news and compared notes on their respective jobs. They were both attached to the secretary's office and both trying for orders for sea duty. Ed Peters said, "They're trying to convince us our work is essential. We're trying to convince them to release us before we acquire whiskers or sink in the social racket of Washington."

Mrs. Forrestal came over with a civilian in tow. Following introductions, she said that he was a local newspaper man interested in hearing about the inspection trip. When she departed, Joan sketched out the itinerary only to discover that he was not interested. Instead he asked her impertinent and personal questions which she politely avoided. She found him aggressive and unattractive, a man who thought of himself as a gift to women. Her friends were successful in rescuing Joan by asking him impertinent and personal questions which they soon regretted. Joan excused herself to join another group.

At dinner, she was relieved to note the newspaper man was at a distant table. She found herself seated between two Naval Reserve officers, one from Pearl Harbor on a temporary assignment and the other on his way to Pensacola. They were interesting, amusing and fun. She told them some of her procurement highlights. They followed her for coffee on the terrace as she noticed her two friends were caught in Mrs. Forrestal's web. When the party began to break up, Ed Peters came up beside her, "Good for you. You iced him out. We'll call you for dinner."

The next day in the main Navy building Joan ran into another New York friend. "Why, Martha Lee Washington! What are you doing here?" It was her former housekeeper who beamed,

"When you went off to war, I took myself off, too. Now I'se a typist."

Dear Martha Lee—she was an excellent cook and laundress. She could do anything around the house. Joan had reluctantly, but she hoped graciously, placed her with friends before she left. Martha Lee had turned them down and enrolled in a civil service typing class. On completion of the course, she had requested that she be sent to Washington where the war was. She had been assigned to the typing pool in the main building and was so busy that future attempts to contact her proved futile.

Later, reminiscing, Joan got carried away with the ardent patriotism that existed in all walks of life at the time. She hoped when the war was over the American people would never relax in a general ennui of patriotism.

On August 26 the Georgetown household was filled with good cheer for Joan's birthday. Mrs. Bagley and Kathleen gave her a beautiful cocktail and buffet which included Kathleen's military friends as well as Joan's. Kathleen had used the occasion to tell her mother of the Parkfairfax move. Those dear friends let the word out so Joan received several presents of kitchen utensils and, to her embarrassment, several bottles of liquor.

Joan was able to move in a few days ahead of schedule. What joy! She bought the bare essentials in the way of furniture and made curtains, covers for twin beds and covers for two single beds doubling as couches in the living room—thanks to the sewing machine borrowed from Heidi. She loved the idea of a full kitchen with a dinette. In her spare moments, she planted a few flowers on the patio.

This development turned into a very happy gathering of friends: Heidi and Bill Woodworth moved in a few doors away; Dick and Debbie Cooper moved in across the road; Jim and Grace Kane (he was a civilian working in the main Navy building) moved in across from Joan; and Commander Bench moved into a building near the Woodworths.

They shared cleaning help and took turns taking and picking up laundry. They pooled food stamps so that once a week someone would collect them, buy meat and cook dinner for all. It was amusing to watch how the men tried to outdo the women in culinary arts.

One Army officer, a friend of Bill's, was a super chef— later when he was transferred, he was really missed. They tried to share car rides when possible to save gas. Here again, she experienced how good, kind and cooperative most people were when needed.

At the beginning of October another invitation was received from Mrs. Forrestal for dinner at her home. Guests were invited for 7:00 o'clock with dinner scheduled for 8:00 o'clock. Joan gathered it was some sort of special occasion as Mrs. Forrestal happily announced the undersecretary would be present.

Joan was introduced to Robert Lovett, Assistant Secretary for Air, War Department, and recognized him as one of the three civilians aboard the Navy flight to Washington from the West Coast. There was no opportunity to mention the incident to him as she was whisked away to be introduced to other guests. Eight o'clock came, eight-thirty and still no undersecretary. The hostess kept her cool and delayed dinner.

Joan was chatting with a Naval officer, Angier Biddle Duke, who eventually became ambassador to four different countries, when shortly before 9:00 o'clock Forrestal rushed in and stood in front of the fireplace to apologize for being late. Obviously he had hurriedly showered and dressed as his fly was unbuttoned.[2] Mrs. Forrestal whispered to Joan, "Do something!" Gosh, he was Undersecretary of the Navy and she a mere female lieutenant. She hesitated and then noticed one of their sons. She slid over to the boy and suggested that he stand in front of his father while he took care of the problem. No matter what anyone might or might not be thinking, the young man handled it well. There was no stir or fuss. It was taken quite naturally. Joan never heard anyone even refer to the incident.

[2]At the time zippers were not used in men's trousers.

These dinners gave Joan the opportunity to know Mrs. Forrestal better and to further admire and respect her. Through the Forrestals she met many important and glamorous people which broadened—sometimes saddened—her horizons. Definitely this dinner was special—the appointments more elaborate, more floral arrangements, more wine glasses at each setting. Their two teen-age sons were present. The guests, in general, were older, more senior, more important. Strangely no one made mention of it being an event of any kind. Joan thought about this for several minutes, coming up with the idea it had to be because the undersecretary was present.

Finding an officer she had come to know, she said, "It's wonderful to have Undersecretary Forrestal here, to see him enjoying himself."

"He doesn't go to cocktail or dinner parties or any social events. He stays at his desk. Captain Gingrich brings him his dinner. He will go to the club at Chevy Chase for a short workout or to play handball but never leaves his desk for too long."

"I've heard of his late hours. To me, he's the greatest patriot of our time. It's good to have him here tonight if for no other reason than to please his wife. She's always charming, but tonight she sparkles."

"She's devoted to him. Not many women would be able to handle it as well as she does."

"She understands and appreciates his accomplishments. I've witnessed how hard she works in connection with the recruiting of WAVES as well as how pleased he is with her efforts."

It amazed Joan how the kitchen staff was able to suspend the dinner for an hour and a half and still serve a superb meal. She suspected Mrs. Forrestal might have guessed the timing. Although the atmosphere appeared a little more solemn, there was plenty of laughter echoing around the room. Guests left earlier than at other parties that she had attended. She believed that was out of respect for the hard-working undersecretary.

CHAPTER IX

CHRISTMAS AND FAMILY

Shortly after this party Joan's mother flew down for almost three weeks. She loved the apartment and was satisfied it was healthy and safe. She took delight in adding a few accouterments. It was like a game with her. She would drop Joan off at the Annex, proceed into the city and wind up at Woodward-Lothrop for something she believed the apartment needed. She then would rush back to set the item in place before going to fetch Joan. Then she would watch for Joan's reaction when she spotted it.

She stocked the kitchen with cooking needs, then took delight in fixing dinner for Heidi, Bill, Ray, Kathleen and Kathleen's mother. It was a great success.

Ray was in top form and amused everyone with an accounting of the first time he took Joan riding in Rock Creek Park. He embellished the tale, laughing at himself until they all cracked up. Joan's mother had tears rolling down her face. He made a date with Pinkie for lunch the next day promising to take her to the stables to show her the horse that Joan had ridden. It was right down her alley. She had a glorious time having Ray to herself, regaling him with stories of Joan, joy for the mother who finds a willing ear. Heidi had a cocktail party for Joan's mother to meet the members of their group. She decided Joan was in good hands with such friends nearby in case of need. When she left, some of the fun went with her.

Luckily, that first night Joan was not alone as she was invited to a small dinner at the home of Artemus Gates, Assistant

Secretary for Air, Navy. She mentioned she had met Secretary Lovett at the Forrestal's and recognized him as one of three men aboard the Navy flight to Washington from the West coast. Secretary Gates felt certain the other men were Henry Stimson, Secretary of War, and John McCloy, Assistant Secretary for Air, War Department, as they had been on the coast at that time investigating aircraft production. "I gathered Secretary Lovett and Secretary Forrestal were close friends," Joan said.

"Yes. Business brought them together in addition to the fact they were neighbors in Locust Valley. On an inspection tour for Union Pacific, Lovett began to look into aircraft production on both coasts. Horrified by what he observed, he wrote a detailed report and showed it to Jim. Bob Lovett was concerned the manufacturers were more interested in custom service rather than mass production which would be needed in wartime. Jim showed the report to Stimson who was so impressed he hired John to become Assistant Secretary for Air."

"They were very busy on that flight, studying oodles of papers and having serious conversations."

"Aircraft production is still very serious."

Joan was cautious not to mention the Marine fighter pilots were training for combat in SNJ planes before the Corsair was available as it had been told to her in confidence; besides, she was sure he was aware of it.

When Thanksgiving rolled around, realizing for some it might be the first time away from home and because it was such a family-oriented time, Joan decided to cook a turkey dinner. She would include Stephanie, Walsh, a few other enlistees and several officers. The evening before, she picked up the turkey, stuffed it and when safely in the refrigerator she set the table buffet style. Returning at lunch time, Thanksgiving Day, she put the bird in a slow oven, prepared cranberry sauce and boiled onions. Later, last-minute fixings were accomplished before her guests arrived.

She was proud of her small patio. As it was warm enough, she served punch and drinks out there. It was a tasty dinner and a successful evening. Everyone happily pitched in for cleanup detail. Joan was particularly pleased they were not alone or homesick on this holiday. She felt satisfied that she had put her apartment to good use.

The next morning, however, she found a note on her desk to see Miss McAfee. Joan went up to Miss McAfee's office not knowing what to expect and was informed that she had broken a very serious Navy rule. Joan was at a loss to understand. Miss McAfee explained that she had invited and entertained enlisted personnel in her home. What a shocker! These were people— human beings—her friends. She worked with them and could see no reason to discriminate. Miss McAfee emphasized the fact it was a rule. She did not like Joan's breaking it and told her so. Joan did not want to break accepted rules. Having to say something, she said she was sorry—deep down she was not. She had not attended any kind of indoctrination school. Perhaps there were other rules she did not know. She'd better find out.

On October 1st, Joan had been promoted to lieutenant, senior grade, a rank equivalent to Army and Marine Corps captain. At about the same time, a letter from John informed her that he had finally made first lieutenant and was pleased about it. She did not have the heart to mention her new rank in her letters.

A week before Christmas Heidi called and asked, "Bill is working late. Will you go to the movies with me?"

"Sure."

"Good. I'll pick you up."

While she waited for Heidi, she was reading a letter from John in which he questioned why she had not told him that she was a full Navy lieutenant, outranking him again. She figured her mother must have told Bob. It was bound to come out. She lost her cool and cried out as Heidi walked in, "Damn it to hell. What difference does it make anyway? If you're in service for a certain time, you get promoted, don't you?"

Heidi stared saying, "What's the matter?"

Joan was quick and short in explaining. Heidi, seeing Joan was upset, said wisely, "He's in an active War Zone and won't have much time to think about it. He'll forget it. You probably worry more about it than he does."

"Did she?" Joan asked herself.

During Christmas 1943, most Naval departments ran on a skeleton staff. Joan was lucky to get four days off. She was luckier still to fetch a ride on a Navy plane to Floyd Bennett Air Base to be home with family for the holidays.

On the flight up, she discovered Congressman Jack Anderson was aboard. He was one of the exceptionally nice, understanding members who never questioned or argued if his constituent could not be commissioned. She listened fascinated as he told her of the activities of his office and the Congress in general. She was amazed to discover that most laws were settled in committee meetings consisting of appointed members. She struggled to comprehend why so few had such power and why the same members usually missed roll call. When he complimented her on how well she handled her difficult job, she assured him that it was a pleasure to take his calls, that they helped to cancel out the few rude and unreasonable ones.

When they landed at the airport, Naval personnel were separated from the civilians. She didn't see him again until they were outside the gate. He was looking for a taxi while she was trying to spot her mother's car. It was very confusing as traffic thundered by at great speed. Had he seen a taxi, it would be unlikely the driver would stop. She offered him a ride if and when her mother showed. They waited about twenty minutes before she saw the car coming along by the curb, proceeding slower than the rest of the cars. She suggested he jump in the back as she got in the front seat.

As soon as her mother was able to get back in the traffic speed, Joan introduced the Congressman and mentioned that he would be able to get either the Long Island train or the subway into New York from their house. Quick as a flash her mother exclaimed, "You wouldn't send the Congressman in by train! He can come home with us, wash up, have a drink and then we will drive him into the city."

"That's a fine idea to go home with you, have a drink and then I can call a taxi."

Mother apparently had a dreadful time to get close to the gate at Floyd Bennett. There was no place to park and naturally, they would not let her through the gate. She kept driving around worried about stopping. Joan was thankful for her patience.

The Congressman and her dad hit if off well. They were on the second drink when Joan's brother, Arthur, arrived with a beautiful girl and a toy bull terrier, "Twerpie." It was evident Arthur had been fortified with several drinks. He brazenly announced, "This is my wife, Margo." Turning to Margo, he said, "This is my family except the kid brother who is off shooting up the Japs."

Hurriedly, Joan introduced the Congressman who took it in stride, having no knowledge of how shocked the family was as none had ever expected Arthur to marry. During introductions the little dog lapped up the Congressman's scotch, which he'd left on the floor by his chair and promptly proceeded to do what appeared to be cartwheels.

The tension was released as they laughed at the dog. Dad offered to make a fresh drink for the Congressman, which he declined and said he really must call a taxi and get into the city. Arthur seized the opportunity to be released from his discomfort and said, "We're going into the city. Be happy to have you join us. We'll drop you wherever you say."

Joan and her parents accompanied them to the car, waved them off and then stood rooted to the spot. Dad broke the spell, "Well, what do you know about that?"

"She sure is a pretty girl," Joan added.

"God help her. I hope she can handle him," Mother said.

Joan laughed, "Can't imagine what the Congressman makes of it. I just hope he gets to town safely."

"You can be sure," Mother interrupted, "he will be the exemplary host and do whatever the Congressman wishes."

"I hope you are right, Mother. We may never know."

Arthur was the middle child, had been hit with polio near the end of his first year at Notre Dame University and eventually suffered an atrophied leg. Being considered a find on the freshman football team, this was no help to his already inflated ego. He was 6'3" tall, had red-blonde hair and pale blue eyes, was athletically coordinated, had a retentive memory, made excellent grades and had been accepted at Notre Dame at the age of fifteen. It was rumored that he spent time at St. Mary of the Woods, a girl's school close by. Naturally, the polio scare caused him concern. He inveigled his parents into allowing him to return East to enroll at Fordham University and live at home.

After college, he got a job at the Brooklyn Union Gas Company and in a short time he was head of Sales. Within two years he was the president of an exterminating company in New York City. A hot romance with a beautiful model was broken up by mother, who claimed she would not make a good wife. This unexpected blow caused a rift in the family. Arthur moved out of the house and took delight in landing women and then abruptly dropping them. To further upset him, when the war came he was unable to enlist as a private because of his disability. Determined to enter the war effort, he got an appointment with an Army colonel who was instrumental in placing him as a civilian with an aircraft manufacturer as head expediter. By Christmas of 1943, he was an officer of the company and a husband.

While Joan helped dad trim the Christmas tree, mother neglected her culinary arts to make numerous telephone calls on Arthur's unexpected announcement. Sitting around after dinner, her mother remarked, "That was some dramatic scene my son put on today. I still can't believe he's married. On the other hand, I hope it will last. I've been disturbed hearing about his shenanigans."

"Margo?" asked dad. "Is that her name? She seems like the type to curb his reins."

"I hope so. And, my baby, Bob. I was praying he'd wait to get married until after the war. They are both too young."

Joan spoke up, "Young men facing war and the unknown are apt to seek some sort of roots they can live and dream about in tense moments. Bob wrote me about the possibility of getting married. I thought about it for a few days, then wrote him he was an extremely intelligent person, athletic, good sense of humor and that Trudy was a very pretty young lady. If she possessed the qualities that mattered to him and that he believed would take him over the long haul—as a grown adult soon to be in combat fighting for his country—I told him I would respect whatever decision he made."

"Oh, Sister, he would have listened to you had you suggested waiting."

"Mother, I understand how you feel. I just could not. It had to be his decision. It's his life."

The next day, Christmas Eve, was traditionally "Open House." Her parents must have done a job inviting the entire neighborhood in addition to relatives. The house was alive with happy folk wandering in any time of the day or evening until time for Midnight Mass. At Mass, Joan found herself fighting back the tears. She was touched by the pride her dad took in introducing her with the big grin and sparkling eyes, "You know my daughter, don't you?" They did. He was showing off his girl in her Navy uniform. She missed John, prayed for his safety and prayed for guidance in handling his moments of unhappiness. She loved him and constantly told him so in every letter. Thank goodness everyone was tired; bed was welcome that night.

On December 26th, she returned to Washington via Eastern Air Lines, not without a crack from her mother, "What, no Navy plane?"

Brother Bob and wife Trudy--newly weds.

CHAPTER X

FORRESTAL AND THE
USS MISSOURI

The draft must have been on the heels of favorite sons as Joan's phone kept ringing; the office was buzzing in spite of the holiday week. The only break in New Year's Day was several of their group met for eggnog at the Woodworths'. Heidi had enough finger sandwiches, dips and crackers that no one needed to worry about dinner, with the result being that they stayed longer than usual.

Joan mentioned her phone was busy with calls about the boys who wanted to avoid the draft. "Have you had any more encounters with Lyndon?" a Lt. Hayes asked.

"No, as a matter of fact, we haven't heard from him for quite a while."

"Scuttlebutt has it he's on the campaign trail mesmerizing or boring whoever will listen to his tall tales of his brilliant Naval service. He's a good storyteller, a better liar—each telling gets bigger, better, more dangerous—clearly indicating his life-threatening experiences beyond the call of duty."

Joan said, "I didn't realize he was in the Navy. He was not in uniform."

"Well, he was." Others gathered to hear the lieutenant as he continued, "He cajoled and pleaded until commissioned a lieutenant commander in 1940 so as to have his draft number counteracted. In early 1942, he and his pal, Tom Connolly, also a lieutenant commander were ordered to the West Coast to visit shipyards in connection with training programs. Word came back they were strutting around in their uniforms, carousing with movie stars, partying and generally raising hell. Johnson was even sitting for a senior Hollywood photographer to get the best angle of his face for portrait photographs. It seems some of his top political advisors were furious and cautioned him his career would be finished if he didn't get into some war action. They knew he passionately wanted to obtain a senate seat." He paused, looking at Joan, and said, "Your friend, Forrestal, convinced the President to include Johnson as one of a survey team going to Australia. He left in early spring with a supply of his pictures. The committee learned war in the area was not going well. Most of the planes were badly in need of repairs after missions against the Japs in New Guinea. Johnson, frantic to get some war action, volunteered to go on a mission. Somehow he loused up and got on the wrong B-26. It was one of twelve planes flying in formation. The plane Johnson was on lost altitude and headed for home followed by a lone zero. Three more zeros joined in the chase and gunfire was hot and heavy. Thus his plane never reached the target. It got back to the base and Johnson had his one-day war story." Lt. Hayes was inundated with questions. He didn't know much more about the incident.

"I'll bet," Joan added, "after he had the action he needed, he had himself reinstated in Congress. That is why he was not in uniform."

About the middle of January, Mrs. Forrestal requested Joan meet her in New York for public relations functions. They stayed at the River Club—that is, they slept there a few hours each of three nights. She was a most efficient woman, also a whirlwind, as they rushed around from one meeting to another held in popular restaurants at lunch or dinner hours, all geared to seeking promotion tactics for WAVE recruiting. The format varied little from previous trips. Joan never ceased to be amazed at Mrs. Forrestal's resiliency and was stimulated being in her presence. The mission was completed and they parted after a luncheon, Joan returning to Washington by train.

There were many messages waiting on her desk. By the time she finished the Navy batch and cleared the paper work involved, it was late in the day when she got to the personal call slips. She was lucky to reach Heidi in her office and discovered her voice was missing its normal, happy lilt as she asked about the trip. "Heidi, what's wrong? You don't sound like yourself."

"Bill's orders for overseas came the day you left. We knew if would happen sooner or later. I have to remind myself it wasn't sooner."

"I'm sorry. I know, you know, Bill—like the rest of the guys—was hoping for action. When does he leave?"

"This Friday. I'm having some of our gang for dinner tomorrow night, sort of a farewell, good luck bit. We want you to be with us."

"Of course. I wouldn't miss it for the world. Bill has been a wonderful friend to me as you have. Why don't I fix salad and dessert? How many will you have?"

"You're a dear," she said. "I've made dessert; salad would be great. There will be nine of us. Incidentally, have you talked with Ray Owens? He's been trying to get you. He thinks he will be going to the Pacific."

"No, not yet. I'll call now. Knowing Ray, he'll still be in his office. I see he's called three times. I better find out what's up. I'll talk with you in the morning."

As she expected, Ray was at his desk. He took great delight in telling her he had been promoted and was given a new assignment as aide to Marine Aviation General Roy Geiger and would be traveling with him to the Pacific. "Have dinner with me tomorrow night. I'll tell you all about it."

"Ray, I can't. Bill got his orders for overseas and Heidi is having a farewell party."

"How about Friday?"

"That's fine."

"How was the trip?"

"It was the usual pitch for recruiting. At the very first luncheon, Mrs. Forrestal had a group of ten men including

111

journalists, public relations experts and advertising people. These men consumed two or three martinis. You know, I've learned to enjoy a martini at dinner. On an official trip of this kind, I do not drink at lunch. What a razzing I took."

"You should have asked for tonic water with a lemon twist."

"My lack of sophistication must have been obvious as the waiter suggested the same thing. I followed his advice for the rest of the trip. This beautiful, intelligent lady easily handled these men to get the results she wanted. Discussions concerning methods of action were sharp, clear and rewarding. Ray, she's an inspiration."

"Friday, I'll do my best to compete."

One thing about being with Heidi, either as an individual for morning coffee or in a group for dinner, she was always full of beans and lots of chatter. The evening of Bill's departure party was no exception; if anything there might have been a little more of the chatter in an attempt to hide her feelings. She had invited what she called the core of the Parkfairfax group: the Kanes, the Coopers, Comdr. Bench, the Army captain and Joan.

By this time the men were anxious for overseas duty and regarded Bill's going as a triumph. Debbie, Grace and Joan knew only too well how much Heidi would miss her Bill in spite of her front which fooled no one. Saying good night and hugging Bill goodbye, Joan realized he'd be gone tomorrow night. She couldn't leave Heidi alone that first night, and so she'd cancel her date with Ray.

Joan should have guessed Ray's reaction—the Marine who took charge of everything. When she explained the situation, he said, "You're right. I'll take you both to dinner."

At dinner, Heidi flooded Ray with questions about the safety of the European Theater, explaining that Bill was assigned as an advisor on the Economic Board. Ray told her what he knew of the situation and quickly changed the subject to the Pacific where he claimed to know more of what was happening. He had nothing but praise for the Seabees—Navy construction men—

who moved into the various Japanese-occupied islands to build airstrips on the perimeters in order for the Army and Marine planes to land. He was well-informed, telling enough for them to understand what John and Bob were facing. Ray, appreciating Joan's thoughts, said he expected to go on several tours of the Pacific war area with the General. He promised to check out her two Marines.

Heidi, quick on the trigger plus her love of photography, said, "Ray, for God's sake, take a camera and get pictures."

They thanked Ray for the dinner and a very informative evening and headed back to Virginia. On the ride home, Heidi commented, "Ray is a nice guy. It's too bad he lives in town. He'd fit nicely into our group. Bill told me Comdr. Bench is not too happy. His father-in-law is not well, and his wife refuses to leave him to live in Washington. Did you know that?"

"No. What a shame. He's such a nice, considerate gentleman. He was in my section for two months in 1942 and was helpful in getting some of our WAVE pilots commissioned. As a matter of fact, at that time, he and his friend, Jack Gifford, took me to dinner to explain the women's pilot situation. They told some weird stories of foul-ups in the Navy. Both of them were full of fun and good humor."

"He does have a wonderful sense of humor—that twinkle in his eye. Bill thinks his wife is unwise in her choice." Heidi sighed and continued, "Bill loved to sit and talk with him, said he had more sense than most of the Navy men he'd met. Of course, he thinks Dick Cooper is a bright young man but doesn't have Ed's experience."

"Last night after your delicious dinner, he was the first one in the kitchen to help clean up. I mentioned Ray would be going on a tour in the Pacific. He had a wistful look as he said he was hoping to go with the Secretary for Air. It seems to me the majority of Reserve officers want to get out where the action is. I guess that's part of why they joined, to fight and get the war over as soon as possible. In fact, there is only one regular Navy officer I've met who prefers his desk job."

Heidi was thoughtful for several moments, then said, "I love this country and its people. They are so very patriotic." She laughed, "Even your Martha Lee had to get into the act."

As they turned onto Heidi's street, Joan asked if she would like to spend the night with her. Heidi tossed her head, "Might just as well get used to the idea of being alone. Bill thinks he will be gone for some time. Good night, dear friend."

On April 28, 1944, Frank Knox, Secretary of the Navy, died. Joan, like her co-workers, was positive Undersecretary Forrestal would be named to the Cabinet post and was shaken to learn Drew Pearson's column indicated the possibility of Lyndon Johnson's being appointed. Although it sent her blood pressure soaring, like many of Pearson's predictions, there was no basis for it, and James V. Forrestal was sworn in on May 19, 1944. He was very popular as evidenced by expressed feelings around the Navy buildings which pleased Joan and confirmed her belief he was a great person.

At the beginning of June, Joan received an invitation to attend the commissioning of the battleship *Missouri* on June 11, 1944, at 3:00 o'clock at the Navy Yard in Brooklyn, New York. It had been hand delivered to her office while she was away from her desk. Stephanie told her a male ensign had left it. Thinking this might be an assignment from public relations, she contacted Lt. Daley to determine if it came from their office. "I don't think so. Wait, I'll check." Coming back on the phone, "No. We know of the event and will cover it, but we did not send the invitation to you."

"Attached is a guest card from Commander W. W. Maxwell to attend a reception in the wardroom following the ceremonies. I don't know him."

"He's the prospective commanding officer. I'd advise accepting right away. It's quite an honor. Whoever sent it expects you to attend."

"OK. If I find out, I'll let you know."

On June 10th, the Naval Air Field at Anacosta called to say a car would be at the main building in D.C. to take her to the airfield to connect with the plane going to Floyd Bennett for the *Missouri* commissioning. "Will many be going?" Joan asked.

"My list shows only a few officers from Bu Ships."

"Thank you."

Getting into the car the next morning, she was surprised to find she was the only female. She didn't recognize any of the men. They were pleasant and excited about seeing the ship, which was the main topic of conversation. Joan admitted she'd never been aboard any ship, let alone a battleship.

The car taking them from the airfield to the Navy Yard pulled up alongside the ship. What an impressive sight! Joan gasped, "Look at the size of it." Her heart was pounding as she took her turn being piped aboard, saluting the flag and the Duty Officer, and waiting at attention until another group was assembled.[3] They were escorted on a tour of the ship which was utterly fascinating. She was amazed at every turn: the efficiency, the planning, the radio and communications station, the boiler rooms, mess halls, kitchen facilities, gunnery equipment, alarm systems, and evacuation equipment. It was onerous to fully absorb or appreciate the magnitude of the whole.

Gathered in the wardroom after the ceremonies, the officers were ecstatic with the ship and being released for sea duty aboard her. One could almost feel their sense of pride.

The return journey to Washington was more relaxed, more friendly. Most of the officers were Bu Ships personnel. Joan began to suspect her invitation had come from the admiral, Chief of Bu Ships, with whom she had a discussion on procurement of WAVES qualified for his Bureau. This had been in 1942 when she was selecting the initial women officers. She remembered his good common sense, his witticisms and his outgoing manner. She resolved she'd send him a note congratulating him on the sleekness of the *Missouri*, how much she enjoyed being aboard and how impressed she'd been.

---

[3] Little did Joan know at the time she was standing on the deck where a year later the Peace Treaty with Japan would be signed.

The Prospective Commanding Officer

Officers and Crew

cordially invite

Lieutenant Marion Enright

to be present

at the Commissioning Ceremonies of the

UNITED STATES SHIP MISSOURI

Sunday, the eleventh of June

Nineteen hundred and forty-four

at three o'clock

Navy Yard, Brooklyn, New York

R. S. V. P.
THE PROSPECTIVE COMMANDING OFFICER
UNITED STATES SHIP MISSOURI
FLEET POST OFFICE, NEW YORK

Invitation to Lieutenant Joan to attend the commissioning of the *USS Missouri*.

The next day, June 12th, was Bob's birthday. Her mother picked that day to fly down for a two-week stay fusing good fun and spirit to Parkfairfax. Everyone saw a lot more of Ray while she was visiting. Following her departure another live wire, Elena Hidalgo, arrived in Washington. Elena was Joan's sophomore sister at Manhattanville; she had hazed and protected the shy freshman. Elena had been born in Mexico, part of the famous Hidalgo clan. She had moved permanently to the United States as a small child. She was of average height with black straight hair which she wore in a French knot, flashing black eyes and a sexy figure. She was interested in everything including art and music.

The day following her graduation she had married Juan Serralles, son of a wealthy family in Puerto Rico. The wedding was a storybook affair: two handsome Spaniards madly in love.

In 1936 Joan and John had gone to Puerto Rico to visit them. If their wedding had been a storybook, their lifestyle was a fairy tale: airplane, yacht, Arabian riding horses, private island complete with house, servants, swimming pool, another house in the mountains, their main house in Ponce, coffee plantation, sugar plantation and Don Q Rum distillery. The entire experience was breathtaking. On the slightest excuse, Joan will tell one incident on herself.

She and John had arrived on the Puerto Rico Line. Anxious to see the harbor as the ship entered, Joan was up, dressed and on the deck at 5:10 A.M. In the excitement of being driven in a pale green, open limousine with a chauffeur and footman in matching pale green uniforms, sitting in the cockpit of Juan's plane as he flew it across the island to Ponce, and being met by a duplicate green limousine which brought them to the main house through vast gardens, Joan forgot about mundane things such as bathroom needs until they were in the house. Elena took her to the bathroom through the suite they would occupy during their visit. Joan estimated the bathroom was about the size of her apartment living room with a sunken tub, glass-enclosed shower, glass door cabinets filled with towels of all colors and sizes, but no toilet. Turning to Elena, she said, "Where's the throne?"

"They're such an eyesore, we keep them out of sight." Pushing a button on the wall, up came the needed equipment. Joan was so startled, she almost forgot her mission.

Following an afternoon and evening of various activities, they arrived back at the house about 3:00 A.M. After bidding their host and hostess good night, they retired to their suite. Not stopping to discard her new dress with its yards of crisp organdy, she entered the bathroom, pushed a button and sat down to a shower of water. She let out a yelp. John rushed in as Joan swore, "I knew that darn plumbing wouldn't work."

"Darling, the plumbing is OK. You pushed the bidet button." He was still laughing as she shed her wet clothes and dumped them in the bathtub.

In the morning they were awakened by a music box installed in the ceiling. Joan decided she should rescue her dress. It was not in the tub. She found it washed, ironed and back in the closet. Her slip, panties and bra had also been laundered and were folded neatly on the dresser. She was delighted but had a creepy feeling when she realized someone had been wandering about as they slept.

They had kept in touch and had not seen each other for a couple of years. Elena phoned from the airport, "I'm here. I have your house and street number but forget whether it's in Alexandria or Arlington."

"Elena! Good to hear your voice. Go powder your nose and meet me out front. I should be there in about twenty minutes. Look for a 1934 beat-up black Chevy." Some nonsense about finding a car or a taxi was promptly dismissed.

Joan's tiny apartment was in an immediate state of disarray and remained that way during Elena's visit. Elena did her best in an effort to be neat—she was just servant spoiled.

Over scrambled eggs and coffee, Elena poured out her problem, "My brother, Eddie, is here in Washington. He's been aboard the aircraft carrier *Enterprise* , which I guess has seen lots of action."

Joan interrupted, "You can say that again. The ship was one of the three carriers to escape Pearl Harbor, being out at sea. As a result, they became the principal Navy weapon at the start of the war. Later they became escort carriers for the big stuff. The *Enterprise* was in most of the battles starting at Midway."

"I believe he said it was in for repairs and he was on leave. He asked me to meet him to sign some papers. Joan, I've had it. I'm finally starting divorce action."

"I'm so sorry, Elena."

"My mother prepared me for the fact Spanish men had mistresses. I fooled myself into believing Juan was different. By the time I found out, I had three children. I closed my eyes until he brought one home. I couldn't take that."

"Oh, Elena. Maybe American men might not have mistresses, but they have their little flings."

"Eddie's New York law firm is handling the action. May I ask him to come here tomorrow afternoon to discuss it, sign papers or whatever. He said he'd take us out to dinner. He's anxious to see you."

"Of course! But you may want to go to dinner by yourselves. Do you want to borrow my beautiful car?"

"Eddie has rented a car. We should have it hashed out by the time you come back from the office. I just want out. He is adamant I get a proper settlement and support for the children."

"He's right you know. Listen to him." It was so good to see her and so sad to learn she was divorcing her handsome Spanish husband. It was wonderful to see Eddie and listen to his hair-raising experiences.

CHAPTER XI

POLITICAL AND PERSONAL TURMOIL

Joan was writing regularly to John and Bob. Letters from overseas were few and far between, which was understandable as they were moving from island to island.

Her office was maintaining its busy pace. The only change in a year and a half was two captains shipped out to be replaced by two coming back from the War Zone. Stephanie, Walsh and Joan had discussed and agreed how fortunate they were with these officers.

The Parkfairfax group had enlarged considerably and spread out from the core so that varied leisure ventures were enjoyed. One Sunday, early in July, gas rations were pooled for an excursion to the battlefield at Gettysburg to honor one Major Gifford of the Pennsylvania Volunteers 106th Regiment, the renowned ancestor of Comdr. Jack Gifford of the Secretary for Air's office. Comdr. Gifford sent Joan a formal order to prepare a report on the battle which she conscientiously obeyed.

Six piled into Heidi's car. None had been to Gettysburg. On the drive to Pennsylvania, Joan read her report and satisfactorily answered their questions. Comdr. Gifford awarded her with a mark of 4.0. Each had contributed to a picnic lunch, which they ate at the site of the 106th Regiment monument until routed by a swarm of yellow jackets. This intrusion was attributed to the fact that Jack's ancestor resented the disturbance and preferred being left in peace. It was a memorable, impressionable experience to walk through the battlegrounds, studying the monuments—yet, a devastating realization of the number of young men killed in a face-to-face attack.

One morning Joan was in Captain Gingrich's office (Secretary Forrestal's aide) when the door was thrown open. The Secretary, who was of slight build, bodily tossed out a much larger Naval officer who muttered something about, "You'll live to regret this. I'll get you."

Captain Gingrich went into the Secretary's office and returned shortly to fill Joan in on the details. His admiration was unbounded as he explained, "Forrestal sure is a gutsy guy! He was on the boxing team at Princeton and is physically no pushover, but his courage in defying the press is, to me at least, frightening. That man you saw tossed out on his can is the controversial columnist, Drew Pearson, who was commissioned by former Secretary Frank Knox, a California newspaperman. Pearson should never have been commissioned in the first place."

"I've read a few of his columns," Joan remarked. "I always found them abrasive and critical to the point I doubted his credibility."

"And so you might. There are a lot of guys around here who will savor this incident and be relieved he's finally out of the Navy. Sorry about the unpleasant interruption. Did we finish?"

"You were looking over the last file but did not give me your decision."

On the bus returning to the Annex, Joan recalled a remark Secretary Forrestal made during that eventful forty-five minutes she shared with him in Boston. "Third party communication is not always reliable."

Maybe so, yet there was much whispering around Washington that this particular columnist was disliked. On occasion he threatened persons who refused to give him information he was seeking. He was arrogant and aggressive; some felt he might be a danger to our security. Joan never asked whether Pearson had gone to the Secretary's office after being decommissioned or whether he had badgered Forrestal who decommissioned him.

Admiral Ernest King and Secretary of the Navy James V. Forrestal. *Official U.S. Navy photograph.*

It wasn't long before rumors flew that the columnist was trying to get something on Forrestal to discredit him, such as accepting bribes on Navy contracts. If this was so, he'd have no success on that score as Forrestal's honesty, integrity and patriotism were known to be unblemished.

Strangely enough, that weekend, at one of Mrs. Forrestal's dinners, Joan sat next to a Mr. Abel who made some cracks about the Secretary's egotism, conceit and lack of human compassion. With one of her best disdaining looks, she remarked, "It is obvious you do not know Secretary Forrestal very well."

He switched to Mrs. Forrestal, "What a shame she held these parties to obtain male attention and companionship she lacks in a husband."

With a frozen grin and an icy voice, Joan said, "I am embarrassed for you in your lack of self-confidence. You seem to find it necessary to attack persons you do not know, or perhaps being a heel makes you feel better about yourself."

Fortunately, Mrs. Forrestal announced coffee was being served on the terrace. Arriving outside, a civilian official joined her, "Did you enjoy your dinner companion on your left?"

Wow! Someone had noticed her reactions, "Not really. He's a very frustrated, unsure human being."

"Perhaps that is what he wanted you to believe. On the contrary, he's very sure of himself and his power. He is one of Drew Pearson's associates."

Dismay showed all over Joan's face. Signals rang in her head. "Don't worry, my dear. I doubt he will bother you. He's after bigger game. He stole Pearson's wife but still works for him." She could only hope the gentleman could not read her thoughts or her fears.

The following morning she phoned Mrs. Forrestal to thank her for an interesting and pleasant evening, suggesting through innuendo that perhaps her parties might be enhanced without the boring man on her left. To Joan's horror, Mrs. Forrestal said, "No, no. You're quite mistaken. He is very amusing and most entertaining. I've been to several parties with him. He's lots of fun."

Joan had no recourse and prayed her fears were unfounded. She was not able to shake off the worry. Sure enough, just a few days later she was awakened around midnight by a phone call from Mrs. Forrestal. She told Joan she was in a telephone booth at the side entrance to the Wardman Park Hotel and asked Joan to come fetch her.

Joan flung on a housecoat and was on her way. She had no trouble finding Mrs. Forrestal. Joan noticed that Mrs. Forrestal had been drinking and was coherent but apprehensive. Joan drove her back to her apartment in complete silence. After a cup of hot, strong coffee she poured out her story.

Some friends had taken her to dinner at the hotel. She'd had lots of fun and several glasses of champagne. One of the men offered to escort her home. Instead he was pushing her into one of the hotel bedrooms. Her normally active mind responded. She laughed, made a silly remark like "not tonight" and fled. He apparently made no attempt to follow her. His mistake was overestimating the amount of champagne that she had consumed.

As she rested on the bed, Joan sat on the edge. Joan was so shaken she let go in telling Mrs. Forrestal how easy it would be to frame her, cause a scandal, ruin her husband's very needed devoted service to his country and she'd be the fall guy. She assured Joan she understood this very well, particularly after the shock she'd been through that evening. An hour later when Joan saw her safely home she felt fairly certain her worry was gone.

Captain Fink and Joan were summoned to appear at a meeting which had been requested by Miss McAfee. It was an awesome gathering: Admiral Denfeld, Chief of Naval Personnel; Capt. Gingrich, Aide to the Secretary; a Marine general in charge of Marine Personnel; several captains; a few lt. commanders; Miss McAfee; and Miss Palmer. Miss McAfee submitted her proposal that WAVES should be sent overseas. There were loud gasps around the table including one from Joan. The men were very much against it and pointed out transportation was too risky and war conditions in Europe were not good. She then suggested they might be sent to Hawaii on a volunteer basis. This possibility was discussed.

Captain Fink turned to Joan and asked how she felt about the idea. She was quick to say she understood the reasoning, but Hawaii was a Recreation and Rest area for service men coming in from the War Zones. With women volunteers, many of whom might be seeking adventure, it could be asking for trouble. She was surprised to feel a sharp heel on her shin. It was evident her thinking was not politic; but it was how she felt, and the men did consider it.

In the end, Miss McAfee won. WAVES were sent overseas to Hawaii. Joan felt Miss McAfee was right in her thinking as she wanted recognition for women and what they were capable of accomplishing. Joan could not fault her for that and Miss McAfee did break the ice for Navy women.

However, Drew Pearson was still carrying on a private war against Forrestal and the Navy in general. Pearson wrote the first objectionable article about the Navy WAVES when, quite naturally, a few women sent to Hawaii became pregnant.

As they returned to their office, Joan mentioned, "Looks like I put my foot in it."

"I don't think so," Captain Fink replied. "I agreed with your reasons. There are bound to be some casualties but she has a point too."

They both noticed an unusual number of females going by. Joan asked Stephanie, "What's going on?"

"I don't know. It's been going on most of the morning. I'll see what I can find out." She intercepted a yeoman to discover that the actor Robert Montgomery was in the department talking with one of the reviewing officers. On his way out, he stopped to thank Captain Fink for the information he received. "I hear you caused a little excitement to our female Navy. I understand their curiosity and can only apologize for it."

Comdr. Montgomery smiled, "Having been at sea duty, away from the gawking public, I had forgotten I was a curiosity.

I haven't seen many WAVES. It was kind of fun. They're very attractive."

That evening, relating the incident to Heidi, she exclaimed, "Did you get his autograph?"

"That would never occur to me. It's not my thing nor, I believe, Stephanie's."

That summer of 1944 on her two trips to the Situation Room at the White House, Joan found the atmosphere intense and the officers uneasy. The war news was disheartening. In Europe the Berlin raid by the B-17 Flying Fortresses was followed by the perilous Utah and Omaha beach landings which were hindered by mines and strong German shore batteries. In the Pacific American ships and planes were attacking the Japanese in the Philippines and Mariana Islands under powerful, hostile conditions.

She grew more and more anxious about her Marines who were somewhere in the Pacific. She couldn't get any news from Ray who was out in the field with the general. On the 6th of September, she was to have dinner with the Coopers. Returning from work, she showered, dressed and was ready to leave when the phone rang. It was John! "Hi, monkey,"—a nickname she had not heard for a time.

"Darling, where are you?"

"In a San Francisco hospital. The old stomach kicked up. They removed two-thirds of my stomach."

"My God!"

"It's OK now. I didn't want to call until it was over. I'm up and about. I should be leaving here in a week or ten days, then I report back to the base for a few days, check in and square things away. The big news, I get an R & R so we'll have thirty days together."

"That will be wonderful. I can't wait."

"I've missed you so much. Boy, have I lots to tell you. I'm working on getting a plane ride from Mojave to Washington. They say it's no big deal. I'll call to let you know where and when to meet me."

"Oh, darling, you must have had a very rough time. I didn't even know you were sick. I haven't received mail for over a month. I couldn't even contact Ray. He's been out in the Pacific with the general. Are you sure you're all right? Please don't hide anything from me. I love you."

"I'm fine. Cross my heart."

It was a hurried call and he was gone. In a daze, she left immediately for the Coopers', hoping to see Debbie before anyone else arrived. Debbie was still in the kitchen when she blurted out the news.

Debbie said, "I've a sister living in Oakland. She's divorced and spends much of her time as a volunteer at the hospital. I'll call her now and have her look up John." She didn't reach her sister until late that night. She gave her the information and asked her to do what she could for John.

The next morning with tears brimming, Joan told Captain Fink. He was a compassionate, terrific person who had seen much of the results of war. He assured her he knew many men who had most of their stomachs removed and were much alive and well years later. She should feel fortunate John was back in the States alive, as serving with the Marines was no piece of cake. She agreed, mentioning she had one more worry as her kid brother was a Marine fighter pilot somewhere in the Pacific. The Captain shook his head, "Your family got into a very dangerous part of the war. I've seen enough of it; now all I want to do is retire and open a delicatessen and sit out front with my hands folded under my apron." He succeeded in getting Joan to relax and promised he'd arrange time off when John arrived on his leave.

Stephanie couldn't help but hear Joan's tale and placed a cup of coffee on her desk. No one in the office ever brought in coffee as the cafeteria was so close. Joan was very touched by this dear girl's thoughtfulness.

The following weeks were full of anticipation awaiting John's arrival. Debbie kept in touch with her sister who said she enjoyed keeping tabs on John, reporting all was well and on schedule. Stephanie started marking off the days on Joan's desk calendar. Someone drew red hearts on the possible days he might arrive. As the days drew closer, every time the phone rang at the office or at home, her heart skipped a beat. The call never came.

She was dictating to Stephanie one morning when she noticed the surprised expression on her face. Following the direction of her eyes, she couldn't believe it. John was standing in front of her desk!

Captain Fink jumped up and welcomed him. The word spread and several officers including Dick Cooper and John Mayer were in the office. Joan felt numb from the surprise and the excitement. She had no idea of what was being said until Captain Fink said, "I'd love to be a part of this happy reunion and take you to lunch."

"Thank you, Captain. You're very kind," John began. "I've been dreaming of this moment for a very long time. I decided to take my wife to lunch at the Wardman Park Hotel, the first place she took me in Washington. I have much to tell her. However, I do appreciate your offer."

"Well, I'll give you two a rain check. Run along. I don't want to see you for several days."

How to describe walking down a Navy corridor with a handsome Marine husband, encountering co-workers who break into broad grins of approval? There is no way. One has to feel it.

They drove out to the hotel. It was too early for lunch. They sat in the cocktail lounge. John was startled but laughed when she asked for a martini. She explained she did not drink at lunch time, but considered this very special. Further, she was a one-drink date. "My little girl has grown up."

He wouldn't talk about the war except in the most general terms. It was clear he had made some lasting friends in his squadron. He respected his commanding officer and was devoted to the Marine Corps. While he was in the hospital, he had plenty of time to think and analyze, to decide what he wanted to do with his future. Unless she had strong objections, he would like to apply for the Regular Marine Corps and make it his career.

As she listened to him, it was evident that he had matured a great deal, that he'd been through some rugged times and that he had his heart set on the Marines. They had been in the bar some time when the waiter announced a table was ready on the terrace. After ordering lunch, John asked her how she felt about his staying in service.

"The idea has never occurred to me; in fact, it is such a new thought I don't know what I think about it. You seem to have given it a great deal of consideration and are convinced it is right for you. If that is what you really want, it is OK with me," Joan assured him.

He waited a minute then went on, "It's a great service with wonderful guys. Living on a base in peacetime would be a very comfortable, very secure way of life with some traveling thrown in occasionally. It's time now to have a child and be a family."

Her mind was racing. The idea of living on a base, subject to the whims of a commanding officer, expected to attend social functions, expected to give teas for the wives, was appalling. It would be a very ingrained existence. Further, neither Joan nor Ray had told him his application had been held because of the ulcer history. With two-thirds of his stomach removed, she didn't see how they could justify taking him into the Regulars. She was struggling with her thoughts. "You look so serious, you're frowning. What are you thinking?" John said.

"First of all, I agree wholeheartedly we should have a child and be a family. It is what I always wanted. To me, it would seem sensible that the first step would be to have you switch into the Regular Corps. Once that was definite, I could become pregnant, a qualification, if married, for an honorable discharge."

He smiled, shook his head, "You don't seem to realize at the end of my leave I have orders to return to California. Living at opposite ends of the country isn't exactly conducive to marital bliss."

She laughed, "That can be fixed. My only official leave on record is the five days before you went overseas. I'm entitled to at least thirty days, maybe more. When it's fait accompli, I'll come flying."

John stayed at Parkfairfax for three weeks before going on to New York to see his family, her family and friends. During those weeks they were a very busy, happy couple. Joan gave a cocktail party to have him meet the part of the group he had not met, as well as to enjoy old friends. Bill was still overseas. He would be missed. It was a pleasant surprise that Ed Bench's wife, Mary, was down for a quick visit and would be at the party. Later, Heidi had a buffet dinner; the Coopers gave a dinner party; the Kanes had a terrific cookout on their patio. John fitted right in with everyone. He mentioned how happy he was to know Joan was surrounded by such friends and was anxious to show his wife off to his friends on the West Coast. Time passed and he was off to New York.

It was all too rosy. Something had to give. It did. John found his father dying. He had no choice but to stay in New York longer than planned. After the funeral, he was unable to return to Washington and flew directly to California. Joan was disappointed and completely unaware she would never see John again. They corresponded faithfully, spoke on the telephone regularly and made the best of what she believed to be a temporary situation.

CHAPTER XII

HEART-TO-HEART
WITH JOHN

Sometime in October, Ray came back from his tours with the general and took Joan to dinner. He proudly gave her a photograph of Bob and himself sitting on a log on one of the Pacific Islands. All he said was they had a fun visit and Bob was fine.

Bob's letter describing the visit was more satisfactory. "I was in my bunk when a sergeant came in to say a Jeep was outside waiting to take me to the general's tent. I had no uniform and after a hectic flying schedule, my flight outfit was no prize. I borrowed a clean coverall and tidied up. Ray gave me a surprise to remember for all time. Can you imagine on a hot island, full of bomb scares and after months of K-rations grabbed on the run, to be led to a table with a linen tablecloth, linen napkin, dishes, silverware and glasses; to be given a steak, fresh vegetables, milk and ice cream? It was unbelievable, a super experience. What a guy to arrange it."

Joan was anxious to tell Ray of John's idea of staying in the Marines to find out his thinking. He was even more horrified than Joan had been and adamant in declaring that he, personally, would never consider it. He also felt John didn't have a Chinaman's chance of having his request approved with his ulcer history and the recent operation on his stomach. All she could do was hope and pray that somehow the application would be approved.

Joan and Ray went riding in Rock Creek Park several times that fall. As Christmas time approached, John indicated there was nothing new on his request. He recommended that she not come out and use up her leave time. He knew she could get home to her family and not be docked any time. Joan went home for Christmas. She could not get rid of a depressed feeling in spite of the love and gaiety provided by her precious parents, many relatives and lots of friends. Her mother sensed her feelings and arranged to fly back to Washington with her for a short visit.

That rascal found Ray's office telephone number in Joan's address book, called and asked what he thought of John's idea. Ray came right to the point, telling her John's request had been turned down. He was surprised that John had not told Joan. "Ray, Joan suspected this would happen. She's been depressed since John's leave. I hate to be the bearer of such information. Let me treat you and Joan to dinner tonight. It might be more official coming from you. Would you be willing to tell her?"

"Sure. The sooner she finds out, the sooner she can handle it. She's a very intelligent, level-headed gal, yet it's difficult to predict emotional reactions in anyone who's in love as she is with this guy. I've had no luck in stealing even a part of her affection."

"Ray, don't say that. She's very fond of you and realizes you've given her many happy times. She's told me how thankful she is for your friendship. I don't know what scenario would have developed if you hadn't commissioned John."

"Wait a minute, Pinkie. Don't forget the Navy was after your daughter. They ordered he be commissioned. I only located the file and put it through."

"I know, Ray. Bless you for that."

"OK. Let's see if we can make this as easy as possible for her. Come to my apartment for drinks. I'll make that one martini of hers a Lulu. Then you can take us to dinner. Where do you want to eat?"

"She likes the little restaurant on Rock Creek."

"Good choice. It's quieter than most. I'll make a reservation."

"But, it's my treat."

"You've got it, Pinkie."

Ray waited until coffee was served after dinner to tell Joan. "Have you heard what John is planning to do now that he knows his request has been turned down?"

"When did he know, Ray?"

"Sometime before the holidays. I gather he didn't tell you. Probably didn't want to spoil Christmas for you."

"How can one spoil something that's already hurting? He wanted it so badly it would be arduous to write about it or even phone. Ray, you're a dear. At least you've prepared me. Thank you."

"I'm sorry you got the word from me."

Joan had little to say as she dropped Ray off at his apartment and proceeded home. She was in bed when her mother put her arms around her, saying, "You know, Sister, and you must believe, no matter what, most things work out for the best. No need my telling you Dad and I tried to prevent your marriage. Over the years we were able to understand, as he is a very sweet, kind, feeling person. I felt so sorry for him at his father's funeral. He wept like a lost child."

"I remember," Joan laughed through her quiet tears. "All you could criticize was 'his hair isn't healthy.' Oh, Mommy, he is a sweet guy. He didn't want children until he felt he could support them. He never could find out what he really wanted to do. Do you remember when we were first married he thought he might like law. He took some courses at the downtown Fordham school. He worked all day and went to class at night while I stayed home nights and typed his lecture notes. It was too much for him. That's when he came down with ulcers."

"Yes. He got that idea from his high school friend, Bill Connors, who went to the same night school and became a lawyer."

"The next dream was to become an actor. It was the fall of 1940 when he joined the acting school at Carnegie Hall and was put into night classes with an older, well-recognized professional."

Her mother interrupted, "Did you tell me that when John was in high school, his brother, Bill, got him into an amateur group at St. Jean Baptist Church? He performed in several plays, didn't he?"

"Yes. He was fairly good, and so handsome all the girls were gaga over him. I thought he was doing well in the program until that weekend of July 4th in Southampton. We were staying with you and Dad. We went to 8:00 o'clock church. When we came out, he suggested we go to Judge's for breakfast. You remember Judge's?"

"Indeed. It was a famous place on the Shinnecock Canal where fishermen gathered to eat a hearty breakfast before setting out in their boats. It was a shack, nothing fancy, clean, giant-size meals. Dad and I would have breakfast there if we were going fishing."

"By the time we arrived, the fishermen were long since gone. The place was unusually quiet. I was unprepared for the flood of inner feelings he poured out to me. He admitted knowing you and Dad did not favor the marriage. He wanted to win your approval by being able to support me. So far he had not been too successful. I was far more successful than he and he was beginning to realize wanting to be an actor was an ego trip. The amateur group he belonged to in the past praised his performances and fussed over him, giving him a false idea of his acting ability. The Carnegie Hall group did not fuss over him. On the contrary, they made it clear he would have to work in small bits for years to allow his name to become known. The coach had given him a stage name, Johnathon. This was the first I'd heard of it. Even after years he would have to be at the right place at the right time to be discovered. He had decided to give it up. He felt that he was getting more recognition at work and should devote his energies in that direction. You mentioned he was like a small child at his father's funeral. That morning I felt he was like a child who had lost a cherished toy. He was naive and vulnerable. I could have wept for him. That would have crushed his pride and killed any self-confidence he was trying to find for himself. I tried to be matter-of-fact and told him he'd given the stage idea an honest try, and if he had not, he might always wonder about it. I also said it was evident he was doing well at the bank and would do better in time. I tried to explain that marriage was a joint effort, and we were pooling our resources, sharing and working together. I believed at the time I had gotten the idea across."

"It sounds like you both had a productive breakfast."

"You know, Mother, when the fact he was actually giving up the idea of acting sank in, I felt an enormous relief—even the lipstick incident could be relegated to oblivion."

"You mean the lipstick Dad found in your car along with a condom?"

Joan looked startled, "Dad never mentioned that. I had a feeling he was seeing one of his classmates. I was glad he was quitting the school. When the war came, he was so anxious to get into service as an officer. He loves the Marines. Maybe it's the first endeavor that has given him a sense of security. I wasn't too happy about the idea of living on a base, but I'd sure go along with it to settle for a couple of kids."

"I wondered why you didn't have a child long ago, particularly since you love children and get along well with them. God is good. You'll still have children. You are certainly young enough. Things will fall into place. Now you must try to sleep. You have to get up early to leave me at the airport."

"I'm so lucky to have you as a mother. You've purged the worst of my worries just by listening to a babbling crybaby."

"Don't forget what a joy you are to Dad and me. Now, good night."

It was early when she pulled into the parking lot at the Annex after returning from the airport. Therefore on entering the building she was surprised to find Stephanie in the corridor. "Hi, Stephanie. We are early birds today. I had to get my mother to an early plane. What's your excuse?"

She looked serious as she said, "Walsh came to see me last night."

"Oh? I could stand a cup of coffee."

"I've already had a cup."

"If you can stand another or watch me drink one, we can sit. You can tell me what's up."

Seated in the cafeteria, Stephanie explained, "Walsh says we have a new skipper. He's a commander and much younger than our previous bosses. I was waiting for you. I didn't want to face him by myself."

"Walsh knows or finds out everything. What else did he say?"

"He overheard it yesterday morning when he delivered some papers to Admiral Denfeld's office. He surmises the commander has been at sea a long while. This might be his first shore duty. He is a commander which in wartime means he's very young."

Noticing Stephanie's worried expression, Joan teased, "What do you want him to look like? Tall, blonde, blue-eyed?"

"I don't care as long as he lets me stay in this job."

"If he doesn't, it means we both go," laughed Joan. "We might as well face it. Let's sink or swim. At least this time there's no surprise like the others."

They were working at their desks when he entered with a cheery "Good morning." They came to their feet, saying in unison, "Good morning, Sir."

"When they gave me this assignment, they did not promise me two attractive WAVES. I'm Charley Duncan. I've come from sea duty. You'll have to bring me up on shore duty." What a smile!

"I'm Joan Evans. This is Stephanie Budd. We will do our best to serve you. Lt. Comdr. Bird is also assigned to this office. He should be in shortly. Yeoman Walsh serves your entire division."

As he went to his desk, Joan knew she liked him and winked at Stephanie. Commander Charles Duncan was average height, straight black hair, dark eyes, Naval Academy graduate, 1933. 1933! That was Joan's class, so he was her age. He was very pleasant, cordial, somewhat reserved.

To Stephanie's relief, he made no changes in the immediate office staff. At first he seemed reticent, shy. Perhaps he couldn't dispose of his sea legs or, more likely, had been in heavy fighting for much too long. It took time to get to know him. When Joan did, she was over-enthusiastic. He was extremely bright, quick in analyzing a situation, and had extraordinary common sense, the latter being, in her estimation, a most important ingredient for a good administrator. In her limited experience this seemed to be lacking in many ring-club officers as compared to the Reserve officers.

She was well aware of the caliber, experience and qualifications of the Reserves found in the many offices along the corridor to the Secretary's office. They came from different, successful business backgrounds. They were men in their forties or older; all were patriotic and willing to serve, believing they had something to offer the war effort. No private corporation could afford the collection.

On January 10, 1945, Joan's mother phoned with the thrilling news that Bob was in the States and would be coming home on leave. Hallelujah! Bob was out of the War Zone. It was just the medicine she needed to pick up her sinking spirits.

Within a day, Bob called, "How are you doing?"

"Bob, is it ever good to hear your voice."

"Did you think it was going to change?"

"Thank God, you can still tease. When are you getting home? How's Trudy?"

"She's fine. I've a proposition for you, hope you can go along with it."

"What have you up your sleeve this time?"

"I've made a commitment to see the parents of one of my less fortunate squadron buddies."

"What a sad experience for you."

"Yes, but think of the heartache his family suffers. They live in Pennsylvania. I've had enough of the hot Pacific Islands. I'm aching to see some snow. Trudy and I thought it might be a

Commander C. K. Duncan and Joan at work. *Official U.S. Navy photograph.*

good idea to spend a weekend at the Inn at Buck Hill Falls, wallow in snow, cold weather and try a little skiing."

"It sounds perfect."

"I can't wait. We should be in New York on the 13th. I'll see if I can get a reservation around the 16th for a few days. Can you get away to join us?"

"I sure can try. We've a new skipper who's been at sea a long time. He's very nice. All I can do is try. Where can I reach you?"

"Time is so short. Better call the family. I may not be in but leave the message. If you can make it, I'll get a room for you."

"Bob, I sure would love it."

When Joan told Comdr. Duncan how happy she was to have her Marine fighter pilot brother home from the Pacific, he said, "They are a wonderful group. Have you seen him?"

"No. He's still on the West Coast. He will be in New York at my parents' home on the 13th."

"Why don't you fly up? I'm sure you'd like to see him."

"You bet. He has a commitment to see the parents of one of his less fortunate buddies. They live in Pennsylvania. He's had enough of the hot Pacific and wants to see some snow. He and his wife are going to Buck Hill Falls for a few days. He wants me to join them for whatever weekend he can get reservations."

"See what plans he can make and join him. We'll put Comdr. Bird to work for a change."

"Thank you, Sir."

"If he gets down this way, I'd like to meet him."

"He's a great guy. You'd like him."

Joan called Heidi to give her the news of Bob and his plans. Joan's enthusiasm must have been contagious as Heidi asked, "Oh, please, may I go with you? We can go up on the train together and share a room. Should I ask Bob?"

"Heidi, he's still on the West Coast. That won't be necessary. I'm to call home to say if I can get away. I'll just leave word that you are coming too so he can get a double room for us."

Early that evening an excited call came from Ed Bench. "How good to hear Bob is back in the States."

"Yes, the family is ecstatic. Weren't you out in the Pacific with Secretary Gates? When did you get back?"

"A few days ago. It was a gruesome trip. The Japs are throwing everything at us including the kamikaze suicide planes. They were first used in the Battle of Leyte Gulf last October. As a result, the Navy and Marine airmen are up front in the islands. I'm relieved Bob's out of there. He'll get leave, then is due for stateside duty for awhile. The pilot training programs are in full force. Let's pray it soon will be over. He won't have to go back. Heidi tells me a trip is planned to go to Buck Hill Falls for some skiing."

"Bob is dying to see some snow."

"Who is going?"

"Bob, his wife Trudy, Heidi and myself."

"Would you and Bob have any objections to Mary and me coming along? Mary can meet us at the Inn. I'll take care of our reservations."

"I think Bob would welcome it. He enjoyed knowing you and will be happy to compare notes on the Pacific action. He is trying for January 16th for three days."

"I'll get moving on the reservation. Let me know if there is any change Can I mention we will be part of your group?"

"Of course. When I call home, I'll mention you and Mary will join us."

When Bob confirmed the reservations, he was delighted that Heidi, Mary and Ed were joining them. "The more the merrier," he said.

Joan anticipated the date. It came at last. She, Heidi and Ed went up by train. Mary met them at the station and drove them to the Inn. It was apparent they were in a mood for a change in routine, a blending of high spirits and sharing. Bob and Trudy were waiting in the lounge. They looked mighty content sipping tea in front of a roaring fireplace.

After greetings and hugs, more tea was ordered. Bob had a very satisfied smile, "We arrived after lunch and went for a long walk in this winter fairyland, kicking up snow. Have I been dreaming of this!"

Ed said, "Our group was there for only three weeks at a time. I know what you mean. It's a combination of heat, humidity and war jitters waiting for attack planes."

"Plus various boobie traps in and around the field," Bob added.

Mary didn't want to listen to any war talk. She went up to bathe and dress for dinner. Bob had arranged for a table for six in the dining room which they would share for their meals. At dinner with Heidi's hilarious stories and Bob's wisecracks, a light tone was established.

Joan woke up before Heidi and dashed to the window to revel in the mountains and the snow scene on a cold sparkling day. Suddenly she laughed out loud at the thought of the last and only other time she'd been to the Inn. "What's so funny?" came a muffled voice.

"Gosh, Heidi. I'm sorry to awaken you."

"Tell me the joke."

"I was reminiscing about the last time I was here in January 1930 when I was a sophomore in college. The mother of a classmate, Claire Gibson, brought us here for a winter vacation. There was a group of Princeton seniors here. Two of them latched onto us or vice versa. Maybe we had our first taste of dating older boys and we were in our element. We skated, went ski-jarring and square dancing. One of the guys suggested we go for a walk after dinner. They would meet us down the path from the Inn's entrance. This erupted into snowball fights and getting one's face washed in snow. In a way of apology, they sneaked in a few kisses."

"You American women are far behind European women. We were kissing boys long before college days."

"We played spin the bottle in the 8th grade. To be sure we were shy and awkward. We improved by the time the junior prom came along. They were always boys our own age. This was big stuff."

"Did Mrs. Gibson catch on?"

"I don't think so. Claire was an only child. Her mother kept a close eye on us. However, the second night we stayed out longer. After that we were given a curfew. It wasn't too bad as the guys left before we did."

Heidi, with a disparaging laugh, "You probably thought you were very naughty."

"I suppose so but it didn't stop us from enjoying it."

The day's plans were discussed as they ate breakfast. Mary and Ed were good skiers. Mary brought their equipment. They were going to try out the slopes. Trudy chose to go to the ice-skating rink. Joan, Heidi and Bob decided to rent skis and try their luck. Bob went off to test his equipment, never having skied before. Heidi had not skied in years and wanted to play around the beginner's slope. Joan agreed she'd do the same, telling Heidi, "John and I went to Lake Placid in 1938 to learn to ski. We arrived by train late in the afternoon. After dinner we went to a Yale-Harvard ice-hockey game. John cheered and hooted and had a great time, but at 1:30 in the morning he was screaming in bed. I couldn't get anyone at the front desk to answer the phone. I ran down to the lobby to find it empty. Fortunately, the man in the next room had been awakened and came out to help. He had a car and suggested he drive us to emergency at the hospital. It was discovered John had a ruptured appendix. A surgeon was contacted and John was operated on within the hour. Luckily we had reservations for two weeks. John was confined in the hospital for ten days. He insisted I spend some time in ski school which I did for two hours in the mornings. I learned to herringbone up a hill and snowplow down."

"What a nasty break for both of you."

"Actually we were fortunate in the doctor and our neighbor who drove me to the hospital twice a day. John enjoyed the attention from the nurses and the girls from the Inn."

Boots buckled and skis in place, they began their ascent. After a few trips down in a snowplow, Joan said, "That's hard on the legs. Those little tykes over there come down parallel."

"Those little tykes also flop down to stop. They don't have too far to fall," Heidi commented. "I'm going to experiment."

They were halfway up when they heard a yell from the intermediate slope. "Good Lord," cried Joan. "It's Bob taking an eggbeater." Joan was terrified. "That clown survived the kamikazes and he's going to break his neck on skis."

Luckily, Bob was coordinated, an athlete who knew how to fall and he laughed it off. Mary and Ed, standing in the lift line, saw him fall and were waiting as he reached the bottom. Ed, assured he was unhurt, suggested he try a lesson or two.

Alone with Bob before meeting for cocktails, Joan asked him about his school chum, Joe Henneberry. She knew instantly from his facial expression she'd made a boo-boo. He did not answer right away. Finally he told her, "You will remember when I left Corpus Christi, I went to the Naval Air Base in San Diego for operational training for combat. When we embarked on the USS Barnes, two fighter squadrons were on board, VMF/217 squadron and VMF/218 which turned out to be the outfit Joe was in. We couldn't believe we wound up in the same mission. We flew as bomber escorts in strikes against enemy-held positions. It seemed unreal—the very first flight, Joe was hit. I watched in disbelief as his plane spiraled into the ocean. In seconds I lost a friend of many years." She asked no more war questions.

When their friends joined them, Ed said, "Anyone object to a sleigh ride? I've rented a sleigh for after lunch tomorrow." The idea pleased everyone. The next afternoon, tucked under fur robes, the driver jingle-belled them around the beautiful snow-covered countryside. During the three days, they enjoyed each other and the outdoors. They ate heartily, slept soundly and were rejuvenated.

CHAPTER XIII

A HEARTBREAKING "DEAR JOAN"

On completion of his leave, Bob was to report to San Diego Air Field. He had obtained the necessary requisitions permitting him to buy a car and obtain sufficient gas rations to drive across the country.

Joan received a jubilant letter about their trip. They found the countryside fascinating and were amazed at how responsive people along the way had been; gas stations refused to take the gas coupons; restaurants and motels treated them like royalty. It was a heartwarming experience and made the time spent fighting Japs worthwhile. He was proud of his country and its people.

Housing outside the base was in short supply. Bob was fortunate to find an apartment overlooking the ocean. Someone had mentioned it to him and was not at all sure the landlady would rent it. A very motherly looking lady answered the doorbell and let out a cry. She mistook Bob for her own son who was in service. Trudy confirmed the fact. The picture of the son was a dead ringer for Bob.

After a friendly chat, hot coffee and homemade muffins, she told them she could not resist renting it to them. Bob admitted he felt shot full of luck and constantly counted his blessings.

He had not seen John although he had phoned Mojave. He was off the base. He would keep trying and arrange to meet somewhere between the bases.

The following month, February, Kathleen Hogan called to suggest lunch in the cafeteria. She called once in a while, so Joan did not suspect devastating news. After selecting lunch, they were barely seated at a table when, with surprise and shock on her face, Kathleen said, "Did you know John was posing as a bachelor and that he is dating all the gals on the base plus a gal from Oakland?"

"Dear Kate, how in the world would I know that?" Joan gasped.

"While you were away with your brother, I was sent on an inspection trip to Mojave. I decided while there to look up John and say hello. You will imagine my surprise when the duty officer answered my inquiry with, 'He's probably off with one of his gals. He's our most popular bachelor.' What are you going to do about it?"

"I don't know. He's wandered before in New York. I played ostrich. I'll probably do the same thing now. He is too darned good-looking and has a way with the ladies," she sighed.

"That's nonsense. You're very good-looking. Men are attracted to you but you're always very much married. Why should it be any other way?"

"Maybe this time I'll write."

"If I were you, I wouldn't waste any time."

This time she didn't play ostrich. She wrote him a very long letter in which she told him she'd heard his request was turned down and that he'd been upset and was dating the entire female contingent on the base for comfort. She tried to convince him he could go back to the bank and not to worry until he had something to worry about. In the meantime, they should thank God he had come back alive and came through an operation. She was looking forward to their plans for a family and suggested taking leave to join him.

The answer was a short letter that he did have something to worry about. He advised her not to come out as he was trying to sort out his problems with no mention of what they might be. Her attempts to reach him by phone were unsuccessful.

145

Heidi became Joan's mainstay. She flooded her with her worries which she took in stride. Heidi told her she was naive, that all men played around and that most came back home. She went out of her way to see that Joan was kept busy after work. At the office, Joan kept her head up, kept her cool; she even had herself believing all would work out, that there were more important things going on around her.

On April 12, 1945, President Roosevelt died. Conversations were suspect of Truman's abilities, but the haberdasher from Missouri turned out to be more astute than expected. The war in Europe resulted in unanticipated losses in fighter and bomber planes. Relief spread through the building when the unconditional surrender of Germany came on May 8, 1945. Hope turned towards the Pacific where action was intense.

On July 6th, she was ordered to New York for three days to report to the New York Herald Tribune in connection with writing an article on the reactions of wives in service to their husbands returning from the war. Holy Cow! Her initial reactions were of joy and relief he was in the States and had successfully come through a serious operation; of sharing a leave enjoying companionship, sexual pleasures and planning a family for the future. And now, what were her reactions? Uncertainty, almost fear about the future. She couldn't instill doubts or disillusion to those wives waiting for their loved ones. She wrote an article on the joys, pleasures and future planning. It was published. On reading it, she hoped, in her case, it wasn't pure fiction.

She stayed with her parents during this assignment. Although her mother asked no questions, she knew her daughter and was not fooled that all was well. "I'm going to fly back to Washington with you for a long visit. There is no worry about Dad. He has many solicitous friends only too anxious to share their home-cooked meals with him when he returns home in the evening."

However, on July 25th her conscience started to bother her. Joan arranged to fly up with her and return later the same day. They took the early flight with Eastern Airlines. They were both reading as they approached La Guardia Airport. The seat belt sign had not been turned on when suddenly the plane dropped, almost immediately turned and went straight up into the air. Passengers and objects of all sorts were thrown about. The stewardess was efficient in trying to get things back in place and trying to determine if anyone had been injured. Nobody was hurt. Everyone was darned scared and badly shaken. The captain apologized and informed them an Army plane had appeared without warning in the commercial flight pattern causing the unexpected maneuvers.

Inside the terminal they discovered the Army plane had crashed into the Empire State Building, demolishing the plane and killing the pilot. They had to feel fortunate it had not crashed into their plane, thanks to the quick reaction of the Eastern Airlines pilot. They were very sad for the tired ferry pilot returning from overseas.

Joan's father was waiting at the airport. His bear hug relieved some of the tension, yet it was difficult to dismiss the incident. They were alerted to the news programs throughout the day. Her visit seemed to be over before it began.

On the plane back to Washington, she struggled with the idea of confiding in Commander Duncan and obtaining his judgment on the feasibility of flying to the West Coast to face the situation and determine John's problems. She would have to weigh carefully the pros and cons. It was a very delicate, very personal dilemma. Perhaps it was unfair to put the commander on the spot and maybe even unfair to John. All her life, God had been good to her. Perhaps she should trust Him to find the right solution.

She had left her car at the parking lot at the Annex. Coming out of the airport, she jumped into a taxi as a Navy man jumped in after her. Cabs had to be shared because of the shortage. She noticed he was an older warrant officer. The service stripes on his sleeve confirmed his many years of service. She also noticed he was very drunk, probably celebrating his return from overseas.

They had gone about a quarter of a mile when his foggy glance seemed to be discovering there was another passenger in the cab. Then all hell broke loose. He was utterly obnoxious and proficient in the use of four-letter words. His gripes were: horse's ass Navy taking goddamn broads into the Navy as officers; they didn't know anything about the Navy; they didn't have a brain in their thick skulls; all the years he had broken his ass for warrant stripes. When he started pounding his fists on the seat, the driver, fearing Joan might get hurt, stopped the cab and ordered him out. Oh, no! It was the so-and-so lieutenant that should get her ass kicked out. The cabbie sized up the situation and told her to get into the front seat with him. She sat huddled on the floor as he sped towards Arlington, hoping to be picked up for speeding—no luck.

The Marine guard at the gate recognized Joan and let her through the gate as she explained the problem. She asked him to help the cabbie who did not favor driving the drunken man into town. The warrant officer got out of the cab, kicked the tires and kicked the gate. He demanded to be taken to the city. The guard called the shore patrol as she dashed to the safety of her car, determined not to budge until that guy was out of sight. The patrol arrived, took down the information from the driver, saw that the man paid his part of the fare and took him off. He must have had past experience with them as he submitted without a whimper. The cabbie offered to follow her home. She assured him she often left the building late without any trouble. She thanked him, saying she'd be fine.

That was her only nasty experience during her time as a WAVE. What a day! It started with the escape from the Army plane and ended with an escape from an intoxicated warrant officer.

She reached her apartment exhausted. She skipped taking her usual bath and barely washed her face and teeth. She fell into bed and went to sleep saying her prayers.

Although in the Land of Nod, for Joan July 25, 1945, was not yet over—the nightmare was soon to begin. It seemed to be in the distance, not connected to her. A bell was ringing. Slowly, she began to realize it was the telephone. She staggered out to the living room and picked up the receiver knowing it was John. "Darling, I'm sorry. You must have been sound asleep. The phone's been ringing for some time. I didn't want to make this call. I don't even want to tell you. I want a divorce. I love you, but I also love someone else. I want to marry her right away. Will you get the divorce?" As he spoke, she was standing against the wall. She slowly slid down until she was sitting on the floor. Joan went numb—all feeling seemed to have left her mind and her body, yet she was trembling. Then she was conscious of the phone and John's voice. "Darling, do you hear me? I want you to do me a favor and get a divorce."

"Yes, John. I hear you," she was almost whispering. "If you want a divorce, I won't contest it. You will have to get it as I never will."

"Come on. I can't get away from here. Please...?"

She replaced the receiver, and, yes, Ma Mere Lecroix, she cried. Ma Mere had been the advanced French Professor at Manhattanville College. She was a short, chubby nun with a large wart at the end of her nose. She wouldn't take any beauty prize, but she was a top teacher and a compassionate human being. She and Joan had become friends when she tried to improve Joan's accent. "Is that Irish face causing trouble?" Graduation day was hot and humid. Ma Mere had been stationed at the door of the chapel to catch the girls wearing only a slip underneath their gown. They were sent back for a dress. When Joan approached, she knew she was caught, but Ma Mere said, "Pass. In life pretty girls will cry a lot." Joan puzzled about the remark but soon forgot it in the excitement of the day. Now it came back loud and clear.

She was still sitting on the floor sobbing her heart out until she felt chilled, stood up and in a daze paced around and around the living room. How could this happen? Why did she hide from the truth when he was at the acting school? Was she so happy and content she trusted him to feel the same? Did she convice herself that because they made such passionate love he could not make love to another woman? Damn! Why didn't she face him? Why didn't she accuse him? She should have told him this behavior was unacceptable. Hell, when Kathleen warned her he was posing as a bachelor, why didn't she get emergency leave and fly to the West Coast? Why didn't she meet him eyeball to eyeball? What did he say? "I love you but I also love someone else. I want a divorce. I want to marry her right away." It was incomprehensible. Dear God, such a short time ago they had three weeks of sharing sheer joy and happiness. Was she so in love with this Adonis she could only believe it was reciprocated? He must have loved her! She wept until she was drained then went to her bed and fell asleep.

She did not hear the doorbell or the knocking at 8:00 o'clock the next morning. It was Debbie. Not getting an answer, she used Joan's key (the original core group had each other's keys for one reason or another, such as cleaning help, picking up or returning laundry, storing meat or vegetables in a refrigerator). She burst into the bedroom. She flung herself on the bed, throwing her arms around Joan crying, "Oh, God. I know. It's my sister. I never should have let her see John. She called this morning to tell me."

They were a crying duet until Joan pulled herself together and sat up in the bed. She shook Debbie by the shoulders, "Please, Debbie, don't cry. You are not to blame. John has roamed before. If it wasn't your sister, it would be someone else. Maybe this time he will be content. I hope so for both their sakes."

"How can you be so magnanimous? I should have known better." The tears flowed again.

"Friends warned me. I was suspicious something was wrong. I did not realize it had gone so far." She was very fond of Debbie, a pretty, charming, gracious person who had merely tried to do a favor for a friend. How on earth could she blame her? She couldn't even blame her sister. "These things do happen. What was it my Dad said? 'No human being has the right to judge another human being. Only a Divine Being knows all the facts.'" Debbie was not convinced. She brought ice in a dish towel to reduce the swelling in Joan's eyes and face. She snapped Joan out of her stupor to the point where she was able to get dressed for work. Joan had heard about the "Dear John" letters being sent to servicemen overseas from their states-bound wives or sweethearts but this was a switch—a "Dear Joan" wake up phone call!

Bill was back from overseas. He and Heidi shored Joan up as did Dick and Debbie. VJ Day came with celebrations everywhere. The war was over, and so was her world. Her dreams of home and family were shattered.

She applied for a release from active duty. Commander Duncan tried to talk her out of it. He argued she'd done a fine job on the commissioning of special cases and now the Bureau would be flooded with requests for decommissioning of favorite sons. He told her he had recommended her for promotion to head the program. He was such a nice guy, but she no longer had the heart to remain. Finally he was convinced and obtained the necessary forms for her.

As she filled out the form, she came to the lines: Name of Spouse, Address of Spouse. She fought back the tears, then suddenly she was angry. They were not yet divorced. She wrote, "John S. Evans, Captain, US Marine Corps, Post Exchange Officer, US Marine Corps Air Station, El Toro, Santa Ana, California."

Her anger provided catharsis for her hurt, making it easier to sever most connections of the past two and a half years. Waiting for the forms to go through channels, she shipped home whatever she wanted to keep from the apartment. She notified the Metropolitan Life Insurance Office that she would be terminating her lease on September 30, 1945.

Finally, she wrote her mother giving her the sad news, suggesting if she could arrange it with Dad, she might fly down to spend a week with her at the Homestead in Hot Springs, Virginia. They could ride every morning, take the hot baths, swim in the salt pool and explore the countryside. She would let her know when to come down.

It was not an easy letter to write. A religious family, they did not believe in divorce. No one on either side of the family had ever been divorced. She was extremely concerned about hurting

151

them and worried about how they would take it. Yet she preferred they hear it from her rather than an outsider.

She mailed the letter and was heartsick remembering how they had tried to protect her, particularly in this marriage. Joan was unequivocally convinced she had a Guardian Angel taking care of her. No one could convince her to the contrary.

Eddie Hidalgo came to Washington. He called to invite her for dinner the very day she received a four-page, small-printed, legal paper with a covering letter from a Mexican attorney requesting she sign and return without delay. Eddie was a capable, brilliant lawyer as well as a gentle, caring person. In the fifteen years she had known him, she had never seen him lose his temper until he read that document. He let go with expletives saying, "Do you know what this is?"

"A request for a divorce. I have not read the fine print. I'm sorry, Eddie, to upset you," she apologized.

"This paper is for a divorce not legally recognized in the United States. Further, it demands you pay all the costs involved, including John's travel and hotel expenses in seeking the divorce."

"If it is not accepted in the States, I don't understand how he can agree to it. He says he wants to get married right away," she exclaimed, bewildered.

"I'll take care of it. He is not going to put this fast deal over on you. If you hear from him or this joker, refer them to my New York office." He stuffed the papers into his pocket, "You and my sister break my heart. Let's forget it and go to dinner."

Commander Duncan was absolutely right. The office was swamped with requests for releases from active duty. In a way, it kept her going. She was much too busy for self-sympathy until she received another blow.

Her check for the August rent bounced, "insufficient funds." She knew she had more money in her checking account than she should have had. She called the bank to discover John had cashed a large check. They had a joint account, but this was unreal as during the war years he had not sent her any money. Fortunately, she had money in a savings account that she could transfer

152

readily. In all honesty, up to that moment, she had not given much thought to money, rather down-played it due to John's feelings about her earning more than he did. The shock of a check bouncing was worse than the embarrassment. She swore it would not happen again. It hasn't. It was agonizing to try to fathom this man she'd loved and was married to for ten years. A call from the White House brought her back to reality and her job.

Her first contact with Norman Bel Geddes, the famous theatrical and industrial designer, was startling, as unique as her future association with him. It came by way of a telephone call from New York. Stephanie informed her a Norman Bel Geddes was calling, person to person from New York. She was sure one of her friends was in a jovial mood that morning. The conversation which followed was to imprint forever on her memory the dynamic personality of this genius. "Hello, I want to talk with Lt. Evans," boomed across the wires.

"This is Lt. Evans," she replied.

"Now see here, young lady. I've wasted enough time this morning putting through this call. Now get me Lt. J. R. Evans."

"I'm sorry, sir. This is Lt. Joan R. Evans." Dead silence followed.

Finally, starting almost inaudibly and ending in a crescendo came, "Well, I'll be damned. It's a woman! I wanted a man. It turns out to be a woman."

"If you called from New York to determine my sex, you've got the answer. There is nothing either one of us can do to change it to suit your wishes."

The deep hearty laugh that later was to become familiar to her, "I guess I'm licked this time in changing the shape and design of things to suit me. I'd like to meet you. When can you come to my office?"

"I expect to be in New York next Tuesday for one day. I believe your office is in Radio City. I could be there after lunch if that is convenient for you."

"That's fine. See you then. Goodbye, Lieutenant."

To say the least, this was a most unusual call. She laughed about it with Stephanie, Walsh and Comdr. Duncan. She wanted to share it with friends until she realized their group had practically disintegrated. Bill was being sent to Japan to serve on the Economic Advisory Board for the revitalization of that country. He and Heidi had gone to Pennsylvania. Ed Bench had already been detached. Ray was again on tour with the general. The Kanes had gone to California to be with their son who had returned from the war. That left the Coopers, but their phone didn't answer. Something unusual had happened, no close friend to tell. Nuts, it wasn't that great anyway.

The following Tuesday she walked into Mr. Geddes' office in New York. His secretary led her through the portals where the geniuses pass. She had never seen Mr. Geddes, and there were three other men in the room. She knew him instantly. His powerful personality seemed to permeate the room. There was no greeting of any kind. She felt like a kangaroo who had accidentally crashed an elegant fashion show. He peered through his oversized, horn-rimmed glasses and turned to address the men, "Well, not only is she a woman and a lieutenant, but she's not hard to look at. I guess she'll do for the job." Turning to Joan, "OK, Lieutenant. I'll pay you what you want. You'll start next week."

She was mesmerized by the man and delighted she'd wasted no time preparing any kind of speech as she wouldn't have remembered a word. Regaining her composure, she stated, "Mr. Geddes, because of your prominence and my insignificance, I am in a position to know more about you than you could know about me." A slight raising of an eyebrow indicated his acceptance of his fame. "However, it would be most helpful to have some idea of the job you have in mind. What you consider it to be worth to you. If we agree, I'd like to examine your books, prospective contracts and the financial status of the corporation before deciding whether or not you need me. Finally, it would be necessary for me to consult with Uncle Sam as to when I will be free to accept any position."

President of the United States of America.

To all who shall see these presents, greeting:

Know Ye, that reposing special trust and confidence in the Patriotism, Valor, Fidelity and Abilities of **MARION RITA ENRIGHT** I do appoint him

A LIEUTENANT COMMANDER

in the Naval Reserve of The United States Navy to rank from the ---- day of ---- He is therefore carefully and diligently to discharge the duties of such office by doing and performing all manner of things thereunto belonging.

And I do strictly charge and require all Officers, Seamen and Marines under his command to be obedient to his orders. And he is to observe and follow such orders and directions from time to time as he shall receive from me, or the future President of The United States of America, or his Superior Officer set over him according to the Rules and Discipline of the Navy.

This Commission to continue in force during the pleasure of the President of the United States for the time being.

Done at the City of Washington this **SIXTH** day of **JANUARY** in the year of our Lord One Thousand Nine Hundred and **FORTY-NINE** and of the Independence of The United States of America the One Hundred and **SEVENTY-THIRD**

By the President

Secretary of the Navy

403939
Relative precedence from 3 October 1945

Joan was promoted to Lieutenant Commander in the U.S. Naval Reserve on 6 January 1949.

During her speech, the emotions portrayed on the great countenance would have been a joy to any movie producer. It almost seemed sacrilegious to have them displayed before such a small audience. He was amazed at her not automatically knowing about the job and incredulous anyone would have to determine his monetary worth; completely dumbfounded that anyone would question his accounts; and finally, annoyance at the inconsideration of Uncle Sam. That was the beginning of an employer-employee relationship that would become a stimulating experience for her.[4]

The trip to New York was necessitated by having to appear at the New York Navy Department in connection with her release papers. She had notified her parents she would go up by train and attend to Navy matters, see about a job interview and be home to have dinner with them before catching an evening plane back to Washington.

When she left Mr. Geddes' office, she hopped the subway home. Excitedly, she related her encounter with Mr. Geddes. She sensed her parents were relieved not to find her depressed. After dinner when Dad was taking the car out of the garage to drive her to the airport, her mother said, "I got your letter. Now that it's over, forget it, find someone worthy of you. Of course, I'll go with you to the Homestead. I'd like to see it again. Let me know when you want me to come down."

Well, what do you know? They had to be upset about the idea of a divorce. They not only accepted it but wanted her to find someone else. No one in the whole world could have more understanding parents. She did love them. One thing was clear: she did not want to marry again.

The papers for release came through. She was to be discharged September 10, 1945, and granted a thirty-day leave. Now she was forced to make final decisions. Realizing she had too much paraphernalia to take home, she decided to drive to New

[4]"Horizons" by Norman Bel Geddes, Little Brown and Company.

York. Heidi and Bill, back from Pennsylvania, were in the throes of preparing their possessions for storage. When Joan mentioned she was trying to find someone who might want the furniture in her apartment, Heidi indicated the Meade family would be moving into Heidi's apartment and was looking for furniture. Mrs. Meade came and decided she could use everything. Joan told her she cold have it the following week with her blessings plus the promise to remove it before September 30th. Mrs. Meade looked horrified and explained, "I just can't take this—twin beds, couches, bookcases, lamps, the rest. I must pay you for them."

Joan, reminded of her former nonchalant attitude about money and her vow to correct it, said, "Whatever you feel it is worth to you is OK with me." They reached a satisfactory figure which pleased both parties.

Her mother was alerted to the change in plans. The day arrived to leave. It was most difficult to say goodbye to Stephanie, Walsh and Comdr. Duncan; even more difficult to close the door of 1752 Preston Drive, the apartment where she had last seen John, where they had planned a future and hoped for a family. The tears came quietly, stopped and came again. She was on the Jersey Turnpike before she snapped out of the depression, realizing she must not cause her parents any further worry. She had made reservations at the Homestead. Many things had to be taken care of before leaving New York.

She advised Mr. Geddes that she'd be able to report to him on October 1st if he still wanted her. How could she believe he'd waste his time seeing her in the first place. Of course, he wanted her. How could she expect him to run his office until October 1— the faker!

Shortly after she arrived at her parents' home, Joan's mother told her John had phoned to give her an address where his clothes were to be shipped, asking specifically for his dinner jacket, trousers and cummerbund. As a reheaded youngster Joan had a temper, but her father had patiently taught her to control such outbursts. Now, to spare her mother, she hid the temper welling up inside her, and said, "O.K., I'll find some boxes and get

157

it over with right away." By the time she arrived at her apartment with the boxes, her anger was erupting. She kicked the boxes across the bedroom floor, threw in helter-skelter his shorts, undershirts, pajamas, socks, sports shirts, sports slacks, sports jackets, dress shirts, three suits, ties and shoes. She stopped to catch her breath and spotted on her dressing table his photograph in its' silver frame with the message, "To my darling with all my love forever."

She wanted to smash that handsome face; instead, she flung it, frame and all, into the box containing his underwear. "There," she said out loud, "all set for the next victim." At this point she found a small box, tossed in the few pieces of jewelry he had given her, including her engagement and wedding rings and placed it on top of the picture. With a feeling of satisfaction, she got a glass of ginger ale and sat down in the living room.

As she simmered down, her head began to take over; she'd retrieve the rings, sell the engagement ring and use the wedding band to fend off embarrassments.

So, he'd asked for his dinner jacket! She had bought it at Tripler's as a present for him. He'd admonished her for spending that kind of money when she should have gone to Roger Peet's-- but he had used the gift certificate! "Well, my fancy one," she thought, "hell will freeze over before I send that to you. I'll keep it for Bob, along with your camel's hair coat and winter Chesterfield, neither of which you'll need in California." She rechecked the closets and his chest of drawers. Finding no forgotten items, she tied up the boxes and sent them COD by parcel post.

Dad refused to let them drive the old Chevy. Mother made a few disparaging remarks about the jalopy and took her Chrysler to be serviced for the trip. Joan discovered that getting her civilian clothes in order had two effects: the relief of getting out of uniform and sadness in finding some outfits that John had particularly liked and often asked her to wear. To avoid unhappy memories, she bought a suit and two dresses. She was flabbergasted at how expensive clothes had become in the years she'd been away.

If she had a magic formula to pick the right person for the trip, it would have to turn up her mother. She knew when to be talkative, when to be funny and when to be quiet. The vacation accomplished what Joan had hoped for—it took her away from any connections that involved John. The physical exercise of riding, swimming and walking was a sedative. Her mother's face lost most of the worried lines of the past three years and she looked much younger. As for Joan herself, she reasoned there had to be some explanation for the unhappy situation. The change in her life must have been predestined. It was time to grow up, face reality, accept fate, recognize her capabilities and extend her energies into a business career. The clouds parted leaving a hazy sun but it was a beginning.

EPILOGUE I

FRIENDS AND FAMILY

Stephanie Budd took advantage of the G.I. Bill of Rights and went to college. Joan has never lost her cherished memories of Stephanie. She was sad that in her disturbed state of mind at the time, she was negligent in not getting her home address. Joan contents herself with the idea that she successfully married and is now happily surrounded by children and grandchildren.

Walsh returned to his job in Boston. He telephoned Joan occasionally for a few years. In spite of her many urgings to come visit her family, he never did. One day the telephone calls stopped. Joan still wants to believe he is alive and well.

Captain Fink retired. He did not open a delicatessen. Joan saw him and his wife several times when she went to Washington. Joan kept in touch until they both died.

Commander Duncan went on to higher accomplishments: he became an Admiral, Commander-in-Chief, Atlantic Command; was Commander-in-Chief, Atlantic Fleet. He well deserved the acclaim he received. Retired, he now lives in Coronado and keeps in touch. Joan received an invitation to attend a reunion of her brother Bob's Marine Fighter Squadron which was held at Coronado. She wrote to Charley telling him she'd be in the area and was hoping for a chance to see him. She not only had a delightful visit to his home, but he took her and five of her relatives to dinner at a fashionable hotel. Charley was still the same person she remembered. It was a nostalgic, memorable evening, thoughts of which would be enjoyed over the years to come. Perhaps she will get out there to see him again, or perhaps he and his wife will come East to visit her—this would be like icing on her Navy memories.

Bill Woodworth was Economic Advisor in Japan for several years until severed from the Army, ordered into the State Department and transferred to Paris in the same capacity. In 1949 Joan flew to Paris for three weeks with Bill and Heidi. Two weeks were devoted to sightseeing and one week to skiing in Davos, Switzerland, where she met Heidi's sister and her doctor husband.

Joan was looking forward to skiing in Davos. She had been to Stowe, Vermont, for a week here and a week there in 1946 and 1947 to learn the basics of skiing. She loved the sport.

Heidi had selected a truly native hotel, The Regina, where all the employees spoke German. Everything was meticulously clean. The furniture was worn enough to be cozy and comfortable. There were many exciting events during the week, but her first experience on the slopes was the most memorable. Heidi and Bill took her down to the Ski Schule where she was tested, rated intermediate and assigned to a guide, Richard Wagner (no relation to the composer). He was a cobbler in the off-season.

She was instructed to meet at the Parsennbahn funiculaire the next morning at 9:00 A.M. There were seven in the group: four men (two Americans and two British), two British girls and Joan. Richard introduced them, led them into the lift which resembled a subway car with no seats, door opening in the middle, and long windows for viewing in all directions. Looking back, the town appeared like a toy village. They changed cars at the halfway station. Joan was surprised to find they were already above the tree line. The virgin white snow fields went on forever. She was unable to distinguish any ski trails.

Reaching the top, stepping out into the snow not too many meters short of the very top of Weissflu Mountain, was like stepping into a celestial world—deep blue sky, mountain ranges on all sides with their peaks extending towards the Heavens. There was two or three inches of new fluffy powder now sparkling in the sun creating a pattern of scattered diamonds. Joan experienced a wonderful lightness, a joy of being alive. All her concerns disappeared in the beauty surrounding her. It was one big snow field as their skis made fresh tracks down a steady, moderate decline, causing them to ski at an easy, manageable speed. It was a glorious feeling of moving in spacious grandeur that could only be created by a Superior Being whose presence was everywhere. It was a striking contrast to the crowded, narrow, hard-packed and often icy ski trails in Stowe, Vermont.

Every so often, Richard would stop, check his troops and continue. After two hours on skis they reached the Parsenn Hutte, a small mountain restaurant where they would spend the next hour and a half—siesta time. Joan felt full of health and happiness until she took off her skis and tried to put her feet on the ground. Her legs shook violently. Her knees knocked uncontrollably. She was frightened and had the awful thought of being taken down the mountain by the ski patrol in a toboggan at the very beginning of her stay in Switzerland. Richard recognized her problem and her fright. He said, "I bet you never on skis such long time, eh? It will go away pretty quick. Come, I help you. Inside we get some turkenblout. That will fix."

Richard was right. She sat down and it went away "pretty quick." He handed her a water tumbler of pink effervescent stuff like a soda. It was ice cold and delicious. She took a healthy slug of it. Richard gasped, "Not so fast, Fraulein. Take easy. Sip slow."

"What is it, Richard?" She asked.

"Maybe little burgundy, little champagne."

It was too late. She'd had three-fourths of the glass. They ate lunch out on a porch soaking up the sun, pestering Richard with questions until they had to move on to keep the schedule to make the train at Klosters.

Joan put on her skis to find her legs were as good as new. Full of joie de vivre and, of course, "maybe a little burgundy, little champagne," she started down the mountain with the marvelous feeling of flying until Richard caught up to her, grabbed her arm and said, "No! No! Fraulein. You must stay behind me. Come I show you." He eased her over a short way. She looked down into a steep ravine. He did not have to warn her any further. She apologized and promised to stay in line. Just as well, as the decline became steeper. They were skiing at a faster rate than in the morning.

About fifteen minutes from the bottom, they came into a narrow, tree-lined path, quite steep. Richard made them go down in the snowplow. It was the first time she fully realized the merit of this terrific invention for controlled skiing.

At the bottom, she removed her skis with some trepidation and was delighted to discover no knocking knees. Within five minutes they heard the whistle of the electric train and watched it pull into the station. Richard took her arm and held her back as her group and other groups boarded. He then helped her onto the train and steered her into a compartment which she would share with Richard and three other guides on the way back to Davos-Dorf. He introduced Joan to his friends and co-workers and proceeded to tell them the knee-knocking experience which he demonstrated standing in the center of the room to everyone's delight. Turning to Joan, he said, "Iss goot, Fraulein, you did vell. Ve give toast to you." He left the compartment to return with five bottles of Heineken's beer. The guides seemed exceptionally pleased with Richard's generous gesture. Joan hesitated. She had never had beer. She tasted it cautiously to find it cold and palatable; it slid down easily. They taught her a German ski song and didn't seem to mind repeating it until she mastered the words and the tune.

Arriving at Davos-Dorf, she thanked them, said goodbye and waved them on their merry way. The crowd of skiers dispersed rapidly, leaving very few people around the station but no Bill or Heidi. She decided to walk back to the hotel when a jolly driver of a horse and sleigh offered to take her home. Heidi had warned her not to take a sleigh unless she was with her as, being an American, they would charge much too much.

Smiling up at him, ignoring Heidi's advice, she said, "Yes, please." He got down, took her skis and placed them on a rack, helped her into the sleigh and wrapped a soft fur robe around her legs. They started up the main street and Joan felt like the lady of all she surveyed. She began singing the German ski song. The driver turned, "Ya, is goot to be young and happy."

"Yes. Please sing with me?" she begged. They sang the song at least three times before reaching the hotel. He jumped down and deposited her skis in the lobby, then reached up to help her. She placed her hands on his shoulders, laughed and said, "OK. My friends told me you would charge me a lot of money. How much?"

"Ach, for you, Fraulein, it is nottin."

"You cannot do that. I must pay you," she protested.

"Ya, I can do that. Today I sing, long time no sing."

She looked at him and said, "Ya, long time I no sing too." She waved goodbye and called out to him, "My friends will never believe me." She raced into the hotel to find Bill and Heidi. Their door was open. They were not there.

She rang for the maid, pantomimed the fact she wanted a hot bath. She was a pretty little thing, all smiles, many "ja ja's." Joan was waiting in her bathrobe when she returned to lead her to the bath. It was a large room in the middle of which stood, on legs, an enormous tub full of hot water. She thanked her, closed the door, flung off her robe and jumped in—and went right out the other side. It was the hottest water she'd ever felt! She pulled the plug, got the water to a bearable temperature and slowly sank down into its warmth. It felt like sheer Heaven. She relaxed and started to sing the ski song. She didn't hear anything, sensed someone's presence and turned to see Heidi and Bill peaking in the door. She sank further down into the tub. They called, "See you later."

She could hear them laughing as she thought, "Wait until you hear the rest of it." Knowing Bill and Heidi had returned made it easier to give up the luxury of the hot tub and dress for dinner. A note on her door said they'd meet her downstairs in the barroom which increased her speed in dressing. When she found them she had to use great restraint to ask about their day before spilling out her exciting adventures. "We had a swell day. The funniest was catching you riding up Main Street in the sleigh. You and the driver were singing, unconscious of the world around you." She started laughing until the tears came.

"You mean you saw me and didn't call to me?"

"You would never have heard us."

"Aren't you going to ask me what he charged me?"

"You looked so happy, Bill and I agreed to subsidize you. We just wish we had had a camera with us. What a picture."

"Well, he didn't charge me anything," she said. Heidi's eyes were wide. "I told him what you said. He laughed and told me it was a long time since he had any occasion to sing. I also told him you wouldn't believe me."

"I believe you," Bill said.

"Thank you, Bill. Maybe Heidi won't believe the rest of my tale. I've never had such an exciting day."

"I'm ready to believe anything at this point," Heidi said.

Joan went back to visit them in 1951. She and Heidi toured much of France, some of Austria and much of Germany where she met Heidi's brother and father to relive some of the horrors the family had suffered during the war. Heidi's father, Dr. DeLorme, was a charming and intelligent person who described how the U.S. Army had rescued him from the concentration camp and helped him regain his home through the Army restitution process. Although Heidi had described how they had damaged his hands to prevent him from practicing his profession of surgery, Joan was shocked at how mutilated they actually were. Heidi's brother, Karl, had been forced into the German Army and tortured because of his father's lectures at Heidelberg against the Nazis. Bill and Heidi returned to the States early in the sixties. When Bill retired, they moved to Virginia. Heidi has died and the last letter to Bill was returned "unknown."

Kathleen and Ed Hogan returned to their beautiful home in Connecticut. Ed died. Kathleen has remarried. She and Joan still see each other and keep in touch.

Dick and Debbie Cooper had two children. Dick continued successfully in business until he died. Debbie lives in Maryland and still keeps in touch.

Ray Owens returned from his tour with the general to find Joan detached from the Navy. He discovered through Heidi of her marriage breakup. Heidi, always the matchmaker, gave him Joan's New York address. After his release, they saw each other a few times in New York. Ray accepted a job as city manager in Portland, Maine. He invited Joan up for a weekend at a friend's fishing camp. His friends were the perfect host and hostess. Ray was the perfect gentleman. She truly enjoyed herself. The following year, Ray was offered the job as city manager of Louisville, Kentucky. He invited her down for the Kentucky Derby. She had been missing Ray, his fun and his company; in her determined way she decided he was no longer on her "safe-shelf." Still unable to accept marriage, she backed off and refused his invitation.

Her mother, learning of Joan's decision, shocked her by saying, "Sister, I do not understand. I'm beginning to believe if Jesus Christ came down you'd turn Him away."

Ray married. Joan still thinks fondly of him and hopes he is well, happy and surrounded with children and grandchildren.

Arthur, Joan's brother, was so successful in his wartime job of expediter, the company asked him to stay on their permanent staff. He decided he wanted to go into his own business and opened a restaurant on the Shinnecock Canal in Southampton, Long Island, catering to the yachting crowd. His wife, Margo, died of a heart attack.

Later he married a gal, Doris, whom he knew from his school days. During his early womanizing period, he had made no bones of the fact he was sterile due to the polio attack. Therefore everyone was startled and most delighted when they had a beautiful daughter. Arthur was dubious about his wife's pregnancy, although his doctor confirmed the fact it was very possible. His wife, who had dark hair and black eyes, considered it a miracle when the little girl was born with red-gold hair and blue eyes. No one could mistake the fact she was Arthur's child. They named her Traci.

Becoming disenchanted with the petty problems of the restaurant business, he sold it and joined two college friends in setting up what would become the Miracle Mile in Manhasset, Long Island. Then they developed shopping centers in various locations, leading eventually to the Mall idea.

In 1968 he was to learn he had lymph cancer. After two years of treatments with various drugs in the States, he went to England and offered himself as a guinea pig for experimental drugs. In 1971 his wife told Joan he did not wish to be around, and he bought a penthouse on Biscayne Bay where he was being cared for by a young, attractive girl. A few months later he went to Stuart, Florida, to stay in the home of a friend as death was imminent. Joan went there immediately.

It had been a year since she'd seen him. As she walked into the strange bedroom she went numb. He was lying half-raised in a hospital bed. The skeletal figure had the red-blonde hair and pale blue eyes emphasizing the dark black color of his skin, a result of the experimental medication. He died that night.

The funeral was held two days later in Stuart. Joan had a vague recollection it was held in an auditorium of a church. It was a cold, eerie atmosphere which left her shivering. Many of the congregation returned to the house where Arthur's friend arranged a buffet luncheon on his porch overlooking the St. Lucie River.

As Joan stood next to Arthur's wife, Doris, she noticed Arthur's once-prized possessions, his 40' boat tied to the dock, his Lincoln Continental and Mercedes over by the garage, now so useless to him. She sensed an indescribable tension as she left the porch. She was conscious of a young girl (someone said she was the girl taking care of Arthur in Miami) and of two strange men no one could identify. As she walked down the driveway, Doris came out of the house screaming, "Ed! They want to take Traci to New York. Please stop them!"

Ed went to Doris and asked, "Who wants to take Traci?"

"That girl and those two men. They can't do it. She is not of age. I'm her mother!" Traci appeared in the driveway and seemed to be in a trance. Was she in shock? Was she drugged? She was insisting she was going to New York. Thank God for Ed.[5]

He took hold of Traci explaining, "Traci, you must stay with your mother who is legally responsible for you because you are still a minor." Ed was forceful and must have reached her, as she listened to him. The girl and the two strange men disappeared. It was several hours before things calmed down, and it was months later before the undercurrents of that day began to unravel.

Doris took her copy of Arthur's will to her attorney who uncovered some strange facts he felt required consultation with the F.B.I. While this was in progress, Doris was holding up fairly well. Traci was back to a normal girl, just turned 16. Joan did not wish to invade their privacy until the following facts were revealed. Arthur had signed a "Power of Attorney" to the young girl. She had obtained possession of the penthouse condominium, both cars and the fishing boat. The Reddington Beach house was in Doris' name and was intact. The New England farm property was in joint ownership and seemed intact. Stocks and bonds in Arthur's name could not be located. There was some question of an organization which procured and trained young girls to take care of terminally ill patients with the purpose of seizing properties, monies and the like. The sad fact was the large portion of his family's support had been bilked.

My God, to think of what might have happened to Traci had Ed not stepped in to prevent her going to New York. The F.B.I., as well as her lawyer, recommended Doris take no action to reclaim her losses in view of the potential danger to herself and her daughter. Quite naturally Doris, in constant fear of unpredictable dangers, decided to sell the Florida house and move to the New England property which she hoped would be safer.

She was settling in when she faced another shocker— someone had forged her signature and secured a substantial mortgage on the property. Eventually, the signature was proven to be a forgery and the bank was forced to absorb the mortgage

[5] Ed was the person Joan finally married.

168

loss. There was no denying a ghost had reappeared. How on earth did Doris keep from breaking down from taking the harsh punishment of such heinous crimes?

She and Traci came through the unbelievable strain of incredible circumstances to become proud, honorable and solid citizens. They live an austere life. They "make-do". They breed, raise, train and sell pedigreed dogs. Traci takes on all sorts of odd jobs, including running steamrollers for road repairs, waiting tables and working as an animal control officer. Joan has the greatest admiration for their accomplishments and the greatest respect for their independence.

The first week in December 1945 brought with it a happiness and joy that remains with Joan to this day. Bob and Trudy came home with their first child, a blonde, blue-eyed baby girl about six weeks old. As Joan held this adorable bundle in her arms, she realized this child could have been hers. She smothered her with the affection that years ago she lavished on the baby's father. "Bonnie" melted the ice she feared was beginning to clog her heart. Surprisingly, the little one responded, releasing her pain and expanding her interests.

Christmas resumed the spiritual joys and human happiness of earlier years. The war was over, people were cheerful and the stores were once again decked with holly. Joan rediscovered the fun of window shopping. She found George Jensen's window displaying handmade, precious infant's clothes. Under the Christmas tree, wrapped and waiting, was probably the most expensive and surely the most beautiful dress the little girl might ever possess. The dress inspired a desire to make pretty clothes for her, later producing a side interest in designing garments, which would become another hobby.

Bob was set on becoming an engineer. He was advised to apply for Rensselaer Polytechnic Institute as it had surpassed M.I.T. in its engineering courses. Bob was accepted and scheduled to start classes in February 1946.

It was fortunate Bob was still at home when Joan received a telephone call from John. She might have slipped back, like the frog in the well in her third grade math class. John sounded hysterical, "Why is Eddie Hidalgo making it so difficult? He's already delayed the divorce for two months. Now he's asking me to agree to alimony payments. I don't even have a job. When I get married, I'll have to support a wife. Will you tell him to omit the alimony?"

Joan took a deep breath, "At the moment I have no need for alimony and will probably never collect it. However, I must go along with my lawyer's wishes as he has my interests in mind."

John snapped, "He sure isn't bothered about my interests. I'll sign this damn paper if you promise not to hold me to alimony."

"I repeat, I have no need for it at the moment and hope to God I never will." Joan didn't. She never collected it and never asked for it.

She was sitting at the kitchen counter. As she replaced the receiver, she discovered she resented the call. She was getting her life back on track, but it appeared he still needed someone to hold his hand and to make life easier for him. He didn't have a job. He'd have to support a wife. He was running true to form as far as supporting a wife! "Well, dear boy," she thought, "you'll have to solve your own problems. You made your bed now lie in it. This time I'm not available, and, further, my checking account is safely in my own name." She sighed, "How long before I hear the last of this Adonis?"

Her resentment was interrupted by Bob." Quit stewing. It's a beautiful winter event. Let's go for a walk."

"Great idea. I'm ready," she said. They hadn't walked long before the cold, crisp air cleared her mind. She smiled up at Bob, "Thanks pal."

"Anytime pal," he answered.

Bob, Trudy and the baby left for Troy to begin his quest for an engineering degree. Joan kept in touch, knew he was doing well and was thrilled to learn he and his family would be back for a visit on his semester break. They stayed with Trudy's parents who lived on the next block. They arrived on a Saturday afternoon. After settling his family, Bob walked over to his parents' house. Joan was lying on her bed reading. Bob threw himself down next to her, letting his tears fall. Trying to hide the alarm she felt, she smiled, "Come on, Bob, it can't be that bad."

"Oh, but it is. Trudy is pregnant again. I've got to get through school. I feel done in."

Realizing his distress and the strain placed on this young man's shoulders, she tried to comfort him, "What's done, dear, can't be undone. You will both have to be more careful. We'll work it out somehow." Joan's heart ached for him. He had been religious from the time he was a kid serving as an altar boy. Since he had come back from the war unhurt, his faith was strengthened further. He tried to abide by the birth control rules of the Church. It was one of those things that turned out extremely well. Karen, his second daughter, was born in September 1946. She is a wonderful person, became a registered nurse and is happily married to a doctor.

In June 1949 Joan and her parents drove to Troy for Bob's graduation from R.P.I. There was a visible change in the graduates. The majority were older, war veterans. Many were married and a number, including Bob, already had small children. They were adults before their time. They had faced a war they had helped win. They would now face a competitive world. As a whole, they appeared serious and ready for the challenge.

Joan's admiration for these young graduates was interrupted near the end of the ceremony when she became aware of the gallant effort of Bonnie, then three and a half years old, who needed to go to the bathroom and was trying to hold on. Well, her generation had guts too. Soon after this urgent problem was taken care of, the graduates dispersed, Bob in their midst. Joan was so proud of him. He had accomplished his goal to acquire an engineering degree. He was tall and good-looking with an open, honest face. He was her kid brother. She loved him dearly and was concerned about the responsibilities he carried on his shoulders, but she had faith in his abilities.

His first job was with Reaction Motors and from there he successfully held other positions in engineering firms. They would have eight children and five are still living. All five have been successful in their chosen fields; all are married with children. Bob retired at age 62 and went back to school to study to become a deacon in the Church. He was ordained by the Most Reverend John F. Whealan, D.D., Archbishop of Hartford, on June 3, 1983, in the Cathedral of St. Joseph. He was assigned to Clayton, Georgia. He is attached to St. Helena's Church where he is kept exceedingly busy with multiple duties. He performs marriages, burials and baptisms; officiates at different services; presides over religious discussion groups within the parish as well as with the clergy of other denominations; takes communion to the housebound; and assists in any way he can with people who need help. The only ecclesiastical duties he is not authorized to perform are the consecration of the Host and hearing of confessions. Trudy has adapted very well to this new way of life and helps whatever way she can, particularly in the "Share and Care" shop.

Joan went down for a week's visit. She was impressed but not surprised at how well thought of and respected Bob is by the parishioners, especially the teenagers who surround him the minute he steps out of his car.

One morning he took her with him into the backwoods where he was taking communion to a wheelchair recipient, as well as some second-hand clothes to one of the sons so he might report for a job interview. Joan knew plenty of poverty existed in the world. She never imagined it to this degree in the United States. As she sat in the car, she could hear the cries of joy he brought to them. Even the mangy, underfed dog wagged his tail as Bob went up the stoop. Within minutes the mother rushed out to the car to greet his sister. The happiness that shone on the face of the toothless, grimy, unkempt, undernourished woman was like a contradiction of the meaning of life. Joan was overwhelmed by the entire setting, realizing she could never be able to handle this reality. She marveled at the gift Bob possessed. He was certainly giving back favors God had bestowed upon him.

That evening Joan told Bob how she admired what he was accomplishing and how proud she was of him. "I came through

Deacon Robert Mulligan
June, 1983

the war years unscathed," Bob said, "and whatever I can do will hardly make up for that. There was much tragedy and much sadness during those years, but there were some laughs too." A silence of several minutes followed until Bob chuckled.

"What is it?" asked Joan.

"One of the funniest things I remember," said Bob, "was walking with you on Constitution Avenue. I was still in a midshipman's uniform, the WAVES uniform was new enough to cause quite a few stares. I spotted three sailors coming towards us. Telling you to go on ahead, I stayed back to watch the reaction. They were utterly confused. But one saluted and the others followed suit. As they went by me, one said, 'What the hell was that?'"

Joan couldn't remember the incident, but joined Bob in laughing about it.

EPILOGUE II

PERSONAL

On October 1, 1945, Joan reported to Mr. Geddes' office. Working with this man was like living in "The World of Tomorrow." Projects his staff considered normal would have been blasted out of any other organization as impractical and impossible. This was no ordinary job, at times it didn't even seem sane. The atmosphere of unique creative genius set a pace which Joan had never encountered and was a godsend for her that first year. It held many inimitable challenges, one of which was her first assignment.

Sitting in his office in an overstuffed chair, Mr. Geddes informed her she would be in charge of a new project. He handed her a sheet listing 150 technical, specially trained personnel requirements, alongside which he noted the initial cost expected for each classification. Before she could reach out to take the sheet from him, he was rattling off that she must rent 1500 square feet of space with a 50-foot ceiling; get rotating spot lights 2 feet in diameter; get this and that kind of camera equipment—all of which must be acquired in two weeks time.

This occurred on her third day in the office. It was obvious the magnetism of this man had taken effect as she wasn't the slightest bit concerned that it was October 1945 in New York City where space, any space, was at a premium; that she had never heard of half the kinds of cameras or lighting equipment he spieled off. The great man had spoken; his way of doing unusual things

175

as routine matters was transmitted to his staff, almost as though it were by a process of osmosis.

Joan's original thinking of space in such proportions was Madison Square Garden, Grand Central Station, skating rinks or tennis courts. Yet an unused pier on the East River turned out to be the place she rented without too much trouble. The highly trained personnel was obtained due perhaps to the lure of the Geddes name plus the availability of men being released from service. The special lighting and camera equipment were on a priority basis at the time, which caused some worry but they were rented on time.

In looking back it seems to have been done easily. Her subconscious recalls a completely hectic, chaotic atmosphere which existed throughout the months that followed in getting the project under way and completing it. The idea was to capture, through photographs of scale model ships, the historic importance of the Battle of Midway in World War II. Although the subjects being photographed were inanimate objects, the scenes were alive with action, excitement caused by the greatest actor, Mr. Geddes. Everyone was working from eight o'clock in the morning until six o'clock in the evening—that is everyone but Mr. Geddes who dashed in several times during the day to check and give instructions.

It didn't take long to learn about the union employees which consisted of the overhead lighting engineers and porters. Obviously the powerful ceiling lights were needed in addition to the standing floor lamps in order for the cameramen to photograph the scenes. One morning the scene was set and models placed, ready for shooting. The overhead lighting men had gone out for coffee. It never occurred to Joan that Mr. Geddes might have been in for some trouble as she climbed the ladders and turned on the lights. A cameraman said the union men would not like her doing that to which she replied she did not like wasting time from a tight schedule. There was much whispering when the lighting engineers returned. They never said one word to Joan,and not once afterwards did they leave the building without checking with her as to when the lights were needed.

One other incident seems so utterly fantastic, it is hard to believe it actually happened. A porter refused to move a potted palm as it was artificial and not a real plant.

The project was two months underway when, one evening, Joan left the pier and returned to the Radio City office to check over some figures. It was about 6:45 P.M. when there was a quiet, gentle knock and Geddes appeared. In a whisper he asked her to come into his office. She knew immediately she was about to face some unusual situation as any other time he wanted her he either boomed through the walls or sent his secretary to fetch her. This was a different approach with no particular element of surprise in it. He was always so unpredictable, each member of his staff accepted almost anything.

She followed him into his office and watched him slump into his chair. Geddes was not tall. He gave the impression of greatness and power. He was meticulous in his personal appearance. An outsider witnessing the scene before her eyes would have observed a small man who appeared very ill with the worries of the entire world on his shoulders, left alone in his grief and sorrow. They would not have known the great genius. His tie was opened, his hair ruffled and he was chalk white with beads of perspiration running down his face.

His office was equipped with special floodlights, lighting fixtures for brilliant lighting effects to match his personality. But this evening one small, low light burned to reflect the tragic nature of the occasion. Way off in the back corner of the office sat a slight man hunched down, almost hidden, in an oversized arm chair. Joan wondered what part he had in this scene as she stepped into her role of the patient, sympathetic listener.

Geddes' voice was so low she had to strain to catch the words that came slowly, interrupted with quick, short gasps and sighs. Mr. Barrymore, the great stage and screen actor, could not have portrayed any death scene more effectively. The substance of his message was that the project would have to be discontinued. He had worked so hard on it; he expected it would have contributed to the history of our country; it could have been a source of pride to our children's children. It would, therefore, be necessary to deprive future generations of the real, true, visual record of the turning point of World War II.

She interposed what she considered appropriate remarks of incredulity, consternation and defeat of this noble purpose, then supplied the cue line, "How can this be?" She discovered, inconceivable as it might seem, money—insignificant, material-istic money—which had been definitely promised by a great man for this great work, was the cause of this disaster. As the last spoken word faded away, the proper moments of silence were held in respect for the death of the project. As she sat down beside him with tear-filled eyes to match his own, the little man in the corner jumped up, went out of the office and called back, "OK, Norman, go ahead with the project. You win. The check will be here in the morning."

The outer door slammed and instantly Geddes was on his feet, his tie pushed back into place, his jacket went on, hair pushed down, normal ruddy color was back in his face and his voice boomed, "Well done. I've already worked out the schedule for tomorrow. We will start with...."

They worked another hour setting up schedules for the next three weeks! The staff was divided into day and night shifts as he ran a twenty-four hour operation. Geddes was everywhere. At the pier, at his office and he set the pace carried out by his staff. Geddes left Joan no time for self-sympathy—in fact her mother joked that he was phoning her at home so often it was a wonder she had time to go to the bathroom or to bed.

After several more uproarious incidents, the photographic record of the Battle of Midway was completed and assembled in an impressive binding for presentation to the Navy Department in Washington. Mr. Geddes insisted Joan accompany him on this mission. Joan made necessary appointments with the Navy and secured train tickets. The night before they were to leave, Joan worked late checking and rechecking the photo sequences. She arrived home exhausted. The next morning her mother awakened her—she had overslept! She tossed on her clothes and gave her mother a hair-raising ride to Penn Station. She arrived on the platform as the train was pulling out. The conductor stuck out his hand and pulled her aboard. She had to walk through eight or nine cars to reach their seats. Mr. Geddes was comfortably settled reading the New York Times. His greeting was, "How about our having some breakfast?"

Good God! Her stomach was in her throat, her heart racing. Well, what else was new?

The presentation was a success. At least the Navy men were intrigued and seemed happy. It had the proper publicity and was then placed in the Navy archives where she hopes it still rests.

With her first assignment completed, Mr. Geddes announced she was to be his Executive Assistant and General Manager. A memo from Mr. Geddes advised he was jotting down a few of the duties she would be handling, thereby freeing him for more important design and creative work. It read:

1. Responsible for public relations, advertising, publicity.

2. Coordination of all contracts as to personnel, production, correspondence.

3. Liaison between clients and himself.

4. Manage the office—organize policies and office procedures.

5. Coordinate various departments. Personnel, hiring, dismissals.

Her only comment was "WOW!" Her family and friends never tired of the funny, unusual stories that occurred over the next year.

One morning, Mrs. Forrestal phoned to say she was coming to New York on a shopping spree and hoped she could stop by to see Joan's office and take her to lunch. Joan and Mrs. Forrestal were in one of the designer's rooms looking at some sketches when Mr. Geddes walked in. This well-groomed, stunning figure took him by surprise. Joan introduced them as he blurted out, "Oh, you're the Navy Secretary."

"No, Mr. Geddes, just his wife," replied Jo Forrestal.

"Well, you'll be interested in seeing my scale model ship collection," he said escorting her into his office.

At lunch she agreed he was a fascinating man. They chuckled at his showing off his ship models—secretary or no secretary—it was a way to cover his embarrassment. They had a good time reminiscing about the war years. It was the last time Joan saw this lovely lady.

Like most artistic geniuses, Mr. Geddes had no concept of financial matters which Joan suspected from the beginning. She tried desperately to forestall bankruptcy. He couldn't believe it until it was too late. By April she prepared what she hoped would be a convincing presentation of the financial situation. He didn't blow, gave her the impression he knew what was going on, appeared lackadaisical, thought everything would be all right. He was up in the clouds. She couldn't reach him. She grasped at a long shot and made a prediction, "Mr. Geddes, if the situation does not change, the company will be bankrupt by the end of the year. I do not want to be around to see the empire fall. I plan to leave the end of May."

He was horrified! All his acting and promises would not change her mind. Joan had the experience of a lifetime working for this man at a time she needed it most. She was sad it had come to an end and was concerned as to what would happen to him.

His bankruptcy came two months earlier than she figured. He was forced to give up his offices and take what was left of his accounts to his apartment, keeping a skeleton staff of three people. To her mother's amazement he still phoned her at home and sent her a Christmas greeting cable from Jamaica, BWI, and, as late as 1954, was asking her to come back to him.

For the next several weeks every free moment, including lunch hour, was devoted to trying to find out what she wanted to do next. Appointments with two Seventh Avenue dress manufacturers opened her eyes—very wide—to dress designing in the garment industry. The reactions of the two different men were almost identical. What they offered, plus the atmosphere, was not her cup of tea. The last manufacturer confirmed it by a slight pat on her rear as she was leaving his office.

An appointment with a Peck & Peck buyer resulted in her buying, outright, one of Joan's designs for $75. She didn't do a heck of a lot better with the lady from B. Altman's. She bought, for $100, her navy circle felt skirt with white, decorated carousel horses. Later this idea was selling everywhere. The horses became poodles, flower baskets, tigers, whatever. Her last attempt in the field of design was with Lord & Taylor. Her appointment was with a male buyer who fancied himself far above talking with an unknown. He bought one of her sketches for $50. It was a lady's white, handkerchief linen shirt with front pleats and black bow tie, styled after a man's evening shirt. A few years later this appeared on the cover of Life Magazine as the latest fashion. Thus ended her desire for a career in clothes design.

She considered the idea of matching people to jobs in an employment agency. Determining the one considered tops in the field, she registered as an applicant and was advised management jobs for women were nil. She was offered a job in the office as an interviewer. The salary was acceptable. She agreed to join the staff on June 1.

The first four months were very satisfying. Her clients were top-notch, the applicants, as a whole, above average. This bubble burst when she was called into the "Boss Lady's" office one morning and was told not to waste time or accept applications from Jews or Blacks. At that time there was no antidiscrimination law. Joan was shocked, and within a short time she resigned from the agency.

The Drake America Corporation had advertised for a male Personnel Director. She was successful in obtaining an appointment with Mr. Andre Maximov, Vice President. In a relaxed fashion he told her the company was primarily an import-export business. Second, they purchased small businesses such as Armstrong Tires, Mark Cross and a few others. They needed someone to formulate, introduce, maintain and develop personnel practices and procedures; to confirm job specifications; procure, screen and select applicants, including department heads; and supervise employees' pension and benefits plans. She began confirming the basic job requirements when he surprised her, "You couldn't be so completely knowledgeable by working in an employment agency. What did you do before?"

"I was Executive Assistant and General Manager for Norman Bel Geddes, Industrial Designer. It was very stimulating although financially insecure."

"We've been thinking in terms of a man. My mind could be changed. How old are you?"

She went to work for Drake America on March 1, 1948. It was an English firm moved to the States. No one had bothered about personnel or policies and internal bickering had broken out. The president was George Artemonoff and vice president was Andre Maximov. Both were aristocratic White Russians who, at age 18, had ingeniously escaped Russia at the time of the Revolution and made their way to the states from South America. They entered Yale University, graduating with law degrees within three years. They were brilliant, fascinating men with a grace and ease that was extraordinary.

Again she encountered unusual experiences. Mr. Maximov was an accomplished pianist. She was invited to dinner at his townhouse where she met talented musicians and listened to electrifying piano duets. She was invited to an Arthur Rubenstein concert at Carnegie Hall. She still nourishes that pleasure.

She went to Mark Cross on Fifth Avenue to meet with Gerald Murphy, President, to inspect personnel records and job requirements. The Gerald Murphy legend was no secret. Joan was well aware of the elegant parties he and his wife, Sara, held for the famous writers Fitzgerald, Hemingway, Dorothy Parker and others in their French "Villa America." She was unprepared for the man. He was a pleasant, polite, likeable person artistically gifted with no sense or desire for the mundane merchandising business, though he had come back from France to try to pull the company together.

Mr. Maximov appeared in her office one morning to inquire if she had any connections in Washington as the import-export business was having problems. It was impossible to obtain cargo releases. Joan felt she might be able to contact one or two Congressmen to determine if anything could be done to speed up the process. She managed to obtain an appointment without much trouble and went to Washington.

The Congressman checked into the situation to find his efforts fruitless as he was told it was a "closed circuit" due to the fact France was at war with North Vietnam and Korea was experiencing rioting. Unfortunately nothing could be accomplished on cargo releases. By December this part of the business took a dive. Thus began the unhappy task of cutting back the staff, Joan included. She left Drake America February 1, 1949, to begin a new adventurous year of her life.

Heidi had written Joan with all kinds of inducements to visit them in Paris. She had never been to Europe and the idea was exciting. She'd been able to save some money and had no job to hold her back. She applied for her passport, made airline reservations and wrote Heidi. Arriving in London to change planes for Paris, she received an unexpected bonus. The plane had mechanical difficulties and was grounded for two days. Expenses for the Hotel Rubens and meals were paid for by the airline. Joan was able to see a bit of London: Westminster Abbey, Claridge's, Parliament, Ten Downing Street and two department stores. She saw a bit of the countryside as she took a train to Bournemouth, a resort town with a most attractive inn, for tea and scones.

The next morning she walked the two blocks to St. James Park to watch the changing of the guards at Buckingham Palace. As Joan watched, enchanted, the A. A. Milne poem kept going through her head,

> "They're changing guards at Buckingham Palace
> Christopher Robin went down with Alice
> Alice is marrying one of the Guards
> 'A soldier's life is terrible hard' says Alice."

The plane to Paris left in the early afternoon. Dear, wonderful, exuberant Heidi waved madly as she came down the ramp. She was dispatched through customs, thanks to Bill's diplomatic status, to be enveloped in Heidi's outstretched arms. It had been four years since they'd seen each other, and they must have looked like a couple of school kids. They caused a few smiles as the porter loaded Joan's skis through the sun-roof opening of the Peugeot.

Joan had been shocked by the fast drivers in Puerto Rico. As they got into Paris, there were fifty times more cars all going at top speed, darting in and out around the numerous bicycles, horns blowing. The chaos was unreal. Joan sat glued to her seat while Heidi chatted away. They were in one of the traffic circles when a much larger car, trying to cut in front, rammed into the side of Heidi's car. Heidi jammed on the brakes and jumped out of the car. A man jumped out of the other car. The two let go with gestures and rapid French. They looked so angry. Suddenly the man handed Heidi a card, wrote something on another card and put it into his wallet as they both broke into smiles and polite goodbyes. All the while this was going on, other cars screeched by avoiding them.

Heidi climbed back into the car. Joan said,"I probably distracted you and caused the accident."

"It was his fault," she shouted. "But what luck. He owns one of the best automobile companies in France. His chauffeur will pick up my car in the morning and leave me one of his cars to drive until this is repaired. He didn't want to report the accident. I don't care. He's a big shot. No need to worry."

"You arranged an exciting introduction to Paris for me. I've never seen such crazy drivers. I was really frightened."

When they arrived at Heidi's apartment, the concierge took care of the luggage. Joan collapsed in a chair on the balcony porch as Heidi fixed tea. It seemed they were trying to condense four years' happenings into the next half hour when the concierge delivered a large box containing two dozen beautiful, long-stemmed red roses. The card read, "My apologies for causing any disturbance to two beautiful young ladies." A separate envelope revealed two tickets to the Christian Dior opening to be held in two days. Heidi whooped and danced around holding the tickets high over her head.

The next day Heidi took Joan to an open market consisting of push carts lined up on either side of a narrow aisle extending for several blocks. Women and men were bargaining in French in loud voices. Two pounds of green beans were dumped into Heidi's canvas shopping bag followed by a whole chicken, head and legs included. On top went oranges and grapes. Joan thought, by comparison, the Fulton Fish Market was a gem.

They walked through the flower market and through the flea market. Joan's eyes were everywhere. Heidi disposed of the contents of the shopping bag at the apartment and took great delight in getting into the long, loaned car to drive to Mont Matre where they had lunch in a popular cafe, Les Deux Maggots. They visited Sacre Coeur Cathedral. Bill was home ahead of them and greeted them with a Cheshire cat grin before he gave them the invitations delivered that afternoon for the opening of Balenciaga, another gift for another collection.

At the Dior opening they found a mad crowd in front of the doors. The odor of perspiration and perfume was so distasteful, Joan lost interest until Heidi talked with a guard and showed him the invitation. It was open sesame—he pushed the crowd aside and ushered them through.

Once inside they were treated royally, given front-row seats and a program listing the models and the costumes. To Joan it seemed as though they were the only ordinary people seated in the front row. The other women were elegantly dressed with five or six ex-husbands' worth of jewelry on display, some accompanied by smart-looking, much older men, one of whom was clutching a miniature poodle. Joan put two and two together to realize they were mistresses accompanied by their benefactors on a buying spree. To Joan they seemed to be phonies, putting on a show of their own, getting what they wanted.

Neither Heidi nor Joan could afford the outfits. They stopped in the lingerie shop where Joan purchased a chemise with a pale green ribbon around the waistline. Years later that ribbon would be tied around the neck of a Labrador puppy to identify her from the rest of the litter.

They went for tea to Rumplemyer's, which Heidi claimed was a must. It was here Joan had her first contact with a lesbian who kept running an umbrella up and down her leg. Heidi caught on immediately and changed tables.

A few nights later they went to the Palais des Sports to watch the Olympic ice skaters. The event was beautifully orchestrated with magnificent costumes. The piece de resistance was to watch and cheer for Dick Button as he took the gold medal for the United States.

The next evening they boarded the train for Switzerland. Joan had a fairy tale enchantment for the country. Watches and clocks were not for her; to her the country meant the hand-carved, charming figures of little girls in Tyrolean dresses, little boys in lederhosen, whimsical animals, flowers on revolving music boxes, hand-embroidered canton smocks and belts, yodeling songs and pretty chalets, majestic mountains and pure air. She wasn't disappointed. Her episodes on the ski trails were unbelievable. She recounted the first one earlier.

There were too many joys to recount here. Her change in attitude is worth telling. On her last ski tour, walking down to the Parsennbahn with heavy skis secure on her shoulder and poles clutched in one hand, a feeling of freedom and independence began to flow through her veins. She was alone but no longer lost—a feeling of walking taller and being able to handle it.

The trip was the greatest, more than she'd hoped for, but returning to the warmth of one's own hearth, to the hugs of parents, to slide into one's own bed was very pleasurable. It also brought back the reality of job hunting. Having been associated with the employment agency, she was aware their listings for the few management jobs usually specified "male." She decided management consultant firms might be a better source. Each firm obtained appointments for interviews for her; each appointment produced a referral interview; often this referral produced a further interview. It was like the domino theory—her hopes would build up, then fall. Along the way she met some capable, stimulating people. Many were to become lasting friends.

This first week of interviews escalated to a high pitch, then dropped off. She found herself with ten free days before a scheduled appointment. She took a break and went skiing in Stowe, Vermont. This spur-of-the-moment idea was a provident decision.

The past two winters she had stayed at Ten Acres, the lodge Bill Woodworth's friend the Army captain had recommended. She called Blanche Blauvelt, the original owner, to discover they had sold their interest and had built a teen-age, college crowd dormitory lodge. Blanche recommended Logwood and offered to make a reservation for her.

On this trip Joan was driving her new Chevy and had lost her queasiness on taking the long drive alone. No more struggling with skis and poles on the train. Janet and Chuck, owners of Logwood, greeted her warmly. Chuck stored her skis, showed her the room, bathroom and dining room. He then took her down to the barroom and introduced her to a most attractive young couple enjoying an apres-ski drink. This is how she met Jean and Gordon Lowe who are still dear friends. They figured prominently in her future happiness. They were from North Adams, Massachusetts. He was a ski instructor and she worked in her father's insurance business. They were expert skiers and asked her to join them. After some slight hesitation about holding them up on the slopes, she accepted and skied with them for three glorious days before discovering they were on their honeymoon. They were a delight and did wonders for her morale. They gave her confidence on the ski trails.

Entering the dining room for breakfast on Saturday morning, she was surprised to find Ed Bench, who had arrived late the night before with his two daughters. The girls had left very early for the milk run at 7:00 A.M. It was such a nice surprise. The Lowes joined them and Joan introduced everyone. She brought them up to date on the fact Ed was one of the Parkfairfax group in Virginia during the war years. The four skied together that day as Ed's daughters were off with their peers. The Lowes, Ed and the girls left early Sunday morning. Joan enjoyed her last two days in ski class before returning to New York.

There was a pile of telephone messages and correspondence waiting for her. The interviews began again and kept her busy. They produced nothing concrete as she turned down offers not in her bailiwick.

At a friend's dinner party she met an eligible bachelor, Paul Somebody-or-other. To her amazement her back didn't stiffen to this matchmaking, which she had previously disliked. He was pleasant, polite and lived in her neighborhood. He asked if she would like to play tennis Sunday morning. She met him at the courts and enjoyed the tennis. He promised to call her and pedaled off on his bicycle. She walked home. Her mother questioned why she had not brought the young man home for lunch. Well now! Was she curious? Would she be "the anxious to marry off daughter" mother? Joan decided it was a bit of both.

This developed into an occasional tennis game. When Paul suggested riding, she was delighted. She found out he was from Bavaria, had been trained with the German cavalry and was an outstanding equestrian. She still did not bring him home.

Her job hunting gained momentum. In June, Joan and her parents went to Troy for Bob's graduation.

Her big break came in July. She was to be interviewed for the office manager's position in one of the top ten law firms in New York. This was her field, her salary range. The management consultant firm notified her an appointment had been set up along with a warning that no woman held this position in that or any other law firm. They had given her a strong recommendation.

The first partner to see her appeared more nervous than Joan. He must have seen her resume ahead of time, yet he kept studying it. At last he said, "I see you worked for Norman Bel Geddes."

"Yes, sir."

"This resume indicates you ran his office."

"More or less, sir."

"Do you mind if I call him?"

"No, sir."

After being questioned as to why he wanted to speak with Mr. Geddes, he was put through to him. Mr. Geddes could easily be heard by Joan. "You want to talk with me about Mrs. Evans?"

"I'm sorry to bother you, Mr. Geddes."

"If it's about Mrs. Evans, you're not bothering me. What do you want to know?"

"Her resume says she was your executive assistant and general office manager...."

"You're damn right she was. I wish she were still with me."

"We're looking for an office manager. We're thinking in terms of a man...."

"She's one of the most capable women you'll ever find. You won't find any man to do the job as well as she will do it."

"You see, sir, we're a large law firm. She'll be responsible to seventeen partners...."

"Law firm! I can't understand why she'd want to bury herself with a bunch of stuffy lawyers. I don't care how many bosses she'll have, she can handle it."

"Then, sir, you don't think we'd be making a mistake to consider her for this job?"

"God, no! You'll be damn lucky if she works for you. She's the one I think is making the mistake."

"Thank you, Mr. Geddes. I think that is all I need."

"Would you like me to write you a letter about her?"

"No. That won't be necessary. Talking with you has been sufficient. Thank you."

Listening to every word Mr. Geddes said, it was hard for her to keep a straight face. However, she did worry that in his efforts to convince the guy she could do the job, he might be killing her off. "Stuffy lawyers," he had said. Ouch! Why hadn't he called Mr. Maximov, her last employer? The famous Geddes name must have struck his fancy and he couldn't resist talking with him. He hung up the phone and excused himself. He wanted to see one of his partners.

He returned and escorted her into the office of another partner. This man was pleasant, asked a few questions and gave her the impression he was much too busy for this nonsense. He escorted her to a third partner's office. The minute they shook hands and exchanged smiles, the chill of the previous encounters disappeared. This man was a trial lawyer, probably the busiest of all. He knew how to interview without making her feel she was on a witness stand. He was interested in her experience, her personality, her spontaneous ability to react to any remark, relevant or not. It seemed sure he accepted her qualifications for the position and was anxious to determine if she could handle seventeen egotistical personalities. She was with him at least forty-five minutes when he asked, "What have you been doing with yourself since you left Drake America last February?"

"My first step was to alert my influential friends and business acquaintances that I was job hunting and send them my resume. Then I contacted two top management consultant firms. Initially I had quite a few prospects, nothing I wanted. The job market seemed to be at a standstill. I had some friends in Paris who wanted me to visit them. I'd never been to Europe, so I just took off and had a glorious time. We even went skiing in Switzerland which was tremendous. Since I've been back, there have been some offers I turned down." She started to chuckle and continued, "You know, sir, I just may have been holding out, waiting for an opportunity like this to present itself."

"I, for one, am glad you did. There is no need for you to start until the first of September. Most of the staff is on vacation during the summer. Would that be all right with you?"

"That would be fine, sir."

"Why don't I see if I can close this out today? I'll be right back."

While she waited, she crossed her fingers and hoped the other two partners would give up the idea of getting a man. She sensed they were confused by the idea of hiring a woman. He returned shortly with the two men in tow. "It's all settled. We agreed we'd like you to come with us at the stated salary, starting the Monday after Labor Day if that suits you." She shook hands with all three, thanked them and assured them she would do her utmost to sustain their confidence.

It was noon when she rode down in the elevator, her heart pounding with excitement. This was exactly the job she wanted. She found a phone booth in the lobby and called the management firm to tell them the good news. She then called Mr. Geddes to thank him. He couldn't understand her working for lawyers but guessed she knew what she was doing and said John wanted to talk with her.

John understood, was delighted, and said, "Hop a taxi, Sweetie, and meet me at the Stork Club for lunch to celebrate."

"Thanks, John. I'm down at the tip of Manhattan. The subway will be faster and cheaper. I have a few quick calls to make. I'll be along." John was Mr. Geddes' sales manager and backed Joan all the way with Mr. Geddes.

She phoned her parents and four or five others. She still had a few good Samaritans carrying the banner for her, but she'd run out of change and would have to contact them later.

Hallelujah! With the job she wanted in her pocket and almost two free months of summer before facing the rigors of a new job, she persuaded her parents to go to Southampton. They had sold the Ox Pasture Lane house at the beginning of the war and were concerned renting a place would be difficult so late in the season. Joan's luck was holding. A friend in the area located a cottage on Little Fresh Pond which she took sight unseen.

Trudy and Bob agreed to Joan's having Bonnie for three weeks. Those weeks spent with Bonnie were a sheer delight. She was a most satisfying, loving little girl. They ran on the beach, played "seagull" and frolicked in the water's edge; Joan held on to Bonnie for pony rides. Bonnie learned to eat shrimp and lobster and to enjoy Tchaikovsky's "Nutcracker Suite" and Prokofiev's "Peter and the Wolf." They danced around the living room to Strauss's waltzes. It could have been a playback to the days she had spent with Bonnie's daddy.

Bob called, all too soon, to let her know they were coming into town to see Trudy's parents. Could she bring Bonnie in? Hard as it was, Joan understood. Her parents and sister Karen missed her. Joan drove Bonnie in, deposited her safely, greeted them and turned right around and drove back to Southampton.

Joan spoke to her parents about the wisdom of buying a house in the area. The result was they went house hunting. The two possibilities Joan liked, her Dad tore apart, "Sister, it would cost a fortune to put this in shape. You'd have to shore it up,

Niece Bonnie--1 1/2 years of age.

insulate it, redo the stairs, then what you would have is a playhouse. No, it's not a good idea."

Down went the momentary vision. The next place was a small barn. It had lovely old, wide boards and hand-hewn beams. As she stood in the middle of it, looking around, she smiled at her father, "You'd have to shore it up, insulate it, put in stairs. Then what would you have?"

"Sister, you're learning. I will guarantee you one thing. Once you own a house your troubles will begin. You should start with a house that does not have too many headaches to begin with."

Down went the idea of converting a barn. Joan decided to try the following year. She had been told she'd have a month's vacation. Not wanting to get into the hassle of Labor Day traffic, they went home the week before. She was anxious to get her teeth into the new job.

When Joan arrived to report to work, the receptionist acknowledged she was expected and made a phone call to announce her arrival. To her delight, down the hall to greet her came the trial lawyer, Mr. Leonard Moore. She was instantly at ease.

He took her on a tour introducing her to the other fourteen partners and their secretaries, to each of the senior and junior associates and to the heads of the various departments. This took time as each introduction was accompanied by some chitchat. Then he brought her to her office.

It was a pleasant room, adequate in size. It contained a desk, a long, narrow table and three chairs. Two filing cabinets would be delivered shortly. As they sat down, he said, "This room has been painted, more or less tidied up for you. In time you may want to change the decor."

"At the moment, sir, it is just fine," she hastened to assure him.

"Three of my colleagues have been trying to manage the firm and take care of their legal work. They haven't done too well with the managing. Their legal work has suffered. I feel strongly you will relieve all of us of a large headache. Unfortunately, I'm in court most of the time so you will report to Mr. Ralph Ray. If you run into any trouble, you can always leave word with my secretary that you'd like to see me. Do you have any questions?"

"Sir, I'm very appreciative of the time you spent to introduce me to the staff. You have made it a lot easier for me when and if I will have to make changes in personnel and procedures. I'm going to wade in slowly until I'm sure of my footing as well as my surroundings. I'll try for acceptance and trust while learning the various functions of the office."

"I'm betting on you," he said as he got up to leave. They shook hands and he said, "Good luck. Yell if you need me."

He had made it clear the firm had never had an office manager, per se. To confirm this, it developed each department had the personnel files for his or her department. She had to tiptoe into this situation. It was imperative for her to know the background of the people she would supervise. There were no job specifications, which didn't matter too much, although she had to get some idea of what employees were expected to do or not do.

In the getting-acquainted period there was glaring evidence of wasted time, wasted motion and waste of supplies. Much had to be done. She did a lot of preliminary digging. By December 1, she had coordinated the personnel files, had some rough idea of job specifications and had some personal contact with each one of the nonlegal staff. She was convinced the one worrisome bottleneck was in duplication. Many clients required briefs to be submitted to the SEC (Securities and Exchange Commission), the CAB (Civil Aeronautics Board) and other government agencies which entailed myriad copies. As a matter of fact, most legal documents required multiple copies. This presented a problem as the stenographic room, consisting of twenty-five stenographers and five typists, was inadequate and needed reorganization.

Electric typewriters were just beginning to make their appearance on the market. The department used standard machines, many of which were of old vintage requiring pounding, making carbons difficult. To complicate this situation, the elderly lady in charge was a hard-working loyal employee of many years standing. A similar situation existed in the filing department, also understaffed and headed by an elderly longtime employee.

There was no pension plan to allow the older employees to retire. These problems highlighted the essential need to update operations. It was evident the entire personnel lacked any sense of an esprit de corps. It appeared the majority were weighed down and bored with tedious, uninteresting "heretofores" plus the burden of making copies. The place needed a shot in the arm, some boost in morale before it smothered Joan.

The Sunday before Christmas, Joan and her mother drove down to the office with a box of Christmas ornaments, Christmas tree lights and a five-foot Christmas tree sticking out of the trunk. Downtown New York was deserted. The lone elevator operator on duty was delighted with the distraction and enlisted the help of the lone porter. They set up the tree on a table in the steno department and decorated it.

The following morning the pleasure created by the tree was worth any effort. The atmosphere was lighter, happier. She waited to see if she'd get any reaction from one or two of the stuffy partners, if they felt it disturbed the serious business at hand. She never found out. However, several of the partners had walked down the hall to surreptitiously glance into the room. It was late in the afternoon when Mr. Moore stuck his head into her office with a grin and the V for victory sign. Perhaps someone had questioned the unusual gaiety. If so, he had straightened them out.

In October Bob and Trudy had their third child, their first son. Joan and her parents had not seen the baby. On Christmas Eve they left almost at daybreak to go to Bob's in New Jersey. They took plenty of goodies and plenty of presents. It had snowed a few days before and a good bit was left around Bob's area. A pair of child's skis and poles for Bonnie provided great excitement. After cursory instruction, that little tyke took off cross-country fashion over the adjoining field. Joan hoped in the not too distant future she'd have a skiing companion. Karen was absorbed with her dolls. Kevin, the new addition, was sleeping peacefully. Joan and Bob enjoyed discussing their respective jobs. They departed after lunch in view of the anticipated holiday traffic.

Joan found progress in the office, although slower than she wanted, was encouraging. Reorganization of the stenographic room was underway. The supervisor had expressed a desire to retire. An arrangement was worked out solely for this individual whereby she would receive a percentage payment each month for an indefinite period.

After a diligent search, a replacement was hired; additional help was obtained; an orderly system of assignments was being worked out; and outdated equipment was being replaced. Investigation to replace the old Multigraph machine with something better proved hopeless at the time. An assistant was hired for the filing department with the idea she would eventually take over. The working atmosphere was more relaxed.

Joan had a hunch she was gaining the confidence of the staff, both legal and nonlegal in what she was attempting to accomplish. She prepared a progress report for Mr. Ray. A week after she submitted it, he sent for her, said he'd discussed it with several partners, and they were satisfied. He mentioned the fact the majority of the partners and the legal staff would be away on vacation in August; therefore would she agree to taking the month of July this year? This suited her fine.

For the past three years, Joan had taken part in the Squadron A evening riding classes of the Seventh Regiment. These classes were suspended during the winter months and resumed in March. Not long after her meeting with Mr. Ray, she attended a class with an Irish master conducting the session. Joan enjoyed it and spoke with him after the period ended. She was fired up and knew she would go to Ireland in July.

It took a few days for preliminary plans to jell in her head. Mother had a brother and his family living in Ballinahowna, near Roscommon, outside of Dublin, whom she had not seen in over forty years. Joan would take her mother, tour Ireland for a week and leave her to visit her family while Joan went off for two and a half weeks to visit Heidi and Bill. Heidi's letters had been coaxing her to come back.

The wheels were set in motion. Any strain felt in the office was quickly forgotten by evening as they cemented their plans and enjoyed the anticipation of the trip. As the departure time drew closer, arrangements were being completed. Her mother had secured a passport; airline reservations were confirmed; letters flew back and forth between Uncle Jim and her Mother and between Heidi and Joan.

Dad reneged on the trip having no desire to go. Nevertheless he handed out advice, issued instructions, checked and rechecked everything. Joan felt he was a bit anxious knowing her mother would be so far away. This thought was confirmed when he drove them to the airport. He could hardly hold back the tears. But as the plane taxied out onto the field, he was waving and smiling.

This episode was super, but that is another story. During the two and a half weeks with Heidi and Bill, Joan likes to share one adventure. Leaving Heidi's home in the Hartz Mountains, they went to Frankfurt to meet Heidi's brother, Karl, who would join them through Bavaria and into Austria. Joan was disturbed by the war destruction in Munich. Most of the old, beautiful buildings were merely facades, yet the famous Glockenspiel with its moving figures remained intact.

Heidi pushed on to the happier surroundings of the Werdenfelser land of mountains. The narrow, winding road, with solid rock on one side and deep drop-offs with no guard rails on the other side, was scary. They rounded one curve to be greeted by the unforgettable sight of the large, castle-like Hotel Sonnebichl nestled into the mountains. It was here they would spend the next three days and nights that were among the happier moments in Joan's life.

Entering the massive portal was like walking into a storybook existence. It was as though all royalty and dignitaries housed there over the years had left an elegance that permeated the patina of the various woods—whether in the paneled walls, the balustrades of the great stairway, or the inlaid patterns of the floors. This same elegance touched the rich, dark colors of soft leathers mixed with the warm tones of exquisite tapestries which made up the furnishings. The crystal chandeliers in the large dining room reflected the table settings of white linens, silver and crystal service which in turn sparkled on the high ceiling.

Karl and Bill shared a room, while Joan and Heidi were in the adjoining room. It was a spacious room overlooking the charming town of Garmisch-Partenkirchen with the wide expanse of mountains behind it. Although the room had lovely, old furniture, the drapes, bedspreads and rugs were of bright colors in contrast to the somber tones of the public rooms.

It was a native German hotel staffed with courteous, helpful German personnel. Dinner that evening was gracious dining at its best with outstanding food. They sat around afterwards bringing Bill and Karl up-to-date on their wanderings until Bill and Heidi announced they were off to bed. Karl asked Joan, "Are you tired or would you care to join me in the salon for an after-dinner drink. I'm not ready to sleep yet." "As a matter of fact, I'm not at all tired. Would love to join you."

The salon was another high-ceilinged room of the same elegance with banquettes along the wall and a few tables placed here and there producing an intimate feeling of privacy. The lighting effect was sheer genius—soft and delicate, with no suggestion of darkness. It was as if it were created by a skylight in late afternoon. A three-piece orchestra was playing unobtrusively in one corner, offering waltz and fox trot selections with perfect rhythm to make the feet respond. Karl ordered Grand Marnier and asked her to dance.

It was a unique, romantic setting. Joan floated on air letting her imagination run wild. One minute she was an empress, the next Cinderella. Returning to their table and liqueur Joan confessed, "This whole setting is an unreal story adventure. It gives me an illusion of being an empress, princess, whatever. I'm having a wonderful time."

"It's just as unreal for me," he admitted. "It's been a very long time since I've been in this atmosphere." He seemed to drift away.

Joan asked, "A penny for your thoughts?"

"You'd never understand what the war years were like for me or my family. Tonight I can forget."

They made light conversation, mostly danced, happy to share each other's company.

It was past midnight when he said, "It is a perfect time for pattisserie and coffee. Would you like that?"

"Do you think I might have some ice cream with coffee?"

He signaled a waiter and appeared to be giving him a complicated description to which the waiter would interrupt with, "Ja, Herr Doctor" as he made motions with his hands. Joan, not understanding a word, sensed the waiter was pleased.

When he left they went back to the dance floor. Twenty minutes later they were still dancing when the waiter signaled. Karl led her to the table. When she was seated, a second waiter appeared with a dish held high above his head. Bowing to them, he placed the dish in front of Joan. It was an unbelievable work of art—an ice cream creation of great beauty. It had three graduated circles, each about one inch high with borders of colored flowers and on the top smallest circle was a beautiful bluebird. Her "Ohs" pleased the waiter who backed away smiling as Joan thanked him. "Oh, Karl! It is a dream. And all ice cream! How did they do it? Do you have a fairy godmother who grants your wishes?"

"Most old hotels have an expert cake and ice decorator on their staff. Your request for ice cream reminded me that a long time ago, on my tenth, or maybe my ninth, birthday, my parents surprised me this way. I decided it would be fun for both of us."

"It will be a cherished memory for me. Thank you, thank you!"

The rest of the tour was "Hans and Gretel", but that too is another story.

Joan returned to Ireland to fetch her mother. Two days later they boarded the plane at Shannon as the entire Gavin family waved them off with a mixture of tears and smiles. The stewardess brought them magazines and a newspaper. The date on the newspaper, July 28, 1950, triggered an unhappy flashback for Joan. It was just over a year ago, on Sunday, May 22, 1949, that Admiral Gingrich had phoned Joan from Washington with the devastating news that Defense Secretary Forrestal had been murdered.

Gingrich had been at Bethesda Naval Hospital. He had witnessed the fact that Forrestal's sash from his bathrobe had been tied tightly around his neck, his face beaten almost beyond recognition. He asked her not to believe the news reports of suicide. He had also gone to the Secretary's office at the Pentagon to check on the diaries only to discover they were missing and had been impounded by the White House. He felt there were too many obstacles placed in the way of his attempts to unearth details. They confirmed the suspicion of a cover-up which had to be coming from a person or persons high up in the federal government.

Joan recalled the forty-five minute session in Boston, on August 11, 1943, when the Secretary was distraught about the infiltration of communists in all phases of government including the highest places. He did not trust George Marshall, even Roosevelt, and others in the State Department and OSS (Office of Strategic Services). His fears were later confirmed when Roosevelt gave in to Stalin at Yalta and when the Truman Doctrine became the Marshall Plan. Joan believed Forrestal personally had prevented Italy from going communistic.

During March of 1948 when the first postwar election campaigning was going on, he started the letter campaign from Italian Americans to relatives in Italy. He contributed his own money and monies raised from his wealthy friends to combat the huge flow of American money to the Russian delegation by the United States Treasury, headed by Harry Dexter White, later identified as a communist spy. He sent two close, personal friends as his representatives to the Vatican.

His campaign against communism was well known. His brilliant mind recognized their devious methods; his patriotism and his vision projected the dangers to the United States. He was devoted to defeating the movement wherever and whenever he could; as long as he was in a position of power, he presented a threat to Russia. Joan believed he had been murdered. It was more difficult to believe it could happen in America.[6] She felt he never should have been forced into the strenuous position of Defense Secretary without a long vacation to ease tensions and exhaustions.

Back in the States, settling into the office routines quickly, her trip faded into the background. It will require effort to summarize the next six or seven years; only incidents of note, for one reason or another, will be shared. Joan's career in management was extremely successful, breaking precedent by holding office in the New York Personnel Management Association, which was about 98% male and establishing a reputation in law office management catapulted by her discovery of a solution to the critical need for better duplicating equipment. She unearthed the

---

[6] In 1966, Cornell Simpson wrote *The Death of James Forrestal* confirming the murder.

Hailoid Corporation in a loft on Sixth Avenue and was so excited about its potential, she rented the equipment for her office. She invited managers from other firms to inspect it, which led to her giving lectures on it. It was successful and later became Zerox. Here she made one of the biggest mistakes of her life—because they felt she had created an interest in the machine they offered her stock at $6.00 per share. Having pushed it so hard, she did not feel it would be ethical to accept the offer. Too late she learned it would have been justified to buy the shares.

Early in January 1951 she had her authority as office manager endangered due largely to stuffy legal interpretation. It was a Monday morning when she picked up the phone to hear Mr. Ray's irritated voice. He wanted to see her pronto. She had hardly stepped inside his office when he said, "Mr. Royce tells me one of his scale model planes is missing from his office. I suggest you call the police to report it."

"Yes, sir. Before I do that I'd like to check to make sure it has not been misplaced."

Mr. Royce's secretary confirmed the fact she and her boss had searched the office without any luck. The daily record sheet indicated two lawyers, three stenographers and a messenger had been working Saturday. The messenger, Tom, a tall, attractive and well-mannered high school senior had been employed for seven months. He had worked full time during the summer months and was now on part time after school and on Saturdays. He was a well-liked, serious employee—still a young man who might be tempted by a model airplane. His mother, a widow, worked as a telephone operator to support three children. Tom was the eldest.

Joan phoned her, chatted a few minutes, then said, "By any chance did Tom bring home a model plane last Saturday?"

"Why, yes," she answered. "I didn't question him about it. Did he do wrong?"

"Let's just say he borrowed it. You see it happens to be a most expensive exact scale model. I'm sure Tom did not realize its value. When he reports for work this afternoon, I'll send him home to fetch it. I will do what I can to see he is not punished and that he keeps his job. Please don't worry. I'll call you back when it is settled."

Her office faced the main entrance hall. She kept watch and called to Thomas as he got off the elevator. When he stood in front of her desk, she said, "Tom, why did you take the model airplane?"

He looked at her and said simply, "I like it. It is beautiful."

"Tom, please sit down." When he was seated, she continued, "That is not an ordinary toy plane. It is an expensive, exact scale model. That's beside the point—whether it cost $5.00 or $5,000, it is Mr. Royce's property. Tom, taking that model is stealing. You could be arrested for it. I'm counting on the fact you were fascinated by it and gave no thought to the act of stealing. I do not want to see you begin life with a police record."

"Please, Mrs. Evans," he interrupted, "I didn't know it was valuable. I was not thinking of the part of stealing."

"OK, Tom. I can understand what happened. Go home, get the model and bring it back to me. Be quick about it. I promise to try to straighten out the matter. If I do, I want you to continue your job here, OK? Off you go."

Once Joan had the model in hand, she went directly to Mr. Royce, giving him the boy's background and family situation. She wanted to convince him of her faith in this young man, of her unwillingness to stamp him for life as a thief and of her desire to retain him as an employee. If she could obtain his cooperation and support, she'd take her chances with Mr. Ray. Mr. Royce, although a shrewd lawyer, was a gentle, compassionate person. He understood perfectly, even admitting that as a young boy he had stolen something or other.

When she finally got to see Mr. Ray, she told him the model had been located and returned to Mr. Royce. She couldn't get away that easily. He pressed her. When she sketched the details, he shouted, "I disagree with you. He should be punished. How else will he learn not to steal?"

"Mr. Ray, this young man has been punished. I guarantee he will never forget the embarrassment he has suffered today."

Fortunately, Mr. Royce appeared. He was senior to Mr. Ray. How much of the conversation he had overheard, she could not tell. He said, "Come now, Ralph, when you have time to think this over you'll reach the same conclusion we reached."

Mr. Ray agreed to think it over and dismissed Joan. She did not hear from him about it. Tom graduated from high school the following June, applied for and was accepted at a law enforcement school, training to be a state trooper. Two years later while she was working on some complicated pension figures, a voice said, "Mrs. Evans." She looked up, all the way up to the 6'3" of a very handsome state trooper who grinned shyly and handed her a box of chocolates.

Strangely enough, Joan sensed she gained respect from most of the partners after this incident. As for the office, organizational improvement was coming along in the various departments. Dead wood was being weeded out and control of supplies was becoming effective. Several associates took the time to mention they appreciated the improvement in the stenographers. Joan was pleased with the results so far.

The first weekend in June, Joan and her mother took off for Southampton. She was dead set on finding a house. She talked with Mr. Day, a real estate agent, who showed her several houses, all of which were much too big. That afternoon they cruised around Southampton and the Water Mill area. She found Water Mill enchanting. She saw a small house not far from the village green within walking distance of the few stores. She phoned Mr. Day. "I've just seen a house that meets all my requirements. It's an old, shingled house. It's small with a nice-sized piece of land, close to the village. It would make a perfect old lady's home for me when I retire. I'd like to show it to you. Maybe you can contact the owner and find out if he would sell, or if not, at least you'd get an idea of what I'm looking for. Would you be willing to meet me at Halsey Lane?"

"That won't be necessary. I know the house. It was originally a stable in the 1800s. It's been rented to a local couple for many years. I also know the owner, Mr. Ives, who lives in the big house north of the cottage. I will check with him. Give me a call about 3:00 o'clock. I'll see what I can do." It seemed an eternity until then, only to be told the owner had hesitated, but decided against selling it.

Off and on during the following week she thought of the house and made up her mind to try a long shot. As long as there had been some hesitation about selling it, she would call on the Ives the next weekend. She bought a bunch of spring flowers and presented herself at their door saying, "I'm the person who had Mr. Day bother you about the cottage. I wanted to bring you these flowers in the way of an apology. Also to ask if you ever consider selling it, would you please give me a chance to buy it?"

"I'm Mr. Ives. Please come in. I'd like you to meet Mrs. Ives. She is not well." They chatted for ten or fifteen minutes. They were a dear, elderly couple who seemed glad to have someone visit them. Mr. Ives asked why she wanted the cottage. She admitted she'd lost her husband during the war, had a good job and was planning for the future. "A small house I could enjoy now on weekends, vacations and when I retire. It would be an ideal old lady's home. Your house is perfect as I could walk to the post office and the stores."

He asked her where she was staying. That evening Joan and her mother went for an early dinner at McCarthy's, a well-known Southampton restaurant. They were in the middle of dinner when she was summoned to the phone. Her landlady told her a Mr. Ives would like her to call him. Her heart was pounding as she asked the operator for the number. Mr. Ives answered, "You brought a little sunshine to Mrs. Ives today. She wondered if you would come to tea tomorrow at four o'clock."

"Of course," she answered. "I'd be happy to come."

This messed up their plans as they always left early on Sundays to get back in time for dinner with her father. She was determined to make friends with the Ives. Her mother agreed and called home to say they'd be late.

On this visit she arrived with tea biscuits which pleased Mrs. Ives. Mr. Ives served the tea, then sat down to join them. He came right to the point, "Mrs. Ives and I have no children. We decided we would like to adopt you and give you the cottage."

Joan couldn't believe her ears. She was astonished by such a request. When the reality of what had been said seeped into her head, her eyes filled with tears. She blurted out, "What a wonderful compliment, but I have a mother and father."

"I guess we figured you were all alone. Maybe they will let us share you, come see us occasionally."

"Oh, yes! My mother has been coming down with me on weekends. May I bring her to meet you next weekend?"

"Please do. It would be better if you phoned first to make sure Mrs. Ives will be feeling all right."

Impulsively, Joan went over and put her arms around Mrs. Ives, hugged and thanked her. She started to shake hands with Mr. Ives who seemed more formidable; instead she hugged him too telling him she'd never forget them and would be privileged to visit them—house or no house.

The following Saturday, she introduced her mother to them. They stayed about forty minutes then departed so as not to tire Mrs. Ives. Fortunately, they went straight back to their room to rest before dinner as Mr. Ives called to say she could buy the cottage. He was not sure when she could take possession as he would have to work out some plan with the tenant. She assured him it didn't matter; she was truly happy and grateful to them for letting her have her dream house.

That is how her life style changed. There were no more trips to Europe. Weekends were spent going to auctions all over New England. Bill Carey, her prewar, scotch-drinking friend, was knowledgeable on Early American furniture and knew which auctions would produce results. He pointed out the better pieces and taught them how to bid.

In the meantime, arrangements were made for the purchase of the cottage. The Bridgehampton Bank approved a mortgage, and Mr. Whiteside, one of her senior partners, had an associate handle the legal side. It turned out the cottage was built in 1744 as a barn. There was some delay clearing the title caused by the fact of a land grant from the King of England to the Halsey family in the seventeen hundreds. The contract of sale was completed on August 27, 1951, one day after her 40th birthday. She took possession on October 5, 1951.

Bill, her fabulous friend, picked up the furniture collected at auctions and stored in her parents' garage and delivered it to the house. Joan borrowed three cots and she and her parents slept there that night.

There are many stories, good and bad, about the restoring of the house and refinishing of the furniture. Joan continued to visit the Ives every weekend and had them to the house for dinner occasionally. They were enthusiastic and encouraging about the improvements. The following summer Mr. Ives died of a heart attack. Mrs. Ives moved to Brooklyn to stay with her sister. The house was sold to a city architect and neighborly relations ceased. Joan kept in touch with Mrs. Ives until she died.

Another happy surprise came along that October. Bob Moore from the management consultant firm proposed Joan for membership in the New York Personnel Management Association, a large organization composed largely of men, with a minuscule percentage of women. She was thrilled to be accepted. Over the next six or more years this organization opened up a terrific outlet for her. It met once a month for dinner presenting an interesting speaker at each session. Bob Moore and Gordon James would save a seat for her at one of the tables and see that she was introduced to some of the members. They sat at tables for eight and swapped management ideas. In fact it was at one of these meetings she discussed the problems of duplication. Someone mentioned having heard of the Hailoid people. He had no information about it. Joan's follow-up on this company has been related earlier.

A few weeks later she was accepted into the Law Office Management Group with one other woman. Days were disappearing for Joan. Christmas with her parents was spent that year at the house in Water Mill.

Sometime in January 1952, Joan received a frantic call from one of the senior partners asking her to come to his office immediately. She found him holding his panic-stricken secretary. He explained, "She just tried to jump out the window. I don't know what's wrong."

Putting her arms around the girl, Joan said, "Kay, will you come with me? I'd like very much to talk to you." Kay clung to her and allowed her to lead her into a vacant office. They sat down on a couch, she started to cry, "I don't know what's wrong with me. I'm up-tight, strung out. I'm scared."

"Look, Kay," Joan began, "you're one of the best secretaries in the firm, a wonderful, capable person. Thankfully your mind is very much intact. This has to be some physical imbalance. Your doctor can take some tests, find out and correct it. Let me call your husband. He can arrange an appointment for you."

"My doctor is in Yonkers. How can I get there?"

"Easy. I have my car in the garage across the street. We can pick up your husband at his office. I'll take you both to the doctor's office."

The doctor diagnosed the problem as the opposite of diabetes and gave her medication. After a week's rest, she was back at work, happy as ever. Joan invited both Kay and her husband, Tom, to a weekend in Water Mill. It was the beginning of a long friendship with the Glenns, lasting until they both died twenty-nine years later.

In May the Water Mill house became an oasis for the exhausted associate lawyer who was head of the tax department. His secretary contacted Joan and told her she felt he was having a nervous breakdown. After satisfying herself this was indeed a possibility, she approached the partner in charge of the department, requesting the associate be given a week off; she would offer her cottage in the country to him, his wife and two small children. This change of scene and rest period was all he needed to get back on his feet.

Joan was thrilled to share her old lady's home for such good purposes. Office personnel were not the only ones who benefited but some very dear friends—that too, is another story.

The next several years were happy, secure ones for Joan. She was attractive, popular and had a good number of male and female friends. Maintaining her vow not to remarry, the men she liked, enjoyed and could trust were placed on what she labeled her "safe shelf." Her independent attitude and good humor seemed to steer her clear of any emotional involvement. Her primary contacts in the office were with men, seventeen bosses, about forty-five associate lawyers, salesmen, repair and service men. Her outside business contacts were also mostly men.

Her activities in the New York Personnel Management Association branched out. Often after meetings Bob Moore, Gordon James and possibly a few others would have a nightcap at the Roosevelt Hotel and dance to the music of Guy Lombardo which they all enjoyed. Under their auspices she took courses in management at the downtown Cornell University Extension School and attended several seminars, some lasting three days or more.

The summer months opened up a new vista for Joan. Mr. George Whiteside, a senior partner, had a summer home across the bay in Water Mill. He appointed her to be secretary of the Water Mill Beach Club. This entitled her to membership without having to pay dues. She loved the ocean and forced herself to take time out from the refinishing and the making of curtains and bed-spreads. She was introduced to many of the members and invited to their parties. It wasn't long before her new friends were unearthing the eligible bachelor.

She was so secure, even smug, with her cottage and her job. She enjoyed her friends' efforts, particularly when invited to various club dances and she had a dancing partner. About this time she met John and Peggy Waters who lived on the next road. Peggy was a Manhattanville girl, about four years after Joan. They were such caring people and did so many thoughtful things. When Joan arrived on Friday evenings, she would find fresh vegetables on the back porch. In the spring she was surprised by tulips they had planted the previous fall. When the tulips died, they planted geraniums. On the odd weekend when she came without her parents, they insisted she join them for a family super.

Peggy invited her to a cocktail party given by a couple celebrating the birth of their first child. The husband was a lawyer, twenty-five years older than his wife, Vickie. Joan can still remember her first sight of Vickie. She absolutely sparkled. She was intelligent with a keen sense of humor and very beautiful. She was twenty years younger than Joan, yet they must have been on the same wave length and became friends. Several years later they shared a weird experience which cemented a friendship that still exists today.

In August while she was on vacation, Bob, Trudy and the three children would spend a week with her. When they went home they left Bonnie, always a joy for Joan. Her parents would arrive for several weeks.

By the spring of 1954, "Ye Olde Lady's Home" was all hers. The mortgage was paid off, a happy, satisfying feeling. By then, she was involved in enough activities to keep her out late on many evenings. Subway travel was relatively safe at the time. To alleviate her parents' concern she rented a small apartment in Stuyvesant Town on 15th Street in the city. This cut down her commuting time substantially and made life a lot simpler for her. Her job was going well and she was well compensated. Many timesaving procedures had been installed. Inventories and supplies were realistic and money saving. Her biggest project now was researching microfilming for the records.

That summer, at a party at Mr. Whiteside's, she met an ideal male companion, Tad Benton. He had been divorced six months earlier under heartbreaking and disillusioning circumstances. He was badly burnt, finished with marriage. They shared a common bond. His family had a summer place in Water Mill. Tad began coming down on weekends. They enjoyed the beach, swimming, tennis, fishing and dancing.

Bonnie was elated when Tad took them and his parents in their large fishing boat to Claudio's in Greenport for a lobster dinner. Tad was a sweet, kind, fun-loving gentleman. Bonnie was devoted to him. Joan thrived on the time they spent together. In the fall they enjoyed duck hunting and in the winter they went skiing. Within a year her parents, his parents, friends in Water Mill and friends in Stowe began to wonder about the outcome. They went merrily on their way ignoring any innuendos.

In October 1956 Joan received an invitation from Anne and Mat Correa to attend a reunion of some of the officers who had been in Washington during the war. Mat had been a Marine officer in Secretary Forrestal's office. He had married a very attractive, well-liked, capable WAVE officer. Joan hadn't seen either of them since she'd been detached from the Navy. It sounded like a fun idea. The invitation stated, "and escort." Tad had been in the Navy, not in Washington, but out on a cruiser. He happily accepted the invitation to join her.

The Correas had done a superb job in collecting a good number of Navy and Marine persons who had worked together. The living and dining rooms were crowded as they made their way around trying to see everyone at once. Joan stopped to tell Mat what a nice idea the party was and to introduce him to Tad. Mat introduced them to a few other Naval officers and said to Tad, "Will you excuse us? I'm going to borrow Joan for a minute. A friend had called to make sure she would be here." He led Joan into a den room full of people and said, "Here's a friend you'll probably remember."

Turning, Joan faced Ed Bench and his big grin. She said, "My, I'm very happy to see you."

"You know, Mat," Ed said, "it must be almost a year since I called this young lady for lunch, only to find what a busy gal she is. I'm still waiting."

"I can believe it," Mat said as he welcomed another guest.

"I really was busy, Ed. Wasn't I leaving for a seminar at Lake George?"

"Something like that. You look very well. Being busy agrees with you."

"I was thinking how well you looked. How are Mary and the family?"

"Mary and I have been legally separated and are proceeding with a divorce."

"Oh! I'm so sorry."

"Don't be. This has been coming for quite awhile. Are you still as busy as ever? What are you up to now?"

"The office keeps me hopping. I've been made an officer of the New York Management Group—the first woman. I've bought a cottage in Water Mill, Long Island, which has me on the go."

"Congratulations on all counts. Will you have dinner with me? I'd like to catch up."

"Honestly, I can't. I'm here with Tad Benton. We're having dinner together. I want you to meet him. You'll like him, he's a nice guy." Finding Tad, she brought him back and introduced him to Ed saying, "Ed's an old friend from the Navy days."

The two men chatted about where they'd been in the Navy and what a good idea the party was until Mat came to take Joan to see another friend. As she excused herself, Ed said, "I'll call you for lunch."

Although no bright lights were flashing and no bells were ringing, her contented, secure life was about to be disrupted. On the Monday morning following the Correa party, Ed Bench phoned for what he called a long-awaited luncheon date. Lunch at Fraunces tavern lasted over two hours. Time simply disappeared. Ed seemed so sincerely interested. She found herself telling him about the house, Mr. Whiteside's many kindnesses, her country friends and her extracurricular business activities. He was cagey on dismissing most of her questions about his doings. She did learn he loved the research part of the investment banking firm and that his oldest daughter was married. He had two grandchildren. Noticing the restaurant was practically empty, she wondered how it could be so late. She had to get back to the office.

"How about lunch again on Thursday?"

"Fine. I'd like that," she answered, giving no thought whatsoever to the possibility she might have another appointment. Ed stopped at the captain's desk to make the reservation.

That afternoon office duties and problems were handled with little effort. By Wednesday she was looking forward to lunch on Thursday. By Wednesday evening she found herself choosing her clothes with particular care. Well, he was a comfortable person, down-to-earth with an extremely keen, practical mind and a marvelous sense of humor. She tossed off her enthusiasm to the fact she had always liked him.

She left the office at noon feeling sure she'd be on time getting back as they would not have so much to catch up on. She was wrong. They reminisced and talked about her brother Bob and the current happenings of the Parkfairfax core group. She asked him if he remembered her SOS when her mother was taken to the hospital with acute glaucoma. He said, "When I arrived at the hospital, you looked so worried, so helpless."

"All I know is if you hadn't shown up, God knows how long she'd have suffered before getting any relief. And Anne, my cousin, you saved that young girl from being butchered."

"I was glad you gave me a chance to help."

"Boy, were you ever a help. I was embarrassed to bother you. Dick Cooper told me how influential you were at the hospital, that you knew the doctors. I did not know where to turn. I am so very grateful to you."

They laughed about the lunch they had enjoyed with Heidi and Bill when they came back for a visit. She told Ed they spent a weekend in Water Mill as they had to see the project that kept her from returning for a tour of Germany. She assured him she was in constant touch with those two beautiful people. She was very late getting back to her desk, but she had learned something. In thinking about how much she had enjoyed lunch, she recalled prior luncheons were always shared with others. Now they concentrated solely on mutual interests, resulting in a more personal contact which was surprisingly pleasant.

Two lunches in one week was unusual. She wondered when and if he'd call again. That weekend Joan and her father were out in the garage in Water Mill refinishing an old Estey organ she and Bill Carey had located in Selden, Long Island, when a young boy delivered an arrangement of autumn flowers. It was from Mr. Warren's nursery in Water Mill, addressed to Joan with no card attached. A telephone call advised the order specified no card was necessary. Her mother was more curious, insisting Joan must know, or that Mr. Warren must have some idea.

That evening Tad and Joan were going to a private dinner party followed by an autumn ball at Seven Ponds Inn. When Tad came, she watched for any reaction to the flowers which she'd placed in a prominent location. They made no impression on him. Come to think of it, Tad gave her presents for birthdays and Christmas. He had never sent her flowers. Bill Carey? He often brought flowers, never sent them. John Krueger? No, dear John would bring a practical present and get a kick out of telling friends, "Can you imagine a young lady turning down a gold bracelet then be willing to accept an electric drill?"

There was only one person she could think of who sent flowers, but she hadn't seen him in over four years. She'd heard he'd married. She gave up.

The party was beautiful with dance music to make the toes tingle. Mr. Whiteside was dancing with Joan and caught her by surprise, "You and Tad make such a good-looking couple. You have such fun together. Many of us are hoping you will marry."

"Mr. Whiteside, you're a dear. Tad and I feel exactly the same way. We do not want to remarry."

"My dear girl, don't waste your life on the past. Second marriages are usually outstanding. Both parties are older, have experience and know what to expect. You know this is a second marriage for me and for my wife. It's been wonderful. Think about it...."

She gave him a hug, "Thank you." Good Lord, at that moment she knew who sent the flowers. As they continued to dance, her head was swimming. No, no, don't get crazy ideas; he's so much older, and very settled in his ways. Mr. Whiteside was leading her off the dance floor and Tad was coming to dance with her. Snap out of it, idiot.

On Wednesday, coming out of the Battery parking garage, Ed was waiting for her. "Hi! I thought I'd have coffee at Schrafft's. Will you join me?"

Looking at her watch to cover her embarrassment, she said, "Yes, thank you. I have time."

As soon as they were seated, he said, "Did you like them?"

She turned and looked directly at him, "They were beautiful. Thank you."

"Did you have a good weekend?"

"Yes. It was fun. The Whitesides invited us to a dinner party followed by an autumn ball. I really love the Whitesides. They've been so darned good to me."

"Us? You and Tad Benton?"

"Why, yes. You remember him. He was with me at the Correas'."

"Oh, I remember him, a nice-looking young man. Do you see a lot of him?"

"Mostly on weekends. His family has a house down the road."

"Anything serious between you?"

"Heavens no. We're good friends. He had a nasty jolt, as I did. It can make one wary." She began to feel uneasy. "Gosh, I must run. Long lunches and coffee breaks may not sit well with my bosses--all seventeen of them," she laughed as she put on her coat.

"Will you have a long lunch with me on Friday?"

"I'm not at all sure it can be a long one. Will you agree to a normal lunch hour?" Why in hell did he pick a Friday? It was a pleasant lunch with light conversation and some serious discussion on world events. He was a stimulating conversationalist. She enjoyed it—it disrupted what should have been a fun weekend.

The next four or five weeks consisted of flowers every weekend in Water Mill; coffee three or four times a week; lunch about twice a week. He did not ask her for dinner or to go dancing. He was comfortable all right, too damn comfortable. He was no longer a "safe-shelf." She was going to have to make a decision to drop it or play it by ear. How could she take a chance on being hurt again? He was getting to her.

By the middle of December she asked her mother, "Are you and Dad doing anything next Sunday?"

"I don't think so. Why?"

"I would like to bring a possible Jesus Christ home for Sunday dinner."

"Sister! That's no way to talk." Then remembering, she broke into a broad grin, "Of course."

Naturally her mother went to town on a very special dinner. She was utterly flabbergasted when Joan walked in with Ed Bench. She was a bit embarrassed at how her mother hugged and kissed him. Mother said, "Ed, it's been a long time. I don't think you've changed a bit. That grin is still the same. Come in and meet father."

"Father, this is Commander Bench, one of Joan's friends from Washington."

Joan said, "Whoa. He's Captain Bench now, Mother. I guess, Dad, you can just call him Ed."

"Welcome, Captain Ed. My wife told me Joan had a group of wonderful friends in Washington."

"She was very popular, sir. She was the prettiest of those original WAVES."

"She was, wasn't she?" (prejudiced parent).

"I worked with her in the same section for a few months. She was also a very capable young lady."

"I hear she's making a reputation for herself in the law firm." (a braggart too).

Joan broke up the trend of conversation by taking drink orders. There was no need to worry about Ed. He remembered Dad was a civilian with the Coast Guard during the war. They were off discussing the Coast Guard, Navy, the war in general. Whew, they seemed to like each other. They also found each other's sense of humor.

The dinner went well. Her mother absolutely refused to let them help clean up the kitchen saying on the next visit (pushing) she'd put them both to work. Driving back into the city, Ed said, "Having known your mother in Washington, I wasn't too worried about her. I worried about your father and hoped he would like me. He's a great person. Your home is full of warmth and affection. Your parents are very proud of you."

"They've been known to bore people about their offspring. Beware," she retorted.

"I was thinking of going up to Logwood for three or four days over Lincoln's birthday weekend. The skiing is usually good then. Any chance you could go up at the same time?"

"That's when I usually go up. I can't think of any reason why not."

"Good. I'll call Janet for reservations. We can drive up together in my car."

"If you talk to Janet, would you please ask her to give me Room 5 if it is available?"

"I don't think I've ever stayed in Room 5. Of course I'll ask her."

"You'd remember it. It's the only room with its own bath and tub. Nothing like a good hot bath after a day's skiing. It's also a double room. I often share it with Roberta Harrington, who also likes the idea of a tub. Did you ever run into her?"

"No. I don't think so." He had pulled up in front of her door. He continued, "I'll be away over the holidays. I may not get back until the first week in January. I'll try to call you. Thanks for a nice day."

"Thank you for coming. Have a nice holiday. Merry Christmas."

"I'll be in touch before then. Where will you be for Christmas? At home or in Water Mill?"

"Bob and his family will be with Trudy's mother. We will all be together at our house for Christmas Eve. Christmas Day, my parents, Bonnie and I will drive out to Water Mill."

An IBM salesman was in Joan's office when Ed phoned the next morning to tell her he'd talked to Janet and made the reservations. Room 5 was all set. He had the same old cubbyhole, no bath. He was off and would give her a ring when he got back in January.

Her mother called in the afternoon. She'd received a HUGE poinsettia plant with a thank-you note from Ed. She was so pleased and asked Joan to give him a big hug for her when she saw him. Joan told her he was off on a trip and wouldn't be back until January.

Lots of things had to be taken care of around the holidays, in the office and at home. She was a busy beaver. Christmas Eve with the family was the usual joy plus the fact she had three nieces and two nephews to keep her busy.

Unpacking the car Christmas Day at Water Mill, Mr. Warren drove in with another HUGE poinsettia plant, no card. Joan and her mother exchanged knowing smiles. It took awhile to find the proper place for it. It was big!

After she had tucked Bonnie in bed, Tad came to take her to his sister's for her customary Christmas night party. The plant was forgotten in the midst of the festivities. It was after 1:00 o'clock when Tad dropped her home. Her mother had left the light on in the living room which seemed to focus on the poinsettia. Joan sat down to admire it and said out loud, "You are very beautiful, but how do I talk to a plant?" She turned off the light and went upstairs. Mr. Geddes' telegram was on her bureau, "Rejoicing beyond the horizon of the New Year." Well, maybe he had a point. The year before he had tried to get her to go with him on a project in South America but wasn't too surprised when she turned him down.

New Year's Eve the office closed at 3:00 o'clock. Joan drove to Forest Hills, picked up her parents and went on through to Water Mill. That night Mary and Larry Doyle, neighbors directly across the bay, had a gala party. Tad and Joan left shortly after midnight as they were getting up early to go duck hunting.

Her father woke her at 4:30 A.M. to tell her he thought the Doyles' house was on fire. Jumping out of bed and looking out the window across Mecox Bay, she realized it was on fire. She immediately told the operator, dressed hurriedly and drove over to find Larry trying to connect a hose and Mary coming out of the house in a sable coat with a large jewelry box which she tossed to Joan. Mary was yelling for Kevin, her three year old son. Kevin and his nurse appeared the same moment the first firemen arrived. The neighbor next door took Mary, Kevin and his nurse into her house.

The Fire Chief advised not to try to rescue anything from the house as he felt the fire was contained in the chimney of the fireplace in the bar room. There was nothing Joan could do. She put the jewelry case in the trunk of her car, returned home and dressed in hunting gear to await Tad.

His labrador was so excited about being in the Jeep with the decoys and going hunting, he jumped all over her. Joan loved it, but it made it more difficult to tell Tad about the fire. He decided to drive past the house to see if anything was needed. Everything was quiet. Three firemen were there to make sure it did not spark again.

No flowers were delivered the next two weekends as the poinsettia bloomed in all its glory. She was beginning to wonder if Ed was back, perhaps too busy to call, when he appeared at the garage. They went for coffee.

"My mother was very pleased with the poinsettia plant. She asked me to thank you as I do for the one you sent to Water Mill. They were both unusually beautiful plants and added to the holiday spirit."

He laughed, "It was good we had a Queens' directory in the office to find your family's address." He was very clever, getting her to talk about her holiday while declaring his was uneventful. Trying to make the Doyle fire the important event, she mentioned the delay of duck hunting. He perked up on the hunting event and asked questions about where they shot, what type of blinds they used, what type of birds came in and finally was Tad a good shot?

Fortunately she had a sixth sense and did not mention the location of that particular shoot which was at Peter Salms' estate in metal, stretch-out blinds, on a private marsh pond complete with butler in the background with coffee, breakfast, whatever. She knew instinctively that would be sissy stuff to Ed. She said, "Yes, by my standards he's a good shot. I take it you enjoy hunting which means you are very good."

He opened up telling her about shooting with his uncle, a dentist, in the Mississippi flyway as a very young boy, which was the beginning of his love for the sport. "Have you any woodcock shooting in the area?"

"I understand there is. Orson Munn, Senior, a friend of mine, claims to know some good alder cover but he won't tell anyone where to find it."

"If he won't tell, he knows where they can be found." He looked at his watch, "I must run. Why don't I call you and see when you are free for lunch next week."

She looked at him. "That will be fine," as she thought, "if you call, I'll be free."

By the end of the day she was looking forward to the Personnel Management meeting and going dancing afterwards at the Roosevelt. Leaving her office, she realized Ed had not called. She began to speculate whether Ed would ever ask her for a dinner date, let alone take her dancing. Did he seem to be more shy than she remembered him during the war? Maybe she was wrong. Time would tell.

The next morning Tad phoned, "Let's go to Stowe over Lincoln's birthday. I haven't skied so far this year."

"Oh, Tad. I told Ed Bench I'd go up with him. You remember him from the Correa party?"

"Yes, your friend from Washington. Are you going to stay at Logwood?"

"Yes. Ed called Janet and made reservations. Why don't you go up anyway?"

"I might. If I do, I'll stay at Top Notch. Dick Boardman, who owns the lodge, has been asking me to stay at his place. I'll give him a ring and let you know if I'm going."

"I hope you do. We can ski together."

That weekend Tad and Joan went for dinner and dancing at the Scotch Mist Inn. He told her he would be going to Stowe, staying at Top Notch and would call her at Logwood.

The following Friday Joan and Ed left New York City around three in the afternoon and stopped for dinner in Manchester, Vermont. They were tired when they arrived at Logwood. Janet greeted them and told Joan that Roberta was there and probably waiting for her in the room. She was not only waiting but flooded Joan with questions about the man who drove her up.

Joan's feminine intuition carried her through the inquiry with vague answers until she was ready for bed.

When Joan appeared for breakfast, Ed and Roberta were engaged in lively conversation. Joan greeted them. Ed stood up and poured her coffee. Roberta wanted to know where they planned to ski and said she'd look for them.

In the car on the way to the mountain, Ed said, "Where did you know Roberta?"

"She was with Geddes for a short time. As a matter of fact, I introduced her to Logwood."

"She's most attractive and seems intelligent. She was with Pan American and knows friends of mine there."

This could be an interesting weekend. Suddenly she remembered Tad and hoped he would call, make it more interesting. They skied the Mountain T'bar area. Ed suggested they watch for "Your friend." She chuckled to herself thinking, "Which friend?" They were having lunch when Roberta caught up with them. They skied together in the afternoon and had fun.

They were putting their skis away downstairs when one of the Logwood ski-bums handed Joan a note, "Mr. Benton phoned at 10:15 A.M., would like you and Ed to join him for cocktails and dinner at Top Notch this evening. Please call." Joan gave the note to Ed. He read it and said, "I don't think we should go for dinner as Janet expects us to be here." She knew that wasn't exactly true. She looked puzzled as he said, "If you wish, we can go for cocktails. Call him and ask if it is all right to come for cocktails, not for dinner."

Top Notch was a new ski lodge up the road. Joan was anxious to see it and was disappointed Ed had not agreed to dinner. She phoned Tad. Of course he was unhappy about dinner but delighted they would come for a drink. Roberta agreed to Joan's using the bath first after a flood of questions as to who the other guy was at Top Notch.

Bathed and dressed, she met Ed downstairs. Top Notch was up on a hill, back from the main road—modern and attractive. Tad introduced them to Mr. Boardman. Joan sat down at the bar while the three men stood. Ed involved Mr. Boardman in conversation while she chatted with Tad. Before they left it was agreed they'd meet at 9:30 A.M. at Big Spruce chair lift and ski together. Ed offered to ask her roommate to join them.

At dinner Joan talked about the new lodge. Ed seemed unusually quiet and begged off after dinner, saying he was tired. He was going to turn in, but not before he asked Roberta to join them in the morning. Actually, it was a good idea to have four skiers as each chair held two people. Roberta was alone. There was no reason not to have her join them.

Ed was up very early the next morning, waxed the skis and had them on the car when Joan joined him. She noticed he had Roberta's skis on the rack too. Was she overly sensitive or did she feel some kind of undercurrent? She fussed with her boots as they waited for Roberta. There seemed to be a lack of any spontaneous flow of conversation. They met Tad as planned, everyone agreeing it was a perfect day.

Ed was the best skier and set a fast pace which Joan and Roberta managed to follow fairly well. Poor Tad took several falls while Ed made sure he was all right, helped him up and brushed him off. The idea struck Joan that perhaps Ed was a bit annoyed at Tad's presence or maybe jealous? No, no, she was way off base. What reason could he have for being upset? It was obvious they liked each other but they had no commitment.

They had a quick lunch together before Joan and Ed started back to New York. Tad and Roberta stayed on for a few more runs. Ed was himself. She knew she was all wet thinking anything was wrong. They made excellent time and stopped in Manchester for coffee and a short break. Happy conversation flowed and all was right with the world. He carried her skis to the elevator saying, "Having been out of the office so much lately, I'll be busy the rest of the week. Maybe we can get together for dinner next week. Let me give you a call."

Riding up in the elevator she thought, "He did say dinner, didn't he?" Indeed, it was dinner. He didn't say where they were going, just that he'd pick her up at 6:30 P.M. in front of the apartment.

Covering her curiosity by chatting about current events of one kind or another, she was surprised when he kept driving west. They were on 9th or 10th Avenue. He was no dope. Noticing her apprehension he said, "Don't worry. I know where I'm going."

He parked the car. They walked around the corner. She spotted the restaurant sign and cried out, "My favorite food! How did you know?"

"How could I forget your enthusiasm at Heidi's Chinese dinner party in Washington?" he answered.

They walked into Ruby Foo's. The maitre d' greeted him by name and with deference. His assistant, a beautiful Chinese girl, expressed great pleasure in seeing him, which Ed returned. He was well-known, must be a frequent customer.

Noting Ed's quick approval, the Chinese girl had escorted them to what Joan assumed was one of the best located tables. The Chinese girl was an exquisite creature whose radiant smile enhanced her delicately carved features. The black satin sheath, fastened by two simple, silver frog closings, was slit up on each side halfway between the knee and the hip, revealing a perfect figure. While they waited for their drinks, Joan said, "Thinking of Heidi's dinner, some time after that you took us to dinner at a Chinese restaurant. Was that a Ruby Foo's?"

He thought a minute, "I really don't remember. It could have been. I think it was over on the south side of Washington. Is that what you remember?"

"Yes, I believe so."

They ate a delicious meal while discussing general topics. Ed had a good head on his shoulders and was endowed with common sense. She respected his opinions and enjoyed the exchange of ideas. As he dropped her off, she said, "That was the best Chinese food. So much better than the place I've been going to on Second Avenue. Thank you, I loved it."

"Thank you, I loved the company. Shall we try it again next Thursday?"

"I'm pretty sure there is a law office management meeting that night. May I check my pad in the morning and call you?"

"I have a meeting in the morning. Better let me call you. We can try for Tuesday or Wednesday."

Joan did have a meeting. They settled on the following Wednesday. Then she had a brainstorm. Her mother had mentioned she wanted to get into the city to do some shopping. Joan would get her to come in and stay over on Wednesday so Joan might invite Ed to see her apartment for a drink before going out to dinner. She was proud of the apartment and wanted Ed to see it. Her mother agreed to go into town with her on Sunday on the way in from Water Mill and stay the week.

The weather in Water Mill was heavenly. The crocus had appeared; buds were starting on the trees; the grape hyacinths were sending out green shoots in the circular leprechaun garden. Spring was in the air and Joan felt full of beans. She and her father worked outside all morning, raking leaves, weeding and edging. They finished lunch and were about to return outside when Tad drove in.

He hadn't been around or called the previous weekend. He explained, "It's so good to be here. I've been stuck in the city. More problems with Marylou. I hope one day it will let up." Marylou was his ex-wife.

Joan knew he was upset. "Tad, I'm sorry. Come in and have some coffee."

"No, thank you. I have to run. Are you going to the Jolliffes'?"

"I told Jane I'd go for cocktails. I'm tired. I'm planning an early dinner here. Then off to bed."

"Do you want me to pick you up?"

"Thank you, no, Tad. I know you. You'll want to stay longer than I do. I'll drive over myself."

"Dad expects me to go fishing with him in the morning. When you leave, tell me to go!"

Sunday night they stopped at the family's house, settled Dad and picked up her mother's suitcase. Driving into the city, she thanked her mother for coming in to stay with her. "I have a dinner date Wednesday with Ed. Your being there will give me a chance to invite him to see you, see the apartment and to have drinks before we go to dinner."

"You told me Ed had gone up to Stowe with you. Have you been seeing much of him since then?" she asked.

"He's been busy. We went to dinner last week. We're having dinner again this week."

"I'm awfully glad, Sister. Dad and I like him very much."

"I like him too, Mother. I'll tell you right now I don't plan to get hurt again. He's legally separated but not actually divorced so I'm playing it by ear. If he gets the divorce, I'll still play it by ear."

"It would be hard for me to see how Ed could ever hurt anyone. He seems very fond of you."

"My dear mother, Ed and I have always liked each other—under very different circumstances. I don't know what he's thinking. I don't know if he'd marry me anymore than I know if I'd marry him. All I can tell you now is he is the first man to hold my interest for a long, long time."

"As far as I'm concerned, that is an encouraging sign," she laughed. "I guess Dad and I worry about you. We won't be around forever. We'd like to know someone will be looking after you."

"For God's sake, Mother. Don't start the 'marrying off daughter' routine. That will kill off anyone. Besides, you're not the type to get away with it."

"Come on, Sister. You're not giving me credit for having any sense. I admit I've been over anxious about you. I think it's your attitude about remarrying that worries me. You've been so stubborn on the subject."

Monday morning she hoped Ed would show for coffee. She was anxious to see if he'd accept the invitation for a drink at the apartment. Her pulse did a dance when she saw him waiting for her. He was delighted her mother was in town and pleased she'd asked him for a drink before dinner. When they parted after coffee, she knew right off Wednesday would be a long time coming. But, like everything else, it arrived on time.

Even her mother surprised her by guessing Ed might ask her to join them and took the precaution of inviting a friend to the apartment for dinner with her, the friend to arrive after their departure.

Joan arrived after work to find the apartment full of cooking smells. Her mother casually announced cousin Ellie was coming to have dinner with her. She was a positive angel with Ed. After all this time she was not surprised, resulting in a normal kiss and hug for him. Ed made favorable comments about the apartment and appeared to be enjoying himself. He stayed longer than Joan had anticipated causing cousin Ellie to arrive before their departure. Only then did he suggest they go on to dinner.

At Ruby Foo's the captain and Mrs. Chang included Joan in their greetings. Dinner was excellent, conversation stimulating and pleasant. Before they left the restaurant, he said, "It looks as though once a week is about right for Chinese food. Shall we come back next week, maybe Thursday?"

This time she'd checked her desk pad, "Thursday is good for me. I'd love it." As he made the reservation with Mrs. Chang, Joan thought, "If this can be called courting, I'm being courted at Ruby Foo's."

Early the next morning a partner from one of the other top law firms contacted her requesting she come to his office to discuss an idea with him. Seated in his office later that afternoon, she was intrigued to find out they would like her to become their office manager, offering twice what she was being paid and extra benefits plus two months' vacation, one in winter and one in summer. This was a tempting offer which could definitely further her career. She was given time to think it over and told the position would not be vacant until the end of the year. They hoped to settle it by the first of September.

Curious to see what Ed's reaction to this would be, she phoned his office to be told he was uptown at a hospital board meeting. They did not expect him back until Monday.

He called Monday saying he was in a hurry and was on his way uptown for a finance meeting at the hospital. Reluctant to talk about the offer over the phone, she did not mention it.

As the week wore on, she began to realize any discussion would have to wait for dinner on Thursday. That day after leaving the office promptly at 5:00 o'clock, she had bathed and dressed when the apartment doorbell rang. The peephole revealed Ed standing in the corridor. Opening the door she exclaimed, "I was expecting to meet you downstairs a half hour from now."

"I was hoping you would invite me for another of your martinis."

"Of course," she spluttered, "please come in."

"I missed our coffee. I missed seeing you," he said giving her the big grin. He had two drinks while she nursed the first one. He was in great form chatting about the enormous problems of the hospital and what was being accomplished to alleviate them. She held back her news of the job offer and listened. Finally he decided they better get going. She was setting down the tray with the glasses and martini pitcher in the kitchen when he came in, swung her around and kissed her. He really kissed her. This was a man who took what he wanted. When he released her, her knees were shaking. She was overwhelmed by her physical reaction. She looked up at him and murmured, "WOW", and made a bee line for her coat, eager for a hasty departure.

In the car on the way across town, she casually mentioned the job offer. He said, "What a compliment to you. Are you going to accept it?"

"I don't know. I'm going to think about it."

Sometime during dinner there was a lull in the conversation. He reached over, took her hand and said, "Would you give up going to Water Mill this weekend and spend the weekend with me? Let me share your apartment with you?"

Her mind was spinning. Her first proposition as a woman. Maybe she should be flattered. Instead she said, "Thank you. That's not my style. Further you're not free to ask me anything, are you? You're not divorced. I've been in management positions for over twenty years. I've known many gals who became involved with married men, widowers, single men, even divorced men who had no intention of marrying them. I've witnessed their suffering, understood their emotions and was always sad they'd been such fools. My advice was constant, break the liaison immediately. They never listened."

He gave a nervous laugh, "I respect your feelings. I just thought we might enjoy each other. I won't ask you again. However, I've been in business a long time too. I've known some men, and some women, whose affairs worked out well for them."

"I'm sure that can happen. I still believe the percentage is minimum." They changed the subject.

At home in bed she could not get to sleep and was furious with herself. For twelve years she'd stayed free, had ducked marriage. Now she had let herself into a proposition. How in hell could she have allowed it to happen? She didn't blame him. Men were like that. Why did he have to be like that? He seemed so special. Tumbling and tossing was ridiculous. She got up, made coffee and stared at the martini glasses. She could feel him kissing her. She said out loud, "Damn, play it by ear, my foot. I've fallen in love with him." Well, she'd fix that. She'd get out of the rat race in the city, find a job in the country and enjoy her house. That's the answer. Now, dummy, finish your coffee and get some sleep. He's probably sleeping like a baby with no thought of you whatsoever."

Although she'd made the decision in the wee hours of the morning under emotional stress, she stuck to it. She handed in her resignation and wrote to Stuyvesant Town canceling her lease. Her friend, Vickie, was a salesperson in a real estate firm in Southampton. Over the weekend she spoke to the firm about obtaining a license and working for them while she looked for a permanent connection. The owner agreed, claiming spring was their busiest time. They welcomed the idea of another salesperson. The necessary forms were filled out. Joan would report May 1.

She used all the tricks in her bag to locate a replacement as quickly as possible, train her or him and get out of the city. She felt guilty as the partners and the whole staff, legal and nonlegal, appeared to be genuinely unhappy at her leaving. The other law firm was surprised at her sudden decision to locate in Long Island and was displeased with her choice.

She avoided seeing Ed until one day, going through applications on her desk and for no reason she could think of, she got up and looked out the window. There on the street, sixteen floors below, was Ed looking up at her. He motioned for her to have coffee. She met him at Schraffts. He wanted to know why she was avoiding him. Why didn't she have more faith in him? He would never do anything to hurt her. After he stopped talking, she told him what she had done and was doing. He was shocked, insisting it was a foolish move. He looked hurt, or did she imagine it? Suddenly she felt she was on the verge of tears. That would be the most stupid thing in the world. She'd learned long ago men hated tears. She excused herself, thanked him for the coffee and left.

For the first time in her conscious memory, she had allowed her emotions to rule her judgment. She hired a woman for her job although she was not at all sure it was the right choice. It was no consolation when the partners approved her selection. Within six months they let her go and hired a man. Throughout the years she had heard men claim it was difficult to rely on women in business. She could amend that: don't trust a woman in love in anything.

Throughout May, June and July the flowers kept coming every weekend. He phoned once a week to see how and what she was doing. Then one Saturday in August he drove into the driveway in Water Mill. She saw him from the kitchen window and went out to meet him. He wanted to talk to her. Was there some place they could go and not be interrupted? Joan called to Bonnie to tell grandma she'd be back in a little while.

In those days it was not a busy village. They were able to park down by the ocean at the public beach. He began, "According to the terms of my separation, the lawyer suggested a waiting period of a year before proceeding further. Until now, I wasn't even interested. It's been two years and you've changed all that. I will start the divorce by the end of this year. Then I will ask you to marry me. If you have no objections to my plan, I want to make a business deal with you. I am building a house outside of Stowe, Vermont, which I hope you will share with me. I cannot be up there to keep tabs on the contractor. I would like you to oversee the construction and plan to decorate it any way you choose. Take your mother up with you if you wish. I shall rent a suite in a motel where you will be comfortable. I will pay you the same rate I would pay an architect or an interior decorator. What do you say?"

She understood the implication of the words, but could not recall the word love anywhere in the formal speech. "When do I start?" her voice was so low she wasn't sure she'd uttered a sound.

"As soon as you can make the necessary arrangements. As soon as I can nail down a suite for you. This time try to trust me. Don't go running off."

"I have one stipulation. You'll have to hold my salary. It would only put me in a higher tax bracket. I'm paying Uncle Sam too much as it is," she laughed.

"Good. Now I know my girl has her sense of humor back again. Let's go back and see what your mother has to say about the idea." What her mother was going to say was something Joan knew by heart: "Thank God."

Returning to the house and observing polite greetings to her parents, Ed said, "I just offered your daughter a job supervising and decorating a home I'm building in Stowe which I hope we will share by next January or February." Addressing her mother he continued, "I suggested she might like you to be with her. I shall make arrangements at the motel close by."

Ignoring the inference, her father piped up, "She did a great job handling the workmen on the addition to this house. I think you've made a good choice."

"I know I have, sir."

"She'll do a good job all right," her mother stated. "She gets a little out of hand once in a while. She knows what she wants and can be stubborn about getting her way."

Quickly, Joan interrupted, "Where's Bonnie?"

"That little bookworm must have gone back to her book," her mother answered as she called to her. When Bonnie appeared, Joan introduced her to Mr. Bench who knew how to chat with an eleven year old girl.

Niece Bonnie, 11 years of age, and Aunt Marion
(Joan) dressed alike!

In spite of her mother's coaxing, Ed would not stay for lunch, saying he had to get back to the city. They went out with him and waved goodbye. Bonnie, looking up at Joan with a twinkle, asked, "Is Mr. Bench going to be another uncle?"

Joan's mother jumped in, "We don't know yet. We'll have to wait and see."

"I hope so. I like him."

That little rascal. Could she have sensed he just might be an honest to goodness uncle.

After church the next morning, Joan and her mother were in the kitchen assembling a picnic lunch to take to the beach. It came as a jolt when she told Joan, "Dad is not particularly well. His eyesight is failing and he chose not to drive the car. I would not like to leave him alone now for any extended time. Perhaps Mrs. Barrett could go with you."

Joan was aware of the eye problem but did not realize it was bad enough for him to stop driving. When he came down to Water Mill, he kept himself busy, always seemed happy, never complained, so she was not aware of his circulatory problems. She guessed Mrs. Barrett would have to do. She was an old friend, recently widowed and an excellent seamstress. This would be a welcome change for her and companionship for Joan. Perhaps she would be willing to make draperies, bedspreads, whatever. It seemed an excellent solution.

In less than two weeks things were in place. Joan and Mrs. Barrett left for Vermont. Joan was thrilled to find Gordon Lowe was working on the construction of the house. He and Jean had moved from North Adams and had built a house on Mountain Road. In the winter months he worked as a ski instructor. Jean worked as an accountant for the Mountain Company. Joan located the building site without any trouble. Gordon showed them around. It was a magnificent spot surrounded by mountains. It had a lovely old apple orchard. Ed owned 200 acres. It was sheer heaven. Joan noticed the building was closed in except for two large chimneys which were in the process of being installed. Gordon led them to the motel, unloaded the suitcases and informed them he and Jean were expecting them for dinner that night. He said he had to get back to the job and knew they needed a rest after the long trip. Joan asked Gordon to notify the contractor, head carpenter, electrician and plumber that she would meet with them at 8:30 the next morning. She wanted him to be present.

The meeting did not go as well as she had hoped. She suspected the intrusion of a "lady boss" did not sit well with these Vermonters. Her opening statement complimented them on the progress of what had been accomplished and advised that Mr. Bench had hired her to keep tabs and to decorate. The first priority was to have the guest bedroom and bath finished as soon as possible.

The contractor balked, indicating Mr. Bench had not specified how the room was to be finished. She simply stated the flooring would be 10" knotty pine boards, the wall 8" tongue-and-groove knotty pine. She would select the stain for the floor and the walls and would stain them herself. (This raised a few eyebrows.) The bathroom fixtures would be off-white or cream colored. She advised the plumber she would stop at his office and select them from his stock or catalog. She met the icy stares, eyeball to eyeball, and was aware of the snickering. Realizing she

231

needed backing, she wound up the discussion saying, "Mr. Bench will be here this weekend which gives us four days to obtain the necessary pine boards and start the guest room."

At dinner the night before, Jean had mentioned the Chellis Collins Furniture Store in Barre as the best place to buy furniture and drapery fabrics. After her session at the house, Joan and Mrs. Barrett headed for Barre. Jean was right. Joan found the furniture she wanted plus the drapery material for the guest room.

Depending on how fast the contractor moved and how soon Mrs. Barrett would have the drapes ready, they could move in and be on the premises. They would have to "make do" with a hot plate for cooking until the kitchen was in place. With Ed's backing, they moved in within three weeks' time.

Two gals alone at night in an unfinished house in the middle of the Vermont mountains had a few jitters they didn't admit to until the strange sounds and noises became familiar and of no consequence. They began to relax and to enjoy the makeshift existence. If anyone thinks he can have a house built and not be present on the site, he must believe in miracles. Even with Gordon's personal interest in having things done correctly, it was a hassle.

From a maintenance standpoint, the interior was to be wood paneling except the master bedroom which would be painted. The painter and Joan crossed swords at first contact. He said he'd never heard of Cohasset stains and couldn't get them. Joan had to order them from Behlan Bros. in New York. He claimed he knew the Wedgwood blue color. He didn't and was thoroughly annoyed when she mixed the paint. Fortunately he had painted only the ceiling which was white and no problem for him. He left his brushes and drop cloths and was to return the next morning to paint the walls. He failed to show at 8:00 A.M. as arranged. At 8:30 A.M. Joan began to paint the walls. When he arrived at 10:45 A.M., she informed him he was fired. They didn't need anyone unable to report to work on time. He was so mad he stalked out leaving his brushes, enabling Joan to finish painting the room.

A few nights later she was horrified to see a flashlight in the orchard and to hear gunshots. She phoned Gordon who calmly said, "Someone is hijacking deer. I'll call the warden. Just don't go outside."

This was repeated three or four times over the next two weeks. The warden assured Gordon he was checking on it. Thank God, Ed came up at the end of the second week. As he drove in the driveway, she went out to meet him. He told her there was a fox in the meadow across the road which should be disposed of as it looked mangy. It took Joan several minutes to even see it—just the two ears and two eyes were sticking up from behind a haystack.

Ed took his gun and crossed the road to the fence as a pickup truck came up the road and stopped to watch. Ed took aim, fired and hit the fox between the eyes killing it instantly. The pickup executed a fast U-turn and sped down the road. Gordon, who had come out to watch, howled, "Boy, that was a hell of a long shot. That was the painter in that truck. Joan had to fire him. We've suspected him of hijacking in your orchard. You want to bet he won't be back?"

He wasn't—no more flashlights or shots in the orchard. She was impressed and proud of Ed's prowess. When he had asked if Tad was a good shot, she guessed Ed was very good. Now she had witnessed just how great he was with a gun. This was a man's man. She knew it and loved it.

There were a few problems with the contractor. He was signing an invoice for pine boards to be used in the kitchen when Joan noticed they were warped and stated flatly they were not acceptable. They were not to be unloaded but returned to the lumber yard. Maybe he decided to fix her wagon as a few days later he took pleasure in advising her that 12" or wider boards for the living room walls were not available. She asked Jean to go down to the lumber yard with her. They climbed a ladder into the loft where such wide boards were stored. They handpicked every one, finding enough 12" to 16" boards in perfect condition.

Not long after that she was shocked to hear the contractor tell Gordon, "Scrap it. He's loaded. Order a new one." She tiptoed

Niece Bonnie--young lady!

down the stairs, waited for him to turn and then looking at Gordon she asked what had to be scrapped. And this man, the contractor, was supposedly a friend of Ed's! This attitude worried her to the point where she telephoned Ed in New York and asked him to bring up all the bills he had paid to date on his next trip. She was not surprised to find each of the itemized bills with mistakes in addition—picayune stuff; a bill of $200 odd dollars with an extra $40 or maybe $60 added on. They were submitted weekly, and in one batch the errors amounted to more than $600; never were the mistakes in Ed's favor. Joan mailed them back to Ed suggesting he have his secretary photostat them, mark the errors and deduct the amount from the next bill after checking it first!

The architect specified two large, raised fireplaces, one in the living room and one directly below in a combination sitting room and office for Ed. It was to be built of field stones, extending from the floor to the ceiling and be 12 feet in width. The mason was a new experience for Joan. He was an artist, a perfectionist. At first she wasn't sure he had a voice or could talk. He would arrive with the stones in his truck after gathering them from the fences around the property. His assistant would spread them carefully on the driveway while the mason would go in the house and stare at the wall space with complete concentration. When the stones were spread out, he would go to check them, ponder ten or more minutes, then point out a particular one which the assistant would place in a separate area. This process was repeated until he had selected six or seven stones when he would nod his head and the assistant would take them inside. A quick glance at the wall, then mortar and stones would fly into place fitting into a perfect pattern. Joan knew this was one process that would take time and could not be rushed or interfered with, so she left him to his art and his cogitations.

Gordon, not realizing Joan was unfamiliar with Vermont deer season practices, failed to warn her that on opening day no one would report for work, nor would they return until they had taken the allotted deer. Most of the men came drifting back within a few days but no mason, which left a gaping hole inviting rain or snow into the house. As each day slipped away, she was grateful they were still dry. He did not get his deer until the very last day of the season. She wondered if he had ruminated too long on each opportunity.

In the middle of December she drove to New York to meet Ed to pick out Witticomb furniture for the living room, sitting room and master bedroom. Ed felt it would be a good idea for Mrs. Barrett and Joan to have his chocolate colored labrador retriever with them for protection and comfort. He delivered "Koko" the next day to her family's house. She became an instant success. She had been in a kennel for too long and was overjoyed to be free with people who petted her. She seemed doubtful when Ed left, yet she settled into the back seat of Joan's car as though she owned it.

Joan's mother drove back to Vermont with her, loved the house and declared it was the first house she'd ever seen framed in mountains. She stayed two days before flying back home. It was a good break for everyone as work for Joan and Mrs. Barrett was suspended. Her mother met Jean and Gordon at long last. They had dinner together at the lodge the night before she departed.

Koko seemed to understand she had been sent to take care of them. She was a bit puzzled when the workmen showed on Monday, and she stayed close to Mrs. Barrett and Joan.

Christmas time was full of combined ingenuity. They placed an 8'x6' sheet rock panel on two sawhorses to make a table, covered it with gay, Christmas cloth and set up red candles. They took two cement blocks on which they placed an 8' plank to make a bench and painted nail kegs bright red and green for stools. They decorated the bare living room with evergreens and made a wreath for the front door. They knew Ed would be coming up, so they invited Jean and Gordon to join them at the first cocktail party held at "Barnes Hill," the name Ed gave to the house.

A few days after Christmas the snows came. Joan began to learn more about living in Vermont. She and Mrs. Barrett had been thrilled with the autumn colors, mesmerized at the electrical storms with lightning bouncing from one mountain to the other and delighted with the complete rainbows which followed. Now they were actually snowed in until Gordon appeared with his Jeep and snowplow. They loved it as it was a true winter wonderland with the pure white snow rarely seen in the city.

Then came the January thaw with the mushy snow and streams of water running down the road in the middle of which the trucks arrived with the furniture and appliances. It took time to clean up the messy tracks on the beautifully stained and polished floors. Gordon told them the thaw came every year in January—too bad it couldn't have been two days later.

As with all things, it passed. They took great delight in arranging and rearranging furniture until it began to look very comfortable indeed. That night they had their first fire in the fireplace. Joan began to miss Ed, wishing he were with them to feel the warmth and comfort of his house. She must have wished pretty hard as he telephoned from Reno. "How's my girl?" he asked.

Joan (Marion Bench) on August 26, 1991, her 80th birthday.

"Ed, it is so warm and cozy here. We have a fire in the fireplace. I've been wishing you were here."

"I've been wishing you were here. There are some wonderful people staying at this ranch who have convinced me to persuade you to fly out as soon as the divorce is final. How do you feel about that?"

"You mean we would be married in Reno?"

"Well, no, just outside of Reno. I've given it a lot of thought. Your church won't marry us no more than my church, which is High Episcopal. I found a very pretty Methodist Church in Carson Valley. The minister, Rev. Silberstein, is a realist. I spoke to him and found him most encouraging, although he insists on meeting with you individually, then meeting with us together. How does that strike you?"

"How thoughtful you are—the religious angle has bothered me a great deal. I'm resigned to the obvious as long as we are married in a church. I don't think God will mind which church."

Ed laughed, "I'm sure He won't, just as I'm sure the minister will approve of you when he meets you. The final papers should be coming through the second weekend in February. Then, my dear, I will see you receive a proper proposal. Think about it. I will be in touch."

"That will be about the time things should be pretty well finished here. I'll check with Mrs. Barrett about staying on here."

The receiver was barely replaced when she was floating around the living room with Koko trying to get into the act. There had been lots of innuendos, but this was the first time marriage had been discussed. He recognized the religious problem and had gone to a great deal of trouble to make it right for them. What a super guy. She couldn't wait for that fantastic man to smother her in his arms.

Ed made all the arrangements. He and two friends from the ranch met her at the airport. As she walked towards him, she let her heart explode. He was so handsome, the blue eyes twinkling, the Bench grin enormous. The four drove to Carson Valley. His friends, Firman Houghton and Joan Keegan, were full of enthusiasm and were so much a part of the plan. They became their witnesses.

At first Joan found the Rev. Silberstein formidable, strict in his questions and carefully analytical. By the time he called Ed into the room, she couldn't quite grasp whether or not she had passed his scrutiny. He questioned them intently as to their feelings towards each other, their religious philosophy and their thoughts of the future. Suddenly the room was overpowered in silence for what seemed an eternity. At last he spoke, "I am convinced you are both aware of the seriousness of marriage and do not regard it lightly, that you recognize and regret the series of unfortunate circumstances in your previous relationships. I believe you have sufficient love and respect for each other to face future adversities." He paused and smiled, "I will be happy to join you in marriage tomorrow at 10:00 A.M."

How could she describe the subdued, yet overjoyed emotions she experienced as they left the rectory.

They drove to the hotel in Gardnerville where Ed had rented a suite. She was deposited in the room with her suitcase, instructed to rest and be ready at 6:30 P.M. when they would return to take her to dinner.

The two Joans liked each other. They would spend the night together. How on earth could anyone expect her to rest? She was bursting with love and felt like a young maiden rather than a mature woman entering her late forties. She wandered around the two rooms, speculating on whether or not this would be the setting of their first night together, when they would offer their complete love. She deliberated, then thought, "Yes, I truly love him and will devote the rest of my life to him."

Deciding to indulge in a hot tub while daydreaming, she was about to run the water when the phone rang. It was Ed, "Are you comfortable, dear?"

"Yes, darling. I was just enjoying the thought of how much I loved you." She actually said it!

"I love you too. Strangely enough, I sensed you felt the same way. I had to call you. I've missed you very much. Try to rest, dearest."

Joan Keegan spent the night with her and drove her to the church the next morning. She was not at all sure if she had ever heard of a bride and groom crying at their own wedding. She witnessed Ed's eyes filled with tears as her tears quietly rolled down her cheeks. This will be hard to believe but will be long remembered: when the minister pronounced them man and wife, his eyes were filled with tears. Joan and Firman were not dry-eyed either. These were tears of exquisite joy to be cherished for a lifetime.

They had lunch together, then went on a sightseeing trip. No matter where they went, there were slot machines: in the airport, drug store, grocery store—everywhere. The majority of people playing the machines did not strike Joan as being able to indulge themselves that way. She did not dwell on the thought too long; she was too happy. She was still in her pale blue wedding dress when Firman took them to a celebration dinner with all the trimmings, including delicious champagne. From the restaurant they drove back to the ranch where Ed introduced his wife to the owner and some guests. He put his suitcases in the car. They said goodbye to Joan and Firman, promising to see each other again, sometime, someplace. They returned to the suite that first night.

Much has been written of the love of a man and a woman. That night they celebrated the love of a husband and wife. The waiting had increased the anticipation, the desire and made physical and spiritual contact very special.

They drove across the country, running into a snowstorm in Texas, purchasing Navajo rugs in Arizona, sharing the joys of being together.

They telephoned Mrs. Barrett, telling her when they expected to arrive at Barnes Hill. She promptly called Jean and Gordon. All were there to greet them on their homecoming. Ed had not seen the finished house. It was a delight to witness his pleasure. Koko knew something was different and went from one to the other to be petted. Mrs. Barrett had made delicious hors d'oeuvres and a special dinner. It was a celebration party in their own home.

They telephoned Joan's parents and Ed's mother. Everyone seemed pleased and happy. Ed, ever thoughtful, complimented Mrs. Barrett on the draperies she had carefully made, on the dinner and on staying at Barnes Hill alone with Koko to take care of the house for them. At this Gordon said, "The farmer's wife, about a quarter of a mile up the road, told me she'd be happy to come help you out with the house, which means she'd like to work for you. I've been told they are very respected in the area. They have three children. He's a dairy farmer."

"That is the best news," Ed said. "I've been hoping we'd find someone. She's close by to keep an eye on it when we are away. Besides, the house is too big for us to take care of. We should find someone for the outside work. Did she say she would come see us?"

"I gather it would be better if Joan stopped by to see her. She'd like the money, but they are very proud people."

"Joan is just the one to handle that. That's a load off my mind," Ed assured Gordon.

Thus began married life as the mistress of their beautiful new home. Joan's meeting with the farmer's wife, Glenola, was mutually rewarding. Glenola is a remarkable woman whom Joan respects and admires. They have remained friends through the years.

Joan's parents lived to see her secure and happy with a man they liked and respected. Her father died suddenly six months after their marriage. Joan had lost a true friend. Ed was her rock of consolation and shared her agony. Two years later Joan's mother, playing tag with Traci, her grandchild, keeled over in great pain. Joan and Ed rushed her to the hospital to learn she had pancreatic cancer. They nurtured her with love and affection for the short time she suffered until death rescued her.

Joan and Ed lived for each other. Their love was absolute. They led a busy, active existence, engaging in sports, participating in community affairs and volunteering as ski instructors in the local elementary school in Stowe, Vermont. They traveled frequently and many friends labeled them "Nomads." They went

Joan and Edward C. Bench arriving at the Robert Carney estate in Southampton, NY, for a dinner and dance in 1958.

to Switzerland, Ireland, all the islands of Hawaii. No matter where they went, they made friends easily and returned with deliciously eventful stories.

They relished the fact that after ten years of marriage they were still mistaken for newlyweds. Following eighteen years of an ideally romantic union, Joan discovered Ed had arteriosclerosis and, two years later, lung cancer. The first illness required a very serious operation after which Joan spent four days and nights by his bedside praying he would make it. The second illness was treated with severe radiotherapy.

Deep mature love and devotion of both during the strain, worry, uncertainties and adjustments of these three years were followed by a miraculous recovery. They had the joy of sharing a further ten years of happiness before Joan was devastated by his death from bleeding ulcers.

With her memories of years of joy, tears, happiness and more tears, Joan is in her eighties. She lives alone in a small country house content to share the lives of her nieces, nephews, brother Bob and his wife, while she enjoys the company of her many younger friends.

INDEX

Anderson, Congressman Jack 104, 105
Advisory Educational Council 4
B-17 Flying Fortresses 127
Bench, Commander Edward 97, 111, 113, 142-143, 157
Bird, Commander Dick 16, 19, 39, 51, 91, 141
Budd, Yeoman Stephanie 69, 72, 82, 91, 102, 114, 121, 126, 128-129, 137-139, 157, 160
Bureau of Naval Personnel 5
Carlin, Virginia 6, 7, 10, 12, 28
Cassini, Comtessa Loiewski 16
Castleman, Captain Kenneth 4, 5, 9, 37
Cheney, Grace 10, 11, 12
Coolidge, Mrs. Calvin (Grace) 84
Cooper, Commander Dick 31
Denfeld, Admiral Louis 78
Duncan, Commander Charles 138, 141, 150, 154-155, 157, 160
Fink, Captain Carl 91
Forrestal, James V. 76, 80, 114, 122, 124, 126
Forrestal, Mrs. James 28, 80-88, 92, 95, 96, 98, 99, 110-112, 125
Geddes, Norman Bel 156-160
Gildersleeve, Virginia 4
Gingrich, Captain 74, 76, 122
Hart, Lieutenant John 35
Jacobs, Admiral Randall 4, 7, 25, 74, 75, 78
Johnson, Congressman Lyndon 72, 74, 114

Kepplar, Captain L.H.J. 86
Knox, Frank 114
Lawton, Captain Andrew 16, 20, 25, 29, 33, 39, 40, 47, 51, 54, 67, 74, 78, 82, 91
Mainbocher 25, 33, 80, 86
Maxwell, Commander W. W. 114
Mayer, Commander John 40, 45
McAfee, Mildred 6, 7, 13, 15, 25, 28, 33, 103, 125-126
Montgomery, Commendar Robert 126
Mullen, Bill and Maggie 5
Owens, Captain Ray 21, 31, 38, 48, 53, 59, 61, 62, 64, 71, 80, 101, 111-113, 117, 127, 130, 133-135, 157
Patterson, Captain T. T. 82
Pearl Harbour 2, 91, 96, 119
Pearson, Drew 114, 122, 124, 126
Rockefeller, Lieutenant John D., III 16, 17, 22, 39, 41, 43, 51, 59
Roosevelt, Eleanor 6, 7, 44, 45
Roosevelt, President Theodore 78, 149
Tunney, Gene 15
Underwood, Captain Herbert W. 85
USS Enterprise 118, 119
USS Missouri 114
White House 51, 67, 69, 78, 94, 127, 156
Women Appointed for Volunteer Service (WAVES) Law 3
Woodworth, Bill and Heidi 16, 25, 27-29, 31, 33, 34, 39-41, 44, 47-51, 53, 61, 64, 65, 70, 97, 101, 111-114, 127, 141, 145, 149, 154, 157, 160